WITHDRAWN

EUROPE 2000

EUROPE
2000

Edited by
Peter Hall

New York   Columbia University Press 1977

Published in 1977 in Great Britain by Gerald Duckworth & Co. Ltd.
and in the United States of America by Columbia University Press

Printed in Great Britain

Library of Congress Cataloging in Publication Data
Main entry under title:

Europe 2000.

Final results of a project conducted by the European
Cultural Foundation.
Bibliography: p.
Includes index.
1. Europe – Social conditions. 2. Europe – Economic
conditions. 3. Twentieth century – Forecasts.
I. Hall, Peter, 1932-   II. European Cultural
Foundation.
HN373.5.E76   1977   309.1'4'055   77-9479
ISBN-0-231-04462-3

CONTENTS

Foreword   xiii

Chapter 1: A new approach to Europe's future   1

Our basic approach   4
Our approach 'to the future: historicism and scenario-
     writing   6
The structure of this book   8

*Chapter 2: Future international scenarios: Europe in a transformed
     world*   10

The world we have left   10
Scenarios for the future:
     (1) Europe suppressed, or survival of the two blocs   12
     (2) One Europe, or Europe united by challenge   14
     (3) A Europe of nations   20
     (4) A Europe of regions, or the revolt of the regional
         periphery   22
     (5) Explosive change in Eastern Europe   27
     (6) Some alternatives and a synthesis   29

*Chapter 3: Future European scenarios: economy and society in a
     changing Europe*   32

Types of history – past and future   34
The economic constraints   35
The demographic constraints   37

Social and political features of political rationality 39
The new power of the state 43
The implications of the international scenarios 45
The new corporatism 46
The dominant scenario – and some variants 46
The dynamics of history: towards a new rationality 47

Chapter 4: Problem landscape of the future Europe 52

Defining mega-problems: needs and their satisfaction 55
Macro-problems:
    (1) Peace, war and security 56
    (2) Growth, stagnation and scarcity 58
    (3) Complexity, social responsiveness and rationality 61
    (4) The unknown hazards 65
Problems of groups in society 66
Group problems: 66
    (5) Urban and regional disparities 68
    (6) The female dilemma 69
    (7) Revolt of the old 72
    (8) The marginal groups
Problems of the individual: 72
    (9) Alienation in industry 72
    (10) Alienation in education 74
    (11) Alienation in the city 76
    (12) Information – overload and starvation
Summary and prospect: mega-problems of the future 77
  Europe: 78
    (1) Peace, war and security 78
    (2) Growth, stagnation and scarcity 78
    (3) Farming, rural life and the natural environment 78
    (4) Urban life and urban environment 79
    (5) Industry for human ends 79
    (6) Access to information 79
    (7) The family – divided and reunited? 79
    (8) Class and inequality 80
    (9) Alienation and a new rationality

Chapter 5: People and land: the regional and rural dimension 82

Urban growth and urban spread 83

Towards agriculture in the year 2000   85
The situation now   85
One view of the future: technical optimism   87
The hypothesis of heavy demand   88
A middle hypothesis: continuation of present trends   89
The major problems of today and tomorrow: 91
  (1) World problems   91
  (2) Problems specific to Europe   91
The challenge of environmental quality   92
The retreat from mountain Europe   97
Four futures for European agriculture: an inquiry among
   the youth of Europe   99

Chapter 6: Urbanisation: towards a human environment in Europe   103

Problem symptoms of modern urbanisation in Europe:
   unification of development trends   105
The basic problems of modern urbanisation in Europe:
   disproportionate exploitation of the environment   108
The chief problem areas of modern urbanisation in Europe   111
Alternative solutions for a future urbanisation of Europe:
   the conflict between values and technologies   111
Coping with future urbanisation in Europe: equilibrium
   between the three components of environmental
   exploitation, or the rediscovery of the Centre   116
Towards human environment in Europe: five spheres of
   action for future urbanisation   119
Towards a dynamic policy of urban renewal   119
Towards an ecologically balanced urbanisation   122
Towards a human-scale built environment   125
Towards a needs-oriented city planning   127
Towards a human environment in Europe through
   planning?   129

Chapter 7: A New role for Europe's industry   132

European industry: its world role   132
European industry and the Third World   136
The multinationals and European industrial policy   136
Regional equity and the role of European industry   139
Internalising industrial externalities   140

Co-determination – a European model?   143
Beyond indicative planning   145
Strategies for improvement   148
European industry in a post-industrial age   152

Chapter 8: Information, education and power   156

New worlds of telecommunication   157
The media   160
The psychological risk   161
Information, technology and education   165
Electronic surveillance   169
Information is power   170
An information policy   172

Chapter 9: Age, sex and gender: the individual and the family   174

The European family: changing role, changing form   174
The revolt of the old   177
Political influence   179
Mobility and the lack of it   180
Work and income   181
Health   182
Housing and social relations   185
Women, children, career and society   188
The woman   193
The man   194
The child   194
The family   195
Society   195
Demands on husbands and wives   197
Demands of families for external resources   197
Time and place of activities   198
The daily round and the local range   199
The long-term period and the wider range   201
Towards a redefinition of the family   203

Chapter 10: Class and inequality   205

Types of inequality   205
Economic inequality   205
Non-economic inequality   206
Inequality between nations   209
Real inequality, perceived inequality and class   212
The nature of class   213
Alternative future scenarios
    Scenario 1: Extrapolation of trends in the 1960s   217
    Scenario 2: A structural down-turn in growth   218
The migrant workers   219
Class polarisation around work and structural marginality   222
Social relations after state capitalism   224

*Chapter 11: The heart of the matter: from alienation to a new
    rationality*   226

Alienation as a force for social change   226
The origin and present nature of alienation   226
Bureaucracy as the organiser of alienation   229
The social consequences of alienation   230
The new consensus: a developing solution?   231
The failure to satisfy needs   233
Towards a new rationality   234
From economic rationality to cultural rationality   237

*Chapter 12: From ideology to utopia: towards feasible solutions for
    2000*   239

Key trends   242
Formative ideas   245
Towards 2000   254
One day in Europe 2000   257
Last words   263

References   263
Index   271

Members of the integration committee of Plan Europe 2000

PETER HALL (Chairman)
Professor of Geography, Chairman of the School of Planning Studies, Dean of the Faculty of Urban and Regional Studies, University of Reading, England

PAUL BARKER
Editor, *New Society*, London

FERNANDO GONZALEZ BERNALDEZ
Professor of Ecology, University of Seville, Spain

LADISLAV CERYCH
Project Director, Project 1 (Education), Plan Europe 2000, Paris

UMBERTO COLOMBO
Professor, Director of Montedison, Milan

JACQUES DURAND
Director, DATAR (Délégation à l'Aménagement du Territoire et à l'Action Régionale), Paris

TORSTEN HÄGERSTRAND
Professor of Geography, University of Lund, Sweden

BERTIL JÖNSSON
Director of Corporate Planning, Volvo, Gothenburg, Sweden

JOSEPH KLATZMANN
Professor of Agronomy, Institut National Agronomique, Paris, France

I.B.F. KORMOSS
Project Director (1974-5) Project 4 (Future of Farming and Environment), Professor, College of Europe, Bruges, Belgium

JOSÉ RAMON LASUEN
Professor, President of Lasuen Associates, Madrid

FRITZ LIENEMANN
Project Director, Project 3 (Urbanisation), Systemplan, Heidelberg, Federal Republic of Germany

RAINER MACKENSEN
Professor of Sociology, Technical University of Berlin, West Berlin, Federal Republic of Germany

PIERRE PIGANIOL
Professor, Director, *Futuribles*, Paris

CRAIG SINCLAIR
Economist, OECD (Organisation for Economic Cooperation and Development), Paris, France

GERHARD STÖBER
Project Director, Project 2 (Man and Industry), Systemplan, Heidelberg, Federal Republic of Germany

Research Officer: GRAHAM CHAPMAN, University of Reading
Editorial Adviser: REG HOLLINGDALE, London
Secretary: MONIKA WHEELER, University of Reading

Contributing Authors: MARIANNE FRANKENHAEUSER (Stockholm), JOHN GRETTON (London), ULRICH HEWER (Heidelberg), KATRIN LEDERER (West Berlin), GEORGE SCHÖPFLIN (London), TONY SMITH (London)

FOREWORD

The European Cultural Foundation here presents the final results of *Plan Europe 2000*. The book is no mere synthesis; it would be quite impossible to summarise the contents of more than twenty published studies. Rather, its aim is to draw attention to the main conclusions on education, industry, urbanisation and agriculture* – and to convey the reflections on these conclusions that the members of the Integration Committee and the researchers themselves have produced.

From 1967 to 1975, more than two hundred experts from ten different countries were engaged in the research work, which was launched by my predecessor, Georges Sluizer. The work could not have been accomplished without immense support from public and private organisations. The Foundation is grateful to all those who made *Plan Europe 2000* possible – in particular to the Netherlands, host country to the institute.

Altogether the contributions totalled Dfl. 4,400,000 (approximately £1 million in late 1976), to which the Foundation added Dfl. 3,000,000 (£750,000) from its own funds. For a private European foundation to make available a total sum of Dfl. 7,400,000 (£1.75 million) was an enterprise requiring a great effort.

In conclusion the Foundation thanks the Chairmen and Members of Scientific Committees, the Directors and research workers of all four research committees, and the Chairman and Members of the Integration Committee responsible for this final report.

The book was edited for publication by Peter Hall, Chairman of the *Plan Europe 2000* Integration Committee, with the assistance of Reg Hollingdale, editorial adviser to the European Culture Foundation. Chapters 1, 4 and 12 were written by Peter Hall; Chapter 2 is based on contributions from Pierre Piganiol, Graham Chapman and

---

* Each of these four areas has been the subject of a separate 'Project'.

George Schöpflin, with final drafting by Peter Hall; Chapter 3 was written mainly by Graham Chapman with contributions by Torsten Hägerstrand; Chapter 5 was drafted by Peter Hall from contributions by Torsten Hägerstrand, Joseph Klatzmann, Fernando Gonzalez Bernaldez, I.B.F. Kormoss and Dan Harris, with reference also to earlier project work (Jansen 1975); Chapter 6 was written by Fritz Lienemann from Project 3 material; Chapter 7 was based on an original draft by Ulrich Hewer plus contributions by Gerhard Stöber, Umberto Colombo, Bertil Jönsson and Pierre Piganiol; Chapter 8 was drafted by Reg Hollingdale from material by Tony Smith, Paul Barker, Marianne Frankenhaeuser and the Project 1 studies; Chapter 9 was largely written by Torsten Hägerstrand; Chapter 10 was mainly written by Graham Chapman, with material from Pierre Piganiol and a contribution from John Gretton; Chapter 11 was drafted by Graham Chapman and Katrin Lederer.

The work of producing this final report was assisted by a grant to the University of Reading by the Social Science Research Council, to whom thanks are due.

RAYMOND GEORIS
Secretary-General
European Cultural Foundation

CHAPTER 1

A New Approach to Europe's Future

Europe has no idea where it's going but it's going there fast. Moreover, our continent, to use Valéry's phrase, seems to be entering the future backwards. Anxiety about the future, anxiety about the unknown, are the root of the present crisis of our society. But anxiety can be a creative force, provided we have the courage to analyse lucidly its causes and to transform it into tangible proposals for action. And to act is to think ahead, to think the future here and now.,

With these words, published early in 1969, the European Cultural Foundation announced *Plan Europe 2000* to the world (European Cultural Foundation 1969, p.5). The project was an ambitious, even an audacious, one: a programme of interrelated studies, drawn up by sixty eminent scholars from the countries of western Europe, which would try to reconnoitre the whole landscape of problems facing European society down to the end of the century, with the aim of probing causes and suggesting possible solutions. These studies were to be undertaken on an international and interdisciplinary basis by researchers from every part of Europe working both in their own universities and institutes and in a central team. The overall scientific direction of the work was to be entrusted to committees of distinguished academics, again chosen to represent the whole range of relevant disciplines and national cultures. And the whole work was to be managed and financed through an Executive Committee of the European Cultural Foundation – a private body, established in 1954 and based in Amsterdam, in which eighteen countries are represented by prominent personalities from the world of culture, the economy and social life.

Plan Europe 2000 was organised from the start in four main projects. Each was designed to stimulate the study of one major group of problems facing Europe – and the world – in years down to the end of the century.

First: *Educating Man for the 21st Century*. Education is a living manifestation of the age of uncertainty. There are doubts about the aims of education, about content, about structures and methods, about the role of education in society – above all in relation to the under-privileged groups of the inner cities. Faced with such doubts, is it possible to develop totally new guidelines for the education of the citizens of the twenty-first century?

Second: *Man and Industry of Tomorrow.* Industry is similarly plagued by contradictions. Is its main purpose to serve strictly economic ends: the production of goods and services in the most economic way by the most efficient methods? Or does it also have to serve a social role for the workers employed in it? What are its responsibilities to the consumer? Are quite new structures of ownership and control needed to reconcile these divergent ends? And will economic crises compel European industry to change directions fundamentally – producing new kinds of goods and services in completely new ways?

Third: *Urbanisation: Planning Human Environment in Europe.* Everywhere, huge urban agglomerations seem to be spreading; everywhere people are voicing the same criticisms of a soulless, alienating built environment. What principles might be developed for a human urban development? How could technology help or hinder? Are there basic physiological and psychological needs that must be satisfied? And how far also is there an ecological imperative to be recognised?

Fourth: *Future of Farming and the Environment.* All over Europe, a technical revolution is transforming rural life and causing an exodus to the towns. What role will agriculture play in late twentieth-century Europe? Will it be further rationalised, to become factory farming in the charge of a few technologists, while much of rural Europe becomes a depopulated wilderness? Or – just as with industry – are there other roles for agriculture, as a way of life and as a guarantor of self-sufficiency in an age of crisis, that European policy-makers should urgently recognise? How do the youth of Europe see such alternative roles for European farming?

Thus there was to be a limited number of studies, concentrating on an agenda of major problem areas. We wanted to know: what can we in Europe put forward in response to these questions? Were we doomed to follow in the wake of North America at a cultural distance of some ten or twenty years? Or could we find that Europe was an original culture, capable of finding for itself forms of human civilisation that might perhaps set an example elsewhere?

These were the four separate themes, or projects. Each was

entrusted to a separate team of researchers, working under a full-time project director, responsible to a scientific steering committee. In turn, these reported to a central scientific committee, representing the chairmen of the project committees, which would guarantee the coordination and integration of the work to the Foundation and to the wider European world. Finally, in the last two years of *Plan Europe 2000* – between July 1974 and March 1976 – the place of this central committee was taken by a wider Integration Committee, specifically charged with the production of this final report.

Now at last more than six years of work are complete. This volume is the final report of *Plan Europe 2000*. It represents the final capstone in the whole research structure, which was from the start envisaged by those who brought the project into being.

It needs stressing that the reader will not find here a simple digest, or abstract, of the main conclusions of the four projects. For that, it is necessary to turn to the separate final reports of the projects, which are published during 1976-7 (Fragnière 1976, Stöber 1977, Lienemann 1977, Kormoss 1977). Rather, this present volume tries to distil from the final project reports – and from a mass of more than twenty other reports that preceded them – the most important general themes that emerge for Europe in the year 2000.

Inevitably, these are problem themes. We do not look forward to some Elysium, where all troubles are ended and mankind lives in perfect peace and harmony. We do think that some human problems – aggression and conflict, the allocation of scarce resources to multifarious wants, ignorance in the face of natural disasters or social problems – will probably remain with man as long as he survives. But we also suspect that other problems which now seem critical may have disappeared or diminished by the year 2000, while quite other questions now invisible or obscure may have come to dominate debate. Thus from the start we wanted to go beyond the transitory problems that loom so large in our time, to try to forecast the very different problem landscape of the future Europe.

Europe 2000 is the collective work of the members of the Integration Committee whose names appear at the beginning of this book. They actively contributed papers and supplied relevant source materials; they invited, read and discussed a series of specially-commissioned contributions from outside experts; they exhaustively criticised drafts of the report in a series of extended meetings during the eighteen-month gestation of the book. The four Project Directors, who were all members of the Committee, played a particular role in supplying successive drafts and summaries of their final project reports. As will be seen from the ascriptions listed in the foreword, most have one or more committee members as principal authors. The final draft of the book was edited for publication by Peter Hall, the Committee's chairman, and Reg Hollingdale, *Plan Europe 2000*'s editorial adviser.

It is perhaps unnecessary to stress that, in a work like this, no member of the Integration Committee could fully commit himself to every word of the book. Throughout our discussions there have been many points of reservation or disagreement. But all members have agreed that the book in this final form should be published as a fair record of our ideas and our arguments.

Our basic approach

Europe 2000 might be a misleading title – in two ways. For it might suggest that this book is about forecasting and what is loosely called futurology. In the narrow sense of both words, in fact, it is neither. In a wider sense, which is the one we collectively use, it is very much about both. To avoid possible confusion, we had better start with some brief definitions.

We do not discuss forecasting in the conventional sense, because there is quite enough of it already. The Central Statistical Office in Britain, the INSEE in France, the Statistisches Bundesamt in Germany* and their equivalents in other European countries, together engage in formidable programmes of forecasting in every sphere of economic and social life. There are forecasts of population, of the workforce, of the course of production and of productivity, of spending for leisure, travel and a variety of consumer goods. One may readily have an estimate of population in 1990 or car ownership in 2005. With all this activity, it would be pointless to set up in competition.

Doubly foolish; for the forecasts have too often proved wrong, sometimes wildly wrong. It might sometimes seem that as good a result could be got by consulting horoscopes or reading tea leaves. Yet despite this fact, there has been too little systematic analysis of the failures of forecasting. If this is done, clear lessons emerge. First, most so-called forecasts are not really such at all, but are mechanical statistical projections based on recent past trends. (Population forecasting provides notorious examples.) They do not go behind trends to causes, and one can see why: it is so difficult. Consider

---

* Throughout this book 'Germany' signifies the Federal Republic of Germany and 'DDR' the German Democratic Republic.

population: factors like abortion and the pill, women's liberation, increasing female participation in the workforce, the economic outlook, social imitation and attitudes towards children are all relevant – not to mention a dozen others. Secondly, in some kinds of forecasts (economic forecasts, in particular) there is a tendency to confuse prediction of the future with exhortation to achieve it; so that such forecasts, especially in low-performance countries like Britain, are perpetually too optimistic. Population forecasts on the other hand may be over-optimistic, or over-pessimistic, depending on the short-term trends they too slavishly follow.

There seem to be various solutions to these dilemmas. One is to abandon all pretension to forecasting and concentrate on short-term adaptive planning. This approach, suggested by operational researchers, is open to the objection that for some purposes we cannot do without forecasts – if only to help expose the full range of possibilities involved in 'planning for uncertainty'. The second approach is to improve the quality of conventional statistical forecasts, especially by viewing models not as firm predictors, but rather as tools for understanding complex interrelationships in a step-by-step process. That is fully compatible with the approach we use here, though it is not our approach. The third possibility is to embrace a great battery of longer-term forecasting techniques ranging from morphological analysis and relevance trees via cross-impact analysis to brainstorming, Delphi methods and scenario writing. Some of these are quantified methods, of great value in analysing relationships between variables in conditions of uncertainty. What they cannot do is to provide any empirical justification – apart from past trends – of the likelihood of one event against another. And that is the justification for the more judgemental kinds of analysis, which have come to be popularly identified with the nascent science (or pseudo-science) of futurology.

That, if anywhere, is where we belong. At any rate, it is where *Europe 2000* began. But during the years of the study – the first half of the 1970s – it has become embarrassingly clear that futurology, like forecasting, was too often wrong in its prognostications. It came to be associated with those bland predictions of the 1960s which almost without exception foresaw continuous quantitative growth extending over decades and resulting in the elimination of poverty, the extension of leisure until the 10-hour week became the norm, and a material utopia where every European family enjoyed two cars and a computer. Such errors can be forgiven in a new science that must learn its way; the trouble is that they tend to persist. The cause, we believe, is that futurology has shared with forecasting a naive belief in the virtue of the quantitative.

One answer to this failure, during the early 1970s, was a new emphasis on constructive futurology: a style that starts by defining desirable futures, and then maps out possible roads to achieving them. Constructive futurology was debated as vigorously within *Plan Europe 2000* as anywhere – as witness, for instance, the contribution of Hake (Hake 1973). But it suffered from one central defect: that it considered the future a blank tablet and the past a closed book. It forgot history, and thus failed to estimate how much novelty could occur in an historical process. Trying to find universal scientific rules, it tried to force the social sciences (and social phenomena) into a straitjacket of rules set by the physical sciences.

Our approach to the future: historicism and scenario-writing

Reflecting on this past experience, in this study we start by emphasising that the future is a continuation of history. We do not claim to forecast or foresee the future, nor do we claim to dictate it. (This we will discuss further in Chapter 3.) Rather, we want to discover as much as we can about it; to initiate a process of mutual education with a European public, so that via the dialectic of debate we can improve understanding. We hope in this way to stimulate further research on alternative futures. We approach the problem as a group of social scientists by trying to harness our resources of imagination. And we do this by starting to write scenarios of future European history.

In Chapter 3, we go on to discuss some basic theoretical problems in this approach – and their practical solution. But before we do this, we need to put Europe within the framework of the future world. In the next chapter, therefore, we start with a look at the world of the recent past, and go on to develop alternative scenarios for the future of international relations.

The method of scenario-writing has been used in many other futures studies. But different futurists have used it in quite different ways, and it is important at the start to distinguish these (Table 1.1). There is a fundamental distinction between *exploratory scenarios*, which start from the present and try to project present trends in a logical fashion into the future, with variations produced by altering the parameters, and *anticipatory scenarios* which start from a realistic desired image or images of the future, described in terms of a number of objectives to be realised. In the sense in which French futurists use the word (France: Datar 1975) only these latter scenarios are truly 'prospective' – though exploratory scenarios may

Table 1.1 Four types of scenario

	Type of Scenario	Aim(s) of Scenario	Premises of Scenario	Procedures used
Exploratory Scenarios	1. Tendential Scenario	Seek to determine a possible future	Suppose that 'heavy trends' are permanent and predominant	Examine the continuation in the future of these trends and the mechanisms which explain them
	2. Framework Scenario	Try to delimit the space of range of possible futures	Suppose that 'heavy trends' are permanent and predominant	Make very varied (extreme) hypotheses concerning the evolution of these trends
Anticipatory Scenarios	3. Normative Scenario	Seek to produce an image of a future that is possible and 'desirable' Establish a procedure relating the future to the present	Suppose that we can determine at the outset a range of possible objectives to achieve	Make a synthesis of these objectives to achieve and relate this image of the future to the present
	4. Contrasted Scenario	Outline a 'desirable' future located at the frontier of possibilities	Suppose that we can determine at the outset a range of possible objectives to achieve relating to the objectives desired	Make a synthesis of objectives to achieve and related this image of the future to the present

Source: France:Datar (1975)

be used to establish the limits of the feasible.

Different scenario writers have used different kinds of scenarios. Thus Herman Kahn's scenarios are decidedly exploratory: history runs unidimensionally and the future resembles the past; causality is linear and quasi-automatic; and alternative values are excluded. At the other extreme Hans Ozbekhan's method uses values specifically to define objectives; the planner is concerned with planning the present in order to reach a preferred future; so a scenario is merely a step in the process of prospective planning. But interestingly, though Ozbekhan's scenario-writing is fundamentally of the anticipatory kind, he also uses exploratory scenarios for preliminary analysis, to serve as an input into later anticipatory scenarios which are finally evaluated and fused into a normative scenario (France: Datar 1975, pp. 43-48).

Our method is also eclectic. The scenarios we now develop in Chapters 2 and 3 are largely exploratory; some assume the continuation of certain heavy trends of the recent past, others allow for parametric variations. They are used to provide a resulting problem landscape of the late 1970s and 1980s, in Chapter 4. But then, by examining the major problem areas in greater detail, in Chapters 5-11, we try to work explicitly towards a statement, not of alternative *values* as such, but rather of a different *rationality* which could provide a sharp break with the exploratory scenarios and their consequences. This is the main burden of the last chapter, which is explicitly concerned with exploratory scenarios.

The structure of this book

The basic structure of this book is therefore simple. In the next two chapters, *Chapters 2 and 3*, we develop our alternative exploratory scenarios – in Chapter 2 for the world in which Europe will find a place, in Chapter 3 for Europe in itself. Building on these, *Chapter 4* tries to outline the problem landscape of the future Europe: the range of problems which we think will arise from a continuation of the present heavy trend. These are problems of the medium term – the Europe of the late 1980s and early 1990s. They take the form of contradictions, particularly between human aspirations and needs on the one hand and existing social and institutional structures on the other. We think that the Europeans of that age will be centrally concerned with these contradictions, and will be devoting time and energy to their resolution. Then, in *Chapters 5 to 10*, we examine each of these problem areas in detail. They bear only an indirect relationship to the four projects of *Plan Europe 2000*; though Chapter

5 draws on the agriculture project, Chapter 6 on the urbanisation project, Chapter 7 on the industry project and Chapter 8 on the education project, these chapters are in no sense summaries of the outcomes of the projects. Rather, they start from the research findings, and represent the Integration Committee's own discussion of these results.

The discussion of these key problem areas, and of others, leads to a general conclusion; that behind all these manifestations is a deeper phenomenon of alienation: which leads to a possible response on the part of Europeans of the 1980s and 1990s in the development of a new form of rationality, a new way of looking at the world. This is the subject of *Chapter 11*. Finally, in *Chapter 12*, we try in a very tentative way to sketch out some possible consequences of adopting such a new world view. Thus we lead from scenarios to medium-term problems, and from deeper analysis of those problems to possible solutions.

One final word of warning and of justification. Chapter 12 contains no 'solutions', in the sense of a prescription for Europe's developing ills. This is because we believe that no single solution can exist. Rather, we are attempting to suggest some ways in which Europeans themselves will come to view their problems. The readers of this book may find our analysis vague or incorrect or positively pernicious, in which case they will want to suggest alternatives. That is the essence of the educative process we want to begin through this book.

CHAPTER 2

Future International Scenarios: Europe in a Transformed World

Our premise, set out in Chapter 1 and now to be developed in the present chapter and the next, is that the future can best be grasped by understanding the past. Historical trends, properly understood, set close limits to the possibilities of human action. The first essential, therefore, is to understand the role of Europe in the world during the recent past – and, in particular, the way in which that role has changed. From this it will be possible to set out a number of divergent but consistent and plausible future scenarios.

The world we have left

For a quarter-century after 1945, international relations were marked by an extraordinary basic stability. Despite superficial signs of perturbation and crisis, the world order remained fixed in the mould which had been set at Yalta in 1944 and at Potsdam in 1945. Those historic meetings divided the world in general – and Europe in particular – into two spheres of influence, dominated by the new superpowers that emerged in the final stages of World War Two. The United States was to dominate the whole of the western hemisphere, the Pacific Ocean and western Europe; the USSR was to hold sway over eastern Europe, her own vast landmass, and a China that was already passing under communist control. Though after 1945 there were crises concerning disputed peripheral areas at the margins of the two spheres – Berlin in 1948, Vietnam in 1954 and again in 1964-72, Cuba in 1961 – the remarkable feature was truly how well the basic division was honoured on both sides; as witness the passivity of the west during the 1968 Russian invasion of Czechoslovakia and the Russian withdrawal of rocket bases from Cuba.

One principal result of that division was the removal of effective international power from Europe. Up to 1914, and even very much up to 1939, the superpowers of the world were the major nation states of Europe: Britain, France, Germany, Russia. Only one of these, peripheral to Europe, kept that status after 1945. The others suffered catastrophic loss of power and influence due to the loss of empire and the wealth that came from it, the destruction and indebtedness resulting from the war, and the defeat and division of Germany. Slowly and painfully, in the decade after 1945, far-seeing European statesmen – Churchill, Schuman, Adenauer – built up a new concept of European cooperation and even European unity. Treaties, conventions, pacts were quickly signed in the areas of military and economic cooperation: the Treaty of Washington creating what later became OECD, the Treaty of Brussels for military cooperation, the convention establishing the Council of Europe, the Atlantic Treaty, and finally the Treaty of Paris establishing the European Coal and Steel Community, all were signed between 1946 and 1951. Clearly, these agreements were designed to rebuild the strength of Europe in both the military and the economic fields. They recognised that this could be achieved only by sinking national differences; in the age of the superpowers, the nation states of Europe could not individually count. And, in the Atlantic Treaty, Europe seemed to be recognising that it must throw in its lot with that of the United States.

But two separate and conflicting concepts of Europe were already emerging. The European Coal and Steel Community had a clearly federal character, giving to its Assembly the kinds of powers normally reserved to a national parliament; the Council of Europe was in essence confederal, depending on unanimous acceptance of its resolutions. And this contradiction between two concepts – one of federal institutions developed for limited and defined purposes, the other of a confederal Europe of nation states – persisted in the two following decades. The 1952 Treaty of Paris, establishing a European Defence Community, foundered in 1954 when the French National Assembly rejected it because of the federal character of its institutions. The 1957 Rome Treaty establishing EEC and Euratom, and resulting from years of preparation by dedicated federalists such as Jean Monnet, soon ran foul of the equally determined anti-federal stance of President de Gaulle. In the Gaullist philosophy, the sole European reality was the nation states; all hint of federalism was denounced and denied; no EEC institution could have power of its own, since that power was reserved to the Council of Ministers representing the states; at most the states should cooperate in matters political, economic, cultural and military. The federalists, still committed to the ultimate ideal of a

European executive and a parliament elected by direct suffrage, compromised because they could see that in the early 1960s the time was not yet ripe.

This alone weakened the development of Europe as a third force. But equally detrimental was the fundamental rift between those who saw Europe as the natural partner of the United States in an Atlantic Alliance and the partisans of an independent Europe – again headed by de Gaulle. The Gaullist view, interestingly, was that the world might move towards federalism – but not on a European basis. Meanwhile, the states should retain their independence in international matters – in relation to the United States as much as to one another.

Thus, right down to the end of the 1960s, Europe failed to restore the place it had held on the world stage before 1939. One reason – the division down the middle of the continent – appeared almost permanent. True, the states of eastern Europe retained their individuality and a substantial measure of independence in the management of their internal affairs; true also, Brandt's *Ostpolitik* led at last by the early 1970s to more normal relations between east and west and to a great increase in trade which, ironically, exposed the states of eastern Europe to the fluctuations of late capitalism. But in larger matters of international relations there could be no doubt that eastern Europe remained and remains part of the Russian sphere. The only prospect of an independent European power, therefore, lay in the west – in the enlarged EEC of the early 1970s. And, for the reasons already given, that power was still merely latent.

Scenarios for the future: (1) Europe suppressed, or survival of the two blocs

We now want to develop alternative scenarios. The ones we set out below seem to us the most plausible. But they are not the only ones; and readers may want to produce alternatives.

For the next quarter century, one plausible hypothesis is that there will be no fundamental change to the familiar world of the 1950s and 1960s: the division of Europe into two spheres of influence, the American and the Russian, will remain. That view has much evidence in support. American world influence, as measured by its military defeat in Vietnam, has been countered by the diplomatic victory in the Middle East; and the fate of the Strategic Arms Limitation Talks still fundamentally hinges upon American and Russian agreement. American diplomacy under

Kissinger has committed itself to a policy of détente, whereby both superpowers could reduce the relative burden of their arms expenditure while at the same time guarding against the development of rival powers. Though this might lead to nominal reductions in the American military presence in Europe, the fundamental division between the two spheres would remain; and it could always be defended, if need be, by an armoury of sophisticated weapons.

But from within Europe itself such a comfortably simple view meets with increasing criticism, and it is interesting that the substance is essentially the same whether it comes from the conservative right or the radical left: that American hold on Europe must weaken because (despite a recent upturn) American economic strength is becoming progressively enfeebled. As a French study brutally put it: 'America is running out of breath while the others grow' (France: Datar 1974, p.16). This study, like many others from French official and unofficial sources, convincingly demonstrates that, while in 1950 the United States was producing 70 per cent of the total GNP of the western bloc, by 1970 the figure was down to 49 per cent and was still falling. Some Marxist critics go further, with a structuralist analysis which argues that America is losing its traditional advantage of economies of scale due to the building-up of the internal European and Japanese markets; while in important fields – such as car manufacture in Europe or electronics in Japan – the leadership in technological innovation has also passed from American hands (Rawthorn 1973, Mandel 1970).

Interestingly, though, there are analysts both on the right and on the left who reject this view. The United States, in their opinion, retains a permanent advantage from its great economies of scale, its massive supplies of natural resources and foodstuffs, its returns from large-scale accumulative investment in the past, and the resulting capacity to withstand almost indefinitely a weak balance-of-payments situation (Krause 1973); and they are supported by evidence that in the late 1970s the American balance-of-payments were again improving. Left-wing commentators add a gloss to this argument: that all national capitalist systems form a cohesive and interpenetrated bloc under the sponsorship of the United States, which also acts as a guarantor against internal subversion (Poulantzas 1973). Thus, though Europe is expanding faster than the United States, this is happening, not despite the Americans, but because of their support; and, in the event of a crisis, European economic and political elites would act in support of American intervention, since they are not united enough to stand on their own.

However, this in turn ignores another fact: the internal political conflict within the United States. Since the Vietnam fiasco, American politicians of all shades have become increasingly suspicious of international commitments that could prove open-ended – as the reaction towards the Angolan situation, in early 1976, clearly demonstrates. If it were necessary to go on pouring funds into a country to save it from communism, the funds might not be forthcoming. As Angola and also metropolitan Portugal show, the problem for the future is less likely to be full-scale armed conflict on the Vietnam model than a combination of extreme civil unrest and guerilla warfare. Such disruption is by no means improbable in parts of Europe in the coming decades, as we shall later try to demonstrate. It represents perhaps the greatest threat to the kind of foreign policy America has tried to pursue since World War Two – and perhaps to the détente itself. For, finally, given the volatile nature of American politics, the likelihood would be a backlash led by a successful politician who stressed America's increasing world isolation and encirclement. And this could logically result in a demand for a return to the fortress concept of the Cold War, especially if, as we later argue, substantial parts of Europe fall to Communist or separatist left-wing governments.

Scenarios for the future: (2) One Europe, or Europe united by challenge

This, in somewhat simplified form, is the essence of a debate that still continues. But a fundamental problem is that both sides are extrapolating from the experiences of the 1960s: the reality of the 1970s is different. Until recently, economic forces seem to have been the determining factors in international relations; and it could comfortably be assumed that economic growth would continue to be the stimulus for national development, as in the past. Neither right-wing nor left-wing commentators seem to have allowed for the possibility of a fundamental shift in relationships due to the rise of such new forces as the major raw material producers or the nations within the east European Soviet bloc. Nor do they seem to have recognised the changes that were beginning to occur in capitalist countries due to pressures from organised labour. Associated with these failures, they have neglected to speculate that in the future individual nation states might react to new challenges in an original way – causing perhaps a fundamental shift in the geography of power.

The starting-point of this scenario is that the countries of the west

Table 2.1 Growth of real GNP in seven major countries

Real GNP

		Weights in total[a]	Average 1959-60 to 1971-72	From previous year			From previous half-year			
							1974		1975	
				1973	1974	1975	I	II	I	II
Percentage changes	Canada (GNP)	3.7	5.0	6.9	2.8	−¼	3.3	−0.5	−2¾	5½
Seasonally adjusted	United States (GNP)	40.0	4.1	5.9	−2.1	−3¾	−3.4	−3.7	−8	5
at annual rates	Japan (GNP)	12.9	11.0	9.9	−1.8	1½	−5.8	3.1	−1	5
Estimates and	France (GDP)	8.0	5.8	6.5	3.9	1	4.3	2.5	0	1½
forecasts	Germany (GNP)	10.9	4.9	5.3	0.4	−2	0.9	−1.7	−4½	3
	Italy (GDP)	4.3	5.5	6.3	3.4	−2¾	6.0	−7.0	−1½	−1½
	United Kingdom (GDP)	5.4	3.1	5.2	−0.2	½	−3.0	5.4	0	−2¾
	Total of above countries	85.3	5.5	6.5	−0.6	−1¾	−1.7	−1.3	−4¾	3½
	Other OECD countries	14.7	5.3	5.3	2.7	1¾	−	−	−	−
	Total OECD	100.0	5.4	6.3	−0.1	−1½	−0.9	−1.0	−4	3¼
	Total OECD excluding United States	60.0	6.3	6.6	1.2	¼	0.8	0.8	−1¼	2¼

[a] 1973 weights and exchange rates.

Source: OECD (1975b)

will face quite new challenges, both externally from the rise of the developing primary producer countries, and internally from the strength of organised labour. Certainly, in the mid-1970s all these countries seemed to be sharing in some degree the melancholy experience of high wage rates, low profits and low investment levels, with no compensation for higher wages bills in the form of higher profitability through increased turnover. The consequence is low growth levels and a balance of payments problem. This is most evident in weak economies such as Britain's and Italy's, as can be seen from Table 2.1. However, low profitability – the first signs of a structural weakness – is now a feature of strong economies such as Germany's. Indeed, because of its dependence on manufactured goods vulnerable to competition, Germany could suffer a structural economic crisis some time in the 1980s.

The orthodox economic view is that this is a temporary cyclical phenomenon – albeit with some odd features which it will be difficult to remedy without great social strain. But many analysts argue that the problem is longer-term and structural: in their view, it becomes progressively more difficult to pass wage rises on to the consumer, so that there are falling rates of profit save in a few cases of pure monopolistic industry. And the traditional Keynesian remedy – injecting money into the public services – proves increasingly ineffectual because it actually reduces demand for the marketable products of industry and thus further cuts profits, as analysis of the disastrous British record clearly shows (Bacon and Eltis 1976). Demand thus no longer serves the function of stimulating the private sector, which can be revived only by the injection of cheap state capital – a remedy now advocated by left-wing Labour Party members in Britain. The danger is that, starting in weak economies, this syndrome will spread throughout the European system via failures of demand for imports from other industrial countries.

In any event, it now appears that some of the more highly developed European national economies – Switzerland, Belgium, Germany – are following the United States and Britain in a well-marked trend: increasingly, instead of exporting manufactured goods they are exporting capital. True, in this regard they are still some way behind: in 1971, for instance, Germany's foreign investment represented only 18 per cent of the value of direct exports, as compared with 195 per cent for the United States or 80 per cent for Britain. But the percentage had doubled in the previous decade, as compared with an increase of only 16 per cent for the United States. True also, a large part of the investment – currently about 60 per cent – goes into other European countries. But about 30 per cent goes to the Third World, and the evidence is that this is increasing as the era of cheap European labour comes to an end. Ford, for instance, has moved its small car division from Germany to Japan. Some observers, such as R.N. Cooper, believe that European countries could, like the United States, exist indefinitely on these investments, obviating the need to produce (Cooper 1973). But this ignores two points: it does not solve the problem of unemployment in the manufacturing plants which may be deserted – particularly by the multi-nationals; and it assumes that the Third World will remain content to pay tribute to the west in this way – a dangerous assumption in the light of the lessons of the 1973-4 energy crisis.

None of this spells the immediate Armageddon of the late-capitalist, welfare-state society of western Europe. But it does suggest that the individual national economies of Europe must confront a far more uncertain future in the late 1970s and 1980s than they did in the entire thirty years after World War Two. Faced with this challenge, they might react by increasing protectionism – a response we examine in Chapter 3. But equally, the new age of crisis could actually act as a fillip to the further development of European cooperation and even unity.

This scenario is based on two postulates. First, it is argued that the very process of economic development in other parts of the world, engendered in part through western capital export – in the Middle East, in parts of South America and South Asia, in Eastern Europe – will create a demand for imports of western goods, especially capital equipment of a sophisticated kind. Secondly, it is posited that Europe can exploit this challenge, in competition with the United States, only if it exploits fully its potential advantages of economies of scale and of technical cooperation. Europe, the argument runs, has a very advanced and sophisticated technology which in many fields could fully compete with the American product – if it could be properly organised. American science-based industry had depended first on the demands of its huge high-income home market, and secondly – especially since World War Two – on the stimulus from defence and space exploration. Europe now potentially has a similar unitary home market; what it lacks is the stimulus to technological leadership. Therefore, it achieves less research and development than, on the basis of its wealth and accumulated knowledge, it should; and where it does venture it too often emerges with expensive failures, as in the notorious case of Concorde. Yet in many fields – in aviation, in information systems, in ocean exploration and exploitation, in atomic or solar energy, in telecommunications – it could play a leading role. And these are the areas where the most advanced industrial nations could retain an unchallenged place in the international division of labour, long after the countries of the Third World have successfully competed in the production of more mundane durable consumer goods like motor cars or television sets. But, as the evidence of failure so far abundantly proves, it cannot be done by individual national efforts: it requires European companies in the fields of aviation, computers, energy. And, on a more mundane level, it needs steady progress in all kinds of technical cooperation and standardisation.

This would suggest a quite striking enhancement of the role of EEC institutions. And the same lesson emerges in the fields of finance and macro-economic management. Here too, Europe has so far failed to play the world role that history, tradition and accumulated expertise would suggest. Though London, Zurich, Frankfurt, Paris are among the recognised top financial centres of the world, it cannot be said that they exert a proportionate influence on the resolution of the world economic crisis of the 1970s. Particularly this has been true of the relations between Europe and the Third World, which must be set on a more stable basis if the world economic system is to be set right. But here there is already a strong suggestion of change: British, French and now Portuguese decolonisation; the entry of Britain into the EEC, which greatly increased the number of ex-colonies interested in an association with the Common Market; the reduction of tarrif barriers agreed at the first conference of Yaoundé; the disequilibrium in the terms of trade between industrialised countries and primary producers which threatened to block possibilities of economic development – all these forces led to the Lomé Agreements of 1975, which are one of the most important developments in international relations of recent years, albeit little recognised. They establish a new basis for relations between Europe and the developing world through the establishment of a European Development Fund, the stabilisation of export earnings to allow better sequencing of development, and industrial cooperation and technical transfers. On these points there is now, apparently, almost total unanimity between the EEC and 46 developing nations in Africa, the Caribbean and the Pacific. Dedicated Europeans see the Lomé agreements as the most important step taken by the EEC since its creation – far exceeding in importance anything achieved in this field by the United States, or the USSR, or the United Nations – notwithstanding the special Drawing Rights, the World Bank, the United National Development Fund, and even UNESCO. The responsibilities of the

Community are no longer restricted to Europe; the EEC is now, apparently irreversibly, a great world power.

If this argument is accepted, it still leaves open some vital unanswered questions concerning Europe's relations with the older power blocs. The Soviet Union realistically appreciates that the possibilities of a widespread communist take-over in western Europe are low; and indeed may not even wish it, since this would multiply its own problems of relating to national communist governments. But it recognises that national communist parties may want actively to foment revolution, and even in some cases to support their cause – as, evidently, in Portugal. A communist take-over by democratic means is a plausible scenario in Italy, Spain and perhaps France – whether Russia wishes it or not. But such regimes might find it advantageous to align themselves economically with the west – even to the extent of a commitment to the EEC. In any event, the USSR needs technical cooperation with EEC nations which alone can provide the managerial and technical sophistication she still lacks. And clearly, it prefers a strong independent Europe to a Europe under American domination. The United States, conversely, must see a united Europe as marginally less open to American economic penetration – though the precise degree of that possibility is hard to gauge. But on the other hand, over a thirty-year period, the United States has associated its own defence, apparently inexorably, with that of western Europe – and vice-versa. However much a united Europe may now seek independence in this regard, its freedom of action is narrowly circumscribed.

In the European federalist scenario, therefore, Europe becomes an economic world power through exploitation of its latent financial and technological capacities. In the process, the old distinction between a federal Europe and a confederal Europe becomes increasingly blurred. There is a major extension of the role of the central EEC institutions by universal suffrage. But the individual nation states are left in full control of the areas they had not surrendered to the Community. The other historic European dilemma – whether it could become completely independent of the United States in a military as well as an economic sense – would still be answered in the negative. But perhaps the relationship might become a more equal one.

Some radical and Marxist critics might see this, at least in part, as utopian: a bureaucratic wish rather than a prediction based on actual historical trends. But, insofar as Europe is moving towards agreement with a substantial part of the Third World, it may represent a feasible answer to the challenge of the mid-1970s

economic crisis. Certainly, many non-aligned nations might prefer
cooperation with Europe to domination by either of the two historic
superpowers; particularly since so many of them are moving
towards their own conception of socialism, very different in kind
either from American corporate capitalism or Russian corporate
communism. Thus one plausible scenario for *Europe 2000* is the
development of a completely new, and very powerful, third force
comprising Europe plus much of the Third World.

The unknown factor is the reaction of the United States. There,
both the major industrial unions and the farm lobby are likely to
react in hostile fashion to the idea of a new economic bloc. The
American multi-national corporations are likely to see a particular
threat. Thus any American government may be driven into reaction.
The most likely form will be a threat to withdraw, or at least reduce,
defence commitments. This could be a serious threat to Germany –
and also to Italy, where the Christian Democrats depend on
American support vis-à-vis the Communist Party. Yet if it reacts in
this way, the United States runs the risk of harming a long-standing
set of relationships. And if it tries to throw more of the economic
burden of NATO on to its European partners, Europe in turn may
react by increasing protectionism.

America has of course other, less direct weapons. The influence of
the multinationals is much greater than their modest 6.5 per cent
share of industrial turnover (in 1971) would suggest, since they have
a large degree of technical monopoly which Europe will not easily
break. But any attempt to use this power might in turn bring forth
reaction from the Europeans. The labour unions are strong, and in
most cases intensely suspicious of what they see as the machinations
of the multinationals. So there is a strong argument for believing
that more protectionism is likely. The question is whether this could
be internalised within a stronger, part-federal EEC, or whether that
body would tend to fragmentation under the pressures. We should
now turn to look at this latter possibility.

Scenarios for the future: (3) A Europe of nations

The starting point for this scenario is the undisputed continuing
strength of the nation state: neither the federal movement on the one
hand, nor the regional movement on the other, has yet significantly
weakened its position. Indeed, its strengths are too often ignored: it
alone has sovereignty, or the legal power of the army, the police and
the courts; it alone represents for most people the largest collectivity
to which they owe allegiance. Doubtless, this position can and may

be eroded somewhat; and we discuss possibilities later. But for the time being, we ask how changes in the international economic relations will affect the responses of national governments and national elites. Here we make a basic assumption: responses to a postulated no-growth situation with increased competition from the Third World and Communist world will not arise due to any fear of external threat; relations between states are too finely balanced for that. There is a common tacit understanding that nations will not precipitate a third world war or the threat of nuclear annihilation; Vietnam, for example, has shown just how prolonged and debilitating a limited war might be. And, as we already noted, the division of Europe into spheres is generally accepted.

Therefore, national governments will respond rather in a short-term, adaptive way to internal influences from pressure groups, which pursue their sectional interests, and adjust to changes in the world economic picture. The most important aim these groups will follow is the protection of the standard of living of their members – particularly their security of employment and their income. So foreign policy will be conducted in large degree according to economic criteria: the stronger the country is economically, the greater its power on the world stage – including the power of economic infiltration.

But one must enter a caveat here, for there is a contradiction. On the one hand, economic factors dominate because of the futility of resorting to arms; but, on the other, pure military strength still carries some weight. Nations with a strong armoury, such as the United States and (on a much smaller scale) France, ultimately carry greater weight than nations having little armed power such as Germany or Japan. And countries such as Germany, or to a less extent Britain, which have stressed economic power rather than arms, may find themselves in a relatively weak position. (Ironically, Britain reduced her arms burden when she found she could not afford it; then the economic campaign for economic strength failed too.) So it should not be assumed that the relative economic decline of the United States will be followed neatly by a decline in international power or status.

This is particularly so because the individual European nation state could not hope to compete with the United States or the USSR, either in armed power or in aggregate economic strength. Indeed, this was one of the strongest reasons for positing the scenario of a united Europe. But no one should doubt that, if they so determined, most countries could retreat into selective protectionism, seeking to protect their own position via bilateral agreements on the model of

Hjalmaar Schacht's policy for the Nazi regime in the mid-1930s. (By these selective agreements, Germany got guaranteed sources of vital foods and raw materials but the primary producers in turn got guaranteed markets. Nowadays, of course, they might not be so desperate to find them.) There is already strong evidence that this could be a likely outcome – such as the dissensions within the EEC, and between the EEC and the United States, on the subject of oil supplies; or the transgressions of the community's agricultural policy by both France and Italy.

But it does not imply a full-scale trade war. Limited agreements among and between European countries may well be necessary to safeguard raw material supplies, and these may be sufficient to keep a somewhat weakened EEC in existence. And there may well be a continuing need for common defence agreements: the remnants of Cold War suspicion, military and arms lobbies, the need for bargaining counters in negotiations with Third World countries and pure prestige considerations should all guarantee that. Therefore, the likely outcome under this scenario is a series of strictly limited bilateral or tripartite agreements dealing with particular commodity exchanges – whether within Europe, or vis-à-vis the outside world – conducted against a constant background of diplomatic manoeuvre between the USA and USSR, which, however, may by then have lost much of its significance for the rest of Europe.

All this assumes that the European nation states remain fully sovereign and powerful entities: but there is the final possibility that the state will be weakened, not from above through the development of federal institutions, but from below through the revolt of peripheral regions. This possibility had become so potentially great by the mid-1970s that it must be taken seriously indeed.

Scenarios for the future: (4) A Europe of regions, or the revolt of the regional periphery

'Centre' and 'periphery' are terms of rich ambiguity. To regional geographers and regional planners they have a fairly limited geographic connotation, referring to the striking differences in post-1945 Europe between the rapid development of the industrial heartland or Golden Triangle (Birmingham-Milan-Dortmund) and the decay of the peripheral rural regions of Europe's coastal peninsulae or mountain frontiers (northern Norway, the Scottish Highlands, Ireland, Brittany, the Massif Central, Ardennes-Eifel, Pays Basques and Pyrenees, Böhmerwald-Bayrischer Wald, Mezzogiorno). To one school of regional development planning, they express also the concentration of political power and entrepreneurial innovation in the metropolitan heartland – a concentration exceedingly difficult for the periphery to break. To Marxist analysts of the new school, they express contradictions in the development of class relations between one nation and another and between one region and another, whereby the older notion of imperialism may be reinterpreted to apply within – as well as between – nations.

Whatever the interpretation, most analysts could agree on certain facts. There is a centre-periphery contrast in modern Europe: the Golden Triangle contains a small fraction of the total area of the enlarged EEC plus EFTA, but it accounts for half its population and more than two-thirds of its total production. And in almost every individual country levels of economic development tend to be lowest in those regions farthest removed from the metropolitan cores. In these distant mountain or peninsular areas, distance has joined with difficulty of access and sometimes with cultural distinctions to hold back development; the poorer the country, the more striking is this distinction, so that the relative difference between Milan and the Mezzogiorno is much greater than that between Oslo and northern Norway. Further, since the peripheral regions of the poor Mediterranean nations are on average much more densely populated than those of the rich north, these differences affect relatively large numbers of people: southern Italy has 40 per cent of the national area and 38 per cent of the national population, but contributed only 25 per cent of the national income in 1968.

Beginning in the 1920s, but even more evident since the late 1950s, a new kind of peripheral area may additionally be identified within Europe: the nineteenth-century heavy industrial region, dependent on coal and steel and heavy engineering, which has lost its economic raison d'être due to the working out of natural resources and the competition of modern industry elsewhere. Britain first experienced this problem and the classic cases – central Scotland, Belfast, north-east England, Merseyside – are still to be found there. The Mons-Charleroi-Liège and the Limburg coalfields of Benelux, the Ruhrgebiet in Germany, and the Pas de Calais in France, are more recent additions. Though some are peripheral in the strict geographical sense, others are ironically located within the prosperous heartland, forming islands of economic distress.

Almost everywhere in Europe since World War Two, active national policies have been developed to aid such regions: the Casa per il Mezzogiorno in Italy, the Assisted Areas programme in Britain, the French *métropoles d'équilibre* designed to aid the development of southern and western France, the *Bundesausbaugebiete* and *Bundesausbauorte* of Federal Germany. And, beginning with the European Coal and Steel Community in the early 1950s, European institutions have increasingly concerned themselves with the problem. But the main impact has been at the national scale, and this is not surprising, for in many cases national political parties draw important regional support from such regions, and in this regard neither the Left nor the Right has a monopoly: the Christian Socialist Party, running-mates of the CDU, have an important base in the mountain areas of the Bavarian-Czech border, the British Labour Party depends on Scottish and Welsh manual workers, the German SDP draws strength from the Ruhrgebiet, the Italian Christian Democrats look to the votes of the Mezzogiorno. It was hardly surprising, therefore, that once the problem was explicit the political parties should have sought to divert aid to these regions. But all the evidence indicates that it has invariably failed to halt economic decline or population drift. And, beginning around 1970, there has been quite a new political factor to contend with.

This is the development of highly militant regional separatist movements in Scotland, in Brittany, in the Pays Basques, in Corsica. Where democratic political outlets are available, they show dramatic gains at the ballot box – as in Scotland. Where they are not, then well organised and tightly disciplined terrorist movements may develop – as in Spain, or, in a more complex context, Northern Ireland. The point is that in every recorded case they seem to command widespread local support. In conventional political terms, they may appear in any part of the political spectrum from extreme left to extreme right; in terms of political backing, they may range from middle class to heavily proletarian; but many of them defy simple analysis in terms of conventional classes.

Not all the peripheries react in this way. In some, the local populations may accept the situation, bought off perhaps by remittances from the centre. Large parts of the depressed peripheries of France and Germany and of the assisted areas of Britain fall into this category – though in the latter, one sign is the existence of a large urban under-class destined for almost permanent high unemployment. Others, such as the Italian south, may actually receive massive assistance at the expense of the high-wage industrial workers at the centre (that is, Europe's Golden Triangle) – in the form of new industry, relative freedom from pollution control and a concentration of new infrastructure. The strength of the reaction seems to depend in part on the sense of regional identity, which will be stronger in areas that were once nations (Scotland), or are highly peripheral and remote (Corsica), or have a strong regional culture (Brittany). It can also be fanned by the presence of valuable raw materials, such as Scotland's oil, or by a reaction to apparent colonisation either from abroad (American capital in Scotland and Ireland) or from the metropolitan heartland (Citroën in Brittany). And lastly, of course, it will relate to the form and the strength of the reaction from the political elites in the national capitals.

This reaction is unlikely to be very welcoming. Central or national political parties will see their traditional bases of power – the Christian Democrats in the Mezzogiorno, the Labour Party in Wales and Scotland – fatally eroded by nationalist movements. Similarly, national high-level bureaucracies will see their authority and power threatened by regional elites. The success of regional movements could in practice only mean the development of autonomous centres of production in the provinces, threatening existing concentrations: the bigger corporations, whether private or public, are hardly likely to look on this threat with equanimity. And, at a time when national politicans and bureaucrats are faced with a loss of power to the institutions of the European Communities, they are not likely to countenance a simultaneous sacrifice in the opposite direction. But it should not be assumed that, conversely, the organs of the EEC would look favourably on the separatist movements: for potentially their autonomy is threatened too, and for the time being they depend totally on the agreement of national elites for the delegation of powers to Brussels, Luxembourg or Strasbourg.

For there is an extremely intractable problem here, and comfortable words like 'delegation' merely tend to obscure it. Power has by definition to be located somewhere: in the final analysis, it cannot be shared. Either, therefore, delegation is a paper exercise, meaning relatively little; or it involves a fundamental transfer of power from the nation states, which have exercised it for periods ranging from one century to ten, back to the constituent provinces from which they were formed. The powers that matter here include foreign policy, fiscal policy, macro-management of the economy, and control over central policy matters in fields such as education, housing or welfare. The experience of federal states, such as Western Germany, shows that some of these powers – especially the last group – may be detached and given to provinces; but there is some evidence even there that the powers of the Länder are weakening (Eversley in Craven 1975, p.54). But most of the peripheral movements are seeking much more than that: they want either the creation of an autonomous state (as in the Basque provinces) or union with another country (as in Northern Ireland). It could be argued, rather cynically, that by divesting themselves of these areas, nation states might strengthen themselves rather than the reverse: for, cases like Scotland apart, they tend to be thinly populated, conspicuously poorer than the heartlands, and a drain on the total national resources. But the political realities already described temper that realism; and they are fortified by a kind of internal domino theory, which suggests that if one area attains devolution the rest of the country may begin to fall apart. This was in 1975 the fear of many British politicians, who saw the English provinces going the way of Wales and Scotland.

The final reaction to the peripheral revolt is difficult to gauge. Centripetal forces are still strong; they could often afford to respond to irritation by rejecting their peripheries – and the economic burden they so often bring. Central elites may withstand even long-continued terrorist campaigns for devolution, as the British experience shows. But in one important sense this is a game the centre can never win. There is an apparently inexhaustible supply of activists willing to dedicate themselves to such causes; and it does not take many to make an army. All the evidence indicates that private armies will be able to make more and more effective and destructive weapons – including, perhaps, nuclear ones by the 1980s and 1990s. There is a risk of escalation, too, because of the obvious attraction of such movements to pure gangster or psychologically-disturbed elements in society. True, the centre will doubtless respond by ever more effective counter-intelligence services and low-intensity operations. But the price, whether in terms of hard resources or in loss of basic freedoms, may be thought too high to pay. Further, these movements can always respond by the alternative of sit-ins or general strikes – which can prove devastatingly effective. And for every political party that needs to retain the periphery because it draws support from it, there is usually another with diametrically opposite calculations. The Italian left would gain from the loss of the Mezzogiorno; the British Conservative party from the loss of Scotland and Wales. Therefore, the likelihood is that at some stage – marked by exhaustion and the electoral victory of one party – the peripheries will gain a substantial measure of devolution, coupled with a tighter degree of control by the central elite over the industrial heartland. After all, in many cases, the centre may feel that it has little to lose by releasing the periphery. Thus Europe 2000 may well be a mosaic of smaller states than Europe 1975. But if so, the problem of the economic weakness of the periphery will remain, and it will express itself as a battle for assistance – probably within the framework of the EEC, if that body survives as an effective resource-allocating entity.

This leads to a further possibility: that the periphery, however, defined, might form some kind of alliance – perhaps loose and informal, perhaps quite solid – against the centre. It could take the form of an alliance of regions. It could take the form of opposition by poor southern Europe to the more prosperous north. One possibility, for instance, could be a split of Spain into its constituent regions, fused with Portugal into an Iberian Federation and perhaps also with the Mezzogiorno into a federation of southern Europe. Such a movement would almost certainly be led by the left-wing groups and would contain a strong demand for fundamental changes in the economic and social order, which, if realised, could result in a break between a liberal (or social democrat) northern Europe and a left-wing (communist with or without fringe groups) south. There could also be left-wing governments, perhaps unaligned with either European bloc though partly integrated within the EEC, in areas like Scotland. This would spell the partial break-up of the EEC and certainly of any attempt to enlarge it. But, as already explained, it might well engender a fierce reaction from the United States; and it is not certain that it would be wholly acceptable to the Soviet Union, which is likely to depend for decades more on the export of technology from a strong EEC. It might, however, suit the aims of Russian diplomacy to keep a strong central bloc within the EEC, while progressively weakening the periphery by means of aid to local separatist movements. This then seems a plausible scenario.

Scenarios for the future: (5) Explosive change in Eastern Europe

The scenarios so far have assumed that Eastern Europe remains a relatively stable bloc under Soviet influence. This could be a wrong postulate. In 1953, 1956, 1968 and 1970, Eastern Europe was torn by popular uprisings which were controlled only by Russian intervention or by major political concessions or a combination of the two. It is always conceivable that in time to come further revolt could bring a major change and even lead to a weakening of Russian influence.

But it must be said that this seems for several reasons unlikely. First, eastern European society is fundamentally very conservative. Social stratification seems rigid, social mobility is slow and many attitudes have been conserved little changed from the late 1940s. This is particularly important in attitudes to the young, who are expected to know their place. Equally attitudes to women would horrify any self-respecting liberationist. By retaining the familiar elements of the intimate environment, these societies have tried to safeguard their adaptation to external changes. Post-revolution conservatism seems to be a powerful force with a long life of its own. Oddly, this seems to be even a barrier to the transmission of official values: it could be an even bigger barrier to the development of unconventional ones.

The spark that set off the Polish revolt of 1970 was working-class discontent at low wages and lack of basic foods and consumer goods. But this itself illustrates the basic embourgeoisement of the manual working class, who now appear to be as thoroughly committed to consumerism as their western European equivalents. The Baltic sea-coast riots toppled the Gomulka government: but the succeeding Gierek regime dealt with the situation by placing greater stress on satisfying consumer demands. And, in addition, authorities throughout eastern Europe connive at a widespread form of corruption whereby equipment and materials from the plant are used for private purposes. Thus the worker can obtain a good living without needing to work hard, and both the foremen and the government look the other way. Meanwhile, as in for example Poland, social security and sickness benefits escalate. Though strikes are illegal, irregular stoppages or go-slows take place.

All these phenomena are tolerated, first by the official myth of the rule of the working class, and secondly because the manual worker is deprived of all responsibility. Party planners are realists, and must recognise economic imperatives; as a result of the energy crisis, Polish miners have become an aristocracy against which the party would find it difficult to take sanctions.

Thus the intellectual and bureaucratic class, which has become an upper-middle-class group with a comfortable life style and bourgeois tastes, exists in uneasy compromise with the great mass of the manual working class. In most east European societies, it has learned how to make accommodations so as to prevent discontent expressing itself in open rebellion. Political dissatisfaction can simply reflect itself in low morale – and consequently in absenteeism, pilfering and poor quality of output. The ruling groups evidently find this a price worth paying for stability – even though it threatens the economic growth to which they are ideologically committed.

There might be a quantum change in this situation if workers' councils attained real power and learned how to use it. Such councils played a crucial role in the Hungarian revolution of 1956 and were prominent in Czechoslovakia about the time of the overthrow of Dubček. But in Yugoslavia, where they have the longest history, they tend in practice to be a device for the protection of workers' living standards, rather like a conservative trade union in western Europe. The evidence, then, is that the manual working class is fundamentally conservative and protectionist, as in the west. Only widespread use of migrant labour could alter this, and up to now this phenomenon has existed only on a miniscule scale in eastern Europe.

All in all, therefore, prospects for fundamental change in Eastern Europe appear almost non-existent. The most likely development is an increasing independence of national communist parties from Moscow: but they are likely to exercise that independence within limits, first because they are conscious of Russian military power, and second because in the last resort they depend on it for their own protection.

More likely, perhaps, is a gradual convergence of economic and social structures between eastern and western Europe. As we shall see in the next chapter, the economies of the west are dominated by increasing corporatism: a relationship between central state planning mechanisms and the relatively small number of major firms which make the great majority of all investments. These firms progressively base more and more of their critical decisions, not on an assessment of the market in traditional terms, but on agreements with the central planning agency to work within a broad framework of investment coordination and state aid. In this way they become by degrees less independent, more completely dependent on state patronage, and less readily distinguishable from the state enterprises of eastern Europe. This greatly eases the development of trading links and even economic cooperation between the two blocs. But, by linking the eastern economies ever more into the western international trading pattern, it increases the risk that the western economies will export recessions into socialist eastern Europe.

Scenarios for the future: (6) Some alternatives and a synthesis

This choice of scenarios has been deliberately selective – perhaps outrageously so. (As we said at the start, we hope that readers will be encouraged to supply others.) It has been Eurocentric, looking at shifts in the international power spectrum strictly from the viewpoint of European statesmen or diplomats. Thus it has ignored a number of developments that do not seem very obviously to affect Europe, such as the rise of Chinese power; and it has considered others only peripherally, from a European stance – as for instance the development of the Third World.

The Chinese arrival on the world stage is likely to have much the same effects on the coming thirty years as in the last ten. It will divert both the earlier superpowers, America and Russia, from their traditional areas of concern or of friction – particularly in Europe. The same goes for the development of the Middle Eastern bloc, where, despite great efforts, neither of the superpowers has been able to achieve a commanding place: a function perhaps of religious and cultural isolation. Here, indeed, a number of factors suggest that Europe may be better placed to forge close links; they include the mutual advantage of exchanging Arab oil for Western technology, the freedom from Israeli involvement either pro- or anti-, and the traditional cultural links such as those of France and Britain with Egypt, or France with the Lebanon, or Britain with the Gulf States. And the rapid development by the United States of the Alaskan North Slope, bringing a high degree of self-sufficiency in oil, will mean less of a seller's market for the OPEC countries by the 1980s – with a greater emphasis on sales to the traditional trading partner, western Europe.

From this mosaic of considerations, some trends stand out as likelier than others. From them, we can perhaps construct a most probable – or at any rate a least improbable – scenario. The superpowers will not retain the monolithic strength of the early postwar years; they will be diverted elsewhere, and for different reasons both are likely to have urgent problems of internal economic development. America will be less concerned with Europe than formerly, but it will not be able or willing to withdraw its military presence; the fundamental dividing line down the centre of Europe will remain, though the currents of trade and knowledge across it will increase. The leading nation states of Europe will continue as the basic units of power, but all – even the strongest – will face fundamental economic challenge arising from the need to compete with the manufactured products and cheap labour of the Third World. They may not rise to this challenge, especially in the cases of greatest structural weakness, such as Italy and Britain. But if they can, it will almost certainly be through technical cooperation under the umbrella of a strengthened EEC, coupled with preferential trade and development agreements with the countries of the Third World. Some of these nations, especially in the Mediterranean south, may acquire communist governments, but these may well prove independent of Moscow and even aligned to the west. At the same time, many nations will face a further – and in some cases very dangerous – challenge from strong political movements in their own mountainous or peninsular peripheries; and, though this challenge will be arduously resisted, the strong probability is that finally the outcome will be partial devolution. (And this could arise in an opposite way if the central powers decided that their peripheries were too troublesome and too economically burdensome.) Some of the new peripheral units, again, could have radical or left-wing governments, leading to a possible change in the political geography of western Europe. Though some may find it expedient to join economic groupings, others may profess a sturdy independence. The most likely Europe of the year 2000, then, is a loose confederation of nation states, including a number of small new arrivals, which have surrendered some of their powers to federal European organs; linked in turn to a loose federation of the countries of the Third World, via a series of trade and development agreements; but with many exceptions. Yet the route from our world to that world is rough and uncharted; and progress along it will doubtless be slow, faltering and treacherous.

CHAPTER 3

Future European Scenarios: Economy and Society in a Changing Europe

Our approach to the future, we stress again, is historicist. True, the whole concept of historicism suffered a massive onslaught in the mid-1950s from Karl Popper and has never quite recovered from it (Popper 1957a). Historicism, in Popper's words, is a viewpoint whereby an observer

> ... will try to understand the meaning of the play which is performed on the Historical Stage; he will try to understand the laws of historical development. If he succeeds in this he will, of course, be able to put politics on a solid basis, and give us practical advice by telling us which political ideas are likely to succeed and likely to fail. (Popper 1957b, I, p.8).

Popper denies that such an attempt is worthwhile because, in his view, 'History has no meaning' (Popper 1957b, II, p.269). But it is important to realise why he thinks this: it is because history as it is now taught is hopelessly selective: it ignores most of human experience and concentrates almost exclusively on the history of power politics. Popper also objects specifically to the conclusion

> ... that history will judge, that is to say, that future might is right; it is the same as what I have called 'moral futurism'. (Popper 1957b, II, p.271.)

Instead, Popper specifically argues for a positive approach to history. We can interpret it with particular attention to the problem of power politics that we may hope to solve in our time – we can interpret the history of power politics from the point of view of our fight for the open society, for a rule of reason, for justice and freedom and equality:

> Although history has no ends, we can impose those ends of ours upon it;

and *although history has no meaning, we can give it meaning.* (Popper 1957b, II, p.278.)

Facts, including the facts of history, have in themselves no meaning; they acquire meaning only through our decisions. Historicism is an attempt, born of despair in the rationality and responsibility of our reactions, to overcome this.

Our view (with individual differences of emphasis) is that Popper's distinction is too crudely dualistic. In any given age people are *to some degree* prisoners of their fate: individuals will find it impossible by themselves to change whole societies or overthrow political regimes; but equally they are not utterly impotent, condemned to stand as spectators on some moving staircase of history – each has some freedom of action, some degree of influence on the course of history. Indeed, Popper seems to come close to saying this himself. We are historicists in this modified sense: we hold that man must understand the forces that operate on the history of his own time in order to understand the limits of his freedom of action and thereby to understand better when, where and how to act.

But here we face a difficulty. This approach must rest on some theory of historical interpretation, and that will depend on the individual historian's concept of knowledge. Broadly, most historical theories deal with a certain common set of interrelationships between economic system, social system, political system, cultural system. They differ in their interpretation of those relationships. For our purpose here, it is probably enough to start with a fairly broad and crude classification: into positivist theories denying any implicit ideological basis and resting on a view of the world that is thought to be objective, historicist theories of cyclical action-and-reaction, and dialectical materialist theories which adopt the same interactive mode but develop from it a concept of revolutionary progression from stage to stage. The sociological models for these approaches are, of course, respectively Durkheim, Weber and Marx.

Such interpretative models must be fitted on to a common set of historical data. But, given the very broad scale at which we are working, this must consist of very general historical categories. Most historians, whatever their ideological persuasion, would probably accept as categories a number of economic systems, such as agrarianism, the free market economy, Keynesianism (the welfare state), various forms called socialist, and perhaps some others. To each of these would correspond social and political systems, though different schools would give some of them different names. They would also differ, quite strongly, in their interpretation of what caused what. For some, facts of economic development would be primary; for others, social values would be basic.

Like any group of social scientists, we would find little ideological common cause among ourselves here. Is it then necessary to develop ten, fifteen, twenty theories of history? We think not; there is a way out, through a concept which has become central to our study and to this book: the concept of rationality.

Types of rationality in history – past and future

Rationality describes the kind of reasoning which the people of any epoch use to describe their world, and thus – consciously or unconsciously – to make their own history and their own future. It is, we think, the nearest approach to a comprehensive historical method: it does not attempt the impossible task of analysing all the social and historical events of an epoch, but rather concentrates on a description of the mode of reasoning typical of that epoch. Yet it is not merely a lowest common denominator of agreement: as well as being descriptive it is analytical. Forms of thought create their own forms of social organisation, just as social organisation in turn creates forms of thinking; we can, therefore, use rationality to discover the patterns whereby men and their institutions have related, in the past and may well relate in the future. Thus it neatly fits a concept of history which is not linear nor circular but rather spiral; in which certain traits reappear, in different guises, but in which the dominant characteristics change, colouring the whole tone of the society.

Certain rationalities – religious, political, economic, scientific – survive from age to age, forming constituent parts of every one. They create institutions – churches, academies, companies – to pursue their ends and defend themselves against change. Yet they too change. It is rare that any way of thinking disappears; but at one time one form will predominate, at another time another. The feudal middle ages were dominated by religious or spiritual rationality, the early capitalist seventeenth, eighteenth and nineteenth centuries by the rise of economic rationality based on a broad belief that the 'objective' laws of supply and demand would serve to structure society as a whole.

After World War One, however, a new kind of rationality began fully to emerge: we call it political rationality. Its central feature is the notion of state intervention in economic processes as seen in the very varying forms of Stalinism, Fascism, Naziism, Keynesianism, the New Deal and the Welfare State. It first attained influence, though not yet complete ascendancy, in western and central Europe at the time of the great slump of the early 1930s; its ascendancy over economic rationality was not complete until after the end of World War Two. At this point, a transitional blend of political and economic rationality seems to have triumphed, using what has been called a 'scientised' outlook (Habermas 1971). 'Scientism', like most ideologies that express a new rationality, implied a belief that history had ended: though it might continue to change within itself, the whole would not again be transformed. It proposed a purely rational and factual view of the world, indeed a scientific view, that would bring forth an underlying harmony in the natural order: political action would guarantee the continued smooth operation of the economic laws of supply and demand. In the economic sphere, Rostow's Five Stages of Economic Development (Rostow 1960) could be used anywhere to achieve a course of continuous and apparently effortless growth. In the political sphere, Bell (1964) confidently announced The End of Ideology.

In the late 1960s and early 1970s, the world saw the rapid disintegration of the comfortable belief in what we can call the scientific-political-economic form of rationality. Groups of the population objected to the idea of growth and tried to demonstrate that if it continued it would lead to disaster. Shortly afterwards, ironically, growth became almost impossible to achieve without rampant inflation. Counter-cultures and drop-out movements opposed to the dominant values of scientific-political rationality began to mushroom; traditional taboos and informal rules, important for the basis of this rationality, began to break down. But in place of this disintegrating rationality there had by the mid-1970s appeared, not the alternative culture expected by observers like Reich (1971) or Rosak (1969), but little more than a cultural vacuum.

The economic constraints

This changed situation did not mean the end of political rationality: it spelt rather a further incursion of political rationality at the expense of economic rationality. Instead of a beneficent technocracy of economic planners expressing some general will or collective interest, there is an increasingly desperate attempt to find some minimal common measure of agreement among opposed socio-economic groups which struggle over the distribution of wealth and power: trade unionists, employers' federations, consumers. These struggles are mirrored on the international level. The changes which have brought this about have arisen through the underlying movement of the world economy, which by the mid-1970s has been displaying a major structural perturbation unparalleled in its post-1945 evolution; but this in turn reflects the impact of political factors, the influence of which must now be traced.

Western Europe, we have already asserted, has reached a stage of late capitalism, or neo-Keynesianism, or the welfare state: in western Europe, though not elsewhere, the terms in our view appear virtually synonymous. For a quarter-century, western European governments have used Keynesian measures to regulate demand and thus to stimulate a high and sustained level of economic growth. In this they were during the 1950s and 1960s remarkably successful. Buoyed by prospects of constantly expanding demand, large corporations in particular showed themselves very willing to raise wages – which further stimulated demand. The result was a phenomenal expansion in real wages and purchasing power for organised workers, as well as increasing social security benefits. But after about 1970, a worm appeared in the Keynesian bud: there was an economic crisis of structural over-production, linked with general decline in demand, dramatically illustrated by Europe's car industries; it was marked by tighter markets, reduced profit margins, lower investment levels and a decidedly lower ability to pass on wage increases in the form of higher prices.

For this there appear to be two chief causes. One is the new power of trade union organisation – which we shall need to analyse in more detail a little later – which has meant that even in a recession wage levels and to some extent employment levels have to be maintained; hence rising industrial costs, and the familiar but puzzling phenomenon of stagflation. True, the link between the rate of inflation and the rate of unemployment has not been broken, but it has been distorted, in that each recession seems to require higher rates of unemployment to reduce the rate of inflation. And, with structural over-capacity, any attempt by government directly to stimulate demand – the traditional Keynesian weapon – is likely to prove inflationary, thus threatening to reduce demand by cutting the disposable incomes of households and the liquidity of companies. Public investment, one weapon in the Keynesian armoury since the early 1930s, is particularly open to this risk.

The other cause, and an equally new factor in the situation, was already noted in Chapter 2: it is increasing international competition – from the United States, from Japan, and now from

Eastern Europe and the more advanced parts of the Third World (such as Brazil and Korea). First in Britain and the United States, then during the 1960s and early 1970s in Germany and Italy, overseas investment has been found increasingly more attractive than investment at home. In these countries, by the mid-1970s, the result has been the same as has long been observed in Britain: an import bill that rises much faster than the returns from exports. True, a large part of this overseas investment has been in Europe – and western Europe in particular has been a prime target for the vast American overseas investment since World War Two. But an increasingly important share – up to one third, in the case of the leading European industrial companies – is now going to Third World countries, where wages are much lower and where environmental resistance to industrial investment is weaker. And it must be remembered that by the mid-1970s industrial wage levels in many European countries had reached American levels, though productivity was in most cases still considerably lower. Coupled with economic growth in the Third World, in eastern Europe and especially in the Middle East, all this spells a severe competitive problem for European industry in the 1980s and 1990s – except perhaps in a limited range of very specialised, skilled, science-based industries where Europe's long industrial lead can still count. When industrial growth can be financed out of primary exports – as in the Middle Eastern case – the threat to Europe is a double one: Europe's own capacity for industrial expansion is reduced by the drain on its balance of payments, while the Middle East countries can build up a powerful, efficient, modern industrial base – as is already illustrated in Iran.

All this does not indicate that Europe is heading for dramatic economic or social breakdown. Indeed, in the short term new markets for capital goods may open up in the Arab world, in South East Asia, in South America and Brazil, while the east-west détente may provide another stimulus. Even in the longer run, Europe has considerable resilience due to its technological capacities and its relative political stability. But it will probably mean quite fundamental changes in the relationship between industry and the state; and thus in the nature of the system.

The demographic constraints

The total number of people living in Europe will powerfully constrain our futures, too: for a Europe of a slow population growth is likely to be a Europe of slow economic change. Most people tend to concentrate their interest on the global consequences of the dramatic increase in the population of the Third World: for Europe a more stable development is assumed, and this is sometimes taken to mean that the population question is not of very vital importance for Europe's future. But this view is mistaken. Change will not come from a natural growth in numbers, because this is probably not going to occur, but an internal transformation of the population structure is almost certain, especially in terms of age balance, with profound social and political effects.

There is a widespread scepticism concerning the reliability of population forecasts, as we already saw in Chapter 1; and this is not without justification. Fertility and migration in particular are variables which are hard to foresee. But predictions have mostly been judged from the absolute numbers they render; and there is also the question of proportions between subgroups. In such matters we tend to be on safer ground: as long as we deal with the prospects of those already born, for example, we had a good chance of accurately calculating how they are going to survive and how the various rates will affect the shape of the population pyramid in years to come. Except for changes produced by large-scale migrations, short-term fluctuations of birth-rates, and violent deaths in times of war, demographic processes are slow, and the future consequences of at least some of them can be discussed well in advance.

The European population is ageing, and the reason is twofold: fertility is declining, so that relatively speaking fewer children are added to the population; at the same time, the mortality pattern has gradually increased the chances of the new-born to survive to an advanced age.

The mid-1960s appears to be the turning-point in European post-war fertility trends. The birthrate was in general already very low, viewed from a global point of view, but it was changing from year to year in various directions in different countries. With 1964 a rapid and uniform drop set in, moving towards a lower level than ever before recorded; in West Germany, by the mid-1970s, the birthrate does not even reach the level required for full reproduction of the population. This convergence of national trends could be interpreted as a general breakthrough of planned parenthood. Birthrates are notoriously difficult to predict, but it is hard to believe that future oscillations will move very far away from the approximate average of two children per woman. From now on, couples will for the first time in history be able to decide the number of children they will have. Investigations among European women concerning what they consider to be the ideal size of a family showed that in Britain the average was 2.9, in West Germany 2.3, and in rural regions of Bohemia 2.5. Women in their twenties indicated the lower numbers, a fact which is of particular significance when future development is under discussion (Van Keep 1971, Pavlik 1971).

Most European women nowadays start having children in their early twenties. If in the future the normal pattern will be to stop having children after the second or sometimes the third child, then clearly the last child will leave home earlier than is the case with today's families. This situation will, of course, lead a growing number of women in their middle years to look for jobs outside the home.

But the implications of a falling birth-rate go wider than this. It means that the growth of the western European home market begins to fall and then perhaps to end altogether. If to this is joined a cessation of growth in per capita GNP, the result could be further crisis in the major European economies. This we think a likely scenario for the 1980s.

Social and political features of political rationality

To understand better what may be entailed by the changes outlined it is necessary to look at parallel changes in social and political relationships – which have already had a profound effect on the course of the European economy.

The most important of these, in western Europe as a whole, is the disappearance (or dilution) of any organised challenge to the liberal-democratic system. Indeed, considering the degree of economic stagnation in these countries in the mid-1970s, the degree of social and political stability seems remarkable. The extra-parliamentary extreme groups have conspicuously failed to make progress since their brief hour of success in the late 1960s – indeed, their increasing resort to terrorism may be the surest indicator of their frustration. The same can be said of the extreme right, which is more and more being squeezed into isolated groups outside the system (as in Italy) or forced to move towards the centre.

This relative stability can be explained only by the success of the traditional left-wing groups – Social Democratic parties in Britain, Sweden and West Germany, the Communist party in France and Italy, and the trade unions – in harnessing discontent in order to make political gains within the system, at the same time moderating it in order not to lose control of the situation. But they can do so because of another relatively recent development: the increased power of the organised working class within the social structure.

This change took place earlier in some countries than in others: in Britain it dates from the success of Labour in the 1945 election, in Germany from the involvement of the trade unions in reconstruction, in France and Italy from the early 1970s.

To a large degree, this results from the changing position of the organised workforce within the system of production. The shift towards more capital-intensive production, the need to maintain a steady rhythm of output, the large amounts of capital tied up in long-term planning, and the ease with which chain production can be disrupted – all these have meant that the workforce could exercise increasingly hard sanctions. The British Labour movement had already learned this in the early 1960s; in France it came with May 1968, in Italy with *L'Autunno Caldo* in 1969. In Britain and Italy in particular, days lost through strikes escalated after the late 1960s; the same was observed in Denmark and Finland; even in Germany the figures doubled during the early 1970s, remaining steadily high thereafter.

But there is one most significant feature about this new power: it has been used in a most conservative way to gain material advantage for labour in the form of higher wages and better working conditions – only rarely have strikes been accompanied by demands for changes in the ownership of the means of production. Bargaining power has increased at the expense of ideology: the unions have become depoliticised, transforming themselves into pure interest groups. Trade union membership in Italy increased by more than 55 per cent between 1969 and 1975, in Britain by 15 per cent between 1968 and 1974. But the object of a strengthened trade union movement has been limited to better wages, shorter hours and improved working conditions – especially the first – and in pursuing this narrow aim the unions have been highly successful. In all countries earnings of manual workers have steadily gained on those for salaried workers; in Britain, for instance, in 1975, manual workers accounted for nearly half of all households with incomes of over £3,000 a year. But the consequence is the further integration of the manual worker into the existing socio-economic system; he has become more reluctant than ever to threaten the viability of the firm which guarantees his standard of living. His strictly non-ideological aim, and that of his union, is to squeeze the maximum share of the resultant gain out of the employer. Even where unions have pursued other aims – such as gaining greater self-determination for their workers – it has not appeared to threaten the present structure, as the cases of LIP and Norton-Villiers-Triumph aptly illustrate.

There is, however, a great deal of puzzling counter-evidence to this thesis: the growing number of wildcat strikes even in countries with good records of labour relations (such as Sweden); inexplicable acts of industrial vandalism; actual hostility to worker participation in some countries (such as Britain). But this discontent has not led to radical demands for changes in the ownership or management of industry; the apparent exceptions, such as LIP in France or Triumph-Villiers in Britain, were born of strictly pragmatic desperation. It might almost be possible to interpret wildcat strikes or vandalism as a visceral reaction against the very stability of the system, which the worker dislikes for reasons he cannot fully specify.

For trade union leaders, there is a stronger sense of ideological identity in the form of demands that the trade unions, as such, be given a special role in national policy-making. This is the essence of the British Social Contract, for instance. But, as the Social Contract so well illustrates, implicit in this new role is an acceptance of gradualism. The trade unions thus begin to find common cause with the large industrial producers – including the multi-nationals – and the political-administrative technocracy; for these groups in the new political centre tend to increase their relative political power vis-à-vis traditional groups, such as the small businessmen, the army and the Church. Italy and France offer particularly good examples of the process. In both these countries the Church has lost ground – as witness the contraception, abortion and divorce issues. And in countries with reasonably stable democratic regimes, the power of the army has suffered similar decline. (Germany offers a drastic example.) Thus the middle class in most European countries has found itself split between a more conservative wing – consisting of the older professions, the small businessmen and in some cases the non-technocratic bureaucracy – and a more radical wing, consisting of the technocracy with its depoliticised, scientific ideology and its new liberal approach to industrial relations.

In many countries the more traditional middle-class group is large in numbers, but ill-organised and too loyal to the system to assert militant sanctions. As a result certain groups – such as sections of the middle class in Britain – have seen their real incomes reduced by inflation; the same has applied on a massive scale to the middle-class retired people living on occupational pensions, which have suffered from inflation. Others have looked to middle-class trade unions to defend their interests; yet others have supported right wing fringes of parties, such as the Christian Democrats in Italy or the CSU in Germany. But it should be noticed that socialist parties, such as the Labour Party in Britain and the SDP in Germany, as well as their French and Italian equivalents, are largely acquiring a middle-class leadership. Perhaps the overwhelming bourgeois influence on the Communist administration of Bologna is a sign of things to come.

The middle class may thus have lost fractionally: but the main victims of the success of the organised labour-technocratic alliance have been the marginal groups, such as the unemployed, part-time workers, the aged, unsupported women, disabled people and the less skilled. As general levels of education and skill rise, these groups – especially the less educated and less skilled – may discover employment at any time increasingly difficult to find, as the American experience clearly shows. But in periods of high unemployment the marginal groups expand greatly in size, especially among younger and less skilled workers, and there is a real possibility then of the development of a violent, dissident, alienated sub-culture – portents of which may already be provided by such varied phenomena as rising juvenile crime rates in almost every country, football hooliganism in Britain, assassinations in West Germany, and political extremism in Italy. Yet great caution is needed in making such general interpretations. There is no obvious logical link between the mindless Saturday afternoon violence around British football grounds and the activities of Baader-Meinhof in Germany: to group them both in an alienated sub-culture is too superficial. All that might be said is that these phenomena result from the satisfaction of material needs unaccompanied by the satisfaction of the need for self-determination.

The point about the marginal groups is that their protests tend to be anarchic and ill-organised politically: they must all essentially depend on charity from the rest of society, represented by the state, and this will wax or wane according to the economic performance of the country concerned, inflation, the concern of the trades union movement, and the middle-class conscience. Especially in a period of recession, these forces may not prove very favourable to the marginals. There is an obvious conflict, in fact, between the interests of the marginals and those of organised labour – which actually may protect itself against inflation if the combined power of the trades unions and the state can guarantee employment. The obvious losers are the marginals, who fail to keep pace with inflation and are the first to lose their jobs. But without the active support of organised labour, the discontent of the marginals can be no more than a temporary embarrassment to governments – as was clearly shown in Reggio Calabria in 1973, when discontent spilled over into open disruption. May 1968 and *L'Autunno Caldo* were probably the last time when, fleetingly, the marginals and organised labour united. It is unlikely to happen again.

Thus contemporary Europe is experiencing a profound shift in the social basis of power. Organised manual labour, following British and Swedish examples, is gaining power and becoming part of the central establishment. The middle class is split; large sections suffer loss of power and prestige, while one section – the technocracy – makes common cause in the centre with labour. Large marginal groups are excluded from power, and are thereby disadvantaged; but they cannot develop a true sub-culture to replace the old class consciousness of manual labour – which is becoming lost as trade union leaders lose contact with a working class they have effectively left. Real power is shared by these workers' leaders and by the technocracy – though this latter group is weakened in a period of economic stagnation, when it can no longer deliver the goods.

This increased power of organised labour has also meant a shift in the criteria used for determining the distribution of the social product among groups. In the growth decade of the 1960s, the principal criterion seems to have been the rate of growth of a given sector: fast-growing sectors such as tertiary industry gained more than stagnant or declining sectors. But by the mid-1970s, a critical new criterion is the bargaining power created by a given group's contribution to the production and maintenance of essential basic goods and services – so that miners and electricity workers count for more than nurses or university teachers. Social status seems increasingly irrelevant to the whole process – and this must further weaken the power of many sections of the middle class. But so long as the middle class retains a near-monopoly of higher education, and this is increasingly required as a passport to more responsible jobs, the process may have limits.

The new power of the state

There is, again, an exception: the new situation requires increasing intervention by the state, which acts as mediator and arbiter to ease social friction. This was already the case in the transitional phase of the 1950s and 1960s, which we characterised as the era of scientific-political-economic rationality; but it is even more markedly so in the recession-ridden 1970s, when a purer version of political rationality seems to have taken root. Indeed, it may be described as the central feature of a society based on political rationality: a central political elite – politicians, industrialists from large firms, union leaders and the bureaucracy – takes an increasingly neutralist stance and a mediating role in order to try to resolve the conflicting pressures of a host of interest groups. The major objective is to maintain political stability and prevent too violent a perturbation of the existing socio-economic order – as seemed to be briefly threatened in France during May 1968 or in Britain during the fuel crisis of 1973-4: the chief means to this end is the maintenance of reasonably full employment in the face of a constant threat of inflation.

All this is perhaps most evident in Britain, due to the particular weakness of its economic position: private industry increasingly looks to the state for help and is not completely dismayed by the idea of nationalisation. The formula being developed in Britain – nationalisation of large industries, workers' cooperatives in smaller industries – may prove to have general application: the question, as the British Labour opponents of EEC membership correctly saw, is how far such policies can be pursued in an open trading situation. Whatever the case, state intervention on this scale involves a fundamental change in ethos in the way the economy is managed. The main criterion is no longer – as in the 1950s or 1960s – profit margins or productivity: maintenance of stability and of reasonably full employment count for far more, and these are fundamentally not economic criteria at all, but political. Economic rationality, and the hybrid form characteristic of the 1950s and much of the 1960s, are increasingly being replaced by pure political rationality.

As the state becomes the arbiter, its servants acquire greatly enhanced power and prestige – and thus provide the outstanding exception to the declining status of the middle class. In every country they become the patrons on which other groups must depend for their share of the national cake. Despite all attempts to prevent it, in European countries the numbers of central and local government officials constantly grow: so does the public sector share of GDP. Similarly, increasing nationalisation means that heads of key state industries become the most powerful economic decision-makers, assuming the role of capitalist corporations in the 1960s. Every new conflict in society demands a new infusion of officials to act as mediators. Ironically, in some cases they may actually do battle with each other on behalf of rival client groups. Thus the reorganisation of local government in England in the interest of greater efficiency added 100,000 new staff to the payrolls because the two levels of local government duplicated many posts. And a ratchet effect occurs, whereby staff once appointed are almost impossible to dislodge if the need disappears or becomes irrelevant. The tentacular bureaucracy is self-justifying and self-perpetuating, and in practice its political masters can do little to limit its growth.

The implications of the international scenarios

At this point we need to put these trends in an international setting. Since World War Two, as noted in Chapter 2, Europe's economic advance has been heavily based on investment in the major industralised and urbanised regions: the axis that extends from northern Italy via the Rhine corridor and the Dutch Randstad to south-east and midland England, plus the Paris region. But it is precisely these regions where the structural economic crisis now bites most deeply: here trade union strength is most concentrated, here are the mass-consumption, mass-production industries that are most vulnerable to competition from outside, here labour costs are rising fastest. The logical result would be a process of natural selection. Those industries that could afford to move out – the more routine mass production industries and the less skilled service industries – would move out: to the older industrial areas where labour was available, to the Mediterranean periphery where cheap labour could be trained, even in some cases to rural areas. Those industries that needed highly skilled labour and specialist services would remain, together with local service industries catering for a high-income population. The main result might be a shift of some kinds of industry towards the Mediterranean seaboard or even to the Third World. Presumably the multinationals would find this economically sensible, and the nations of southern Europe might welcome the resultant development. For, even if communist regimes took over there, they might be enthusiastic about importing the multinationals' technology and organisational skills.

The process is in fact already happening: assembly industry such as car manufacture, as well as heavy industry requiring tidewater and relative freedom from interference on ecological grounds, have been investing heavily in southern Europe. And nationalist pressures in northern Europe might encourage the process – at any rate for foreign-owned multinationals which might face nationalisation there. The problem is that the theory demands for northern Europe a very rapid compensatory development of leading industries – using new technology, very highly skilled labour to produce goods with very high value added – as well as non-routine services, and it is doubtful whether governments dominated by trade union interests would be able to make the necessary structural adaptations fast enough. The result could be that these countries, including even Germany, will come to depend on manufacturing industries that are not competitive in world markets, plus returns from investment abroad. Either nationalistically, or through manipulation of EEC policies, these countries would then seek to minimise their resulting losses through a combination of trade restrictions and aggressive marketing of their subsidiaries' products in overseas markets – especially perhaps in the USA. This was a likely scenario we already developed in Chapter 2.

The new corporatism

If this account of current underlying trends in Europe is at all plausible, it leads to a striking conclusion: that the European economy and society are moving towards a new version of the corporate state witnessed between the wars in Italy and Germany. This is the conclusion from the analysis by R.E. Pahl and J.T. Winkler (Pahl and Winkler 1974). In proposing it here, we want to rid the idea of certain connotations. Such a state would not necessarily, or even probably, have the features we associate with a Fascist state: but its essential socio-economic relations would be similar – in particular massive state intervention, a wholesale restriction on free competition through an encouragement of planning agreements with large corporations, the increasing importance of political rather than economic-rational considerations in planning decisions, and nationalistic autarky.

The question is whether corporatism could come into existence through a willing consensus, as Pahl and Winkler think. It could certainly not be achieved through agreement between the large corporations and the state alone, with suppression of trade unions: organised labour, and its expression through liberal democracy, are far too strong for that, provided they use their power with moderation. (This is why a repetition of the Fascist state of the 1930s is hardly conceivable.) But it could happen through agreement between large businesses (excluding foreign-owned multinationals), trade unions and the technocratic bureaucracy, united against the multinationals behind a protectionist philosophy.

The dominant scenario – and some variants

In this chapter, we have evolved what we can call a dominant scenario. It assumes that Europe economically challenges the United States, but that it is threatened in turn by competition from outside and even from its own developing regions. It assumes governments of a liberal democratic cast, dominated by alliances between the technocratic bureaucracy and organised labour, with a decline in the power of the traditional middle class and a large, relatively powerless marginal population. It assumes that such governments increasingly resort to protectionism, either on a national basis or through manipulation of the policies of supranational groups such as the EEC.

It can be called a broadly social democratic-nationalistic-corporate scenario. In putting it forward as the most plausible, we want to stress that it is only one of a number of alternatives – some nearer, some farther in spirit. One, which we can call *neo-capitalist*, is essentially the surprise-free future of the middle 1960s: it assumes continued growth and the further development of the consumerist society. We think that this scenario is less likely than ours, which indeed can be regarded as an historical progression from it – the surprise-free future of the 1970s, if you like. Another, which can be called *authoritarian*, assumes a very large degree of central state control over the whole economy through a bureaucracy allied with a single dominant political party: it is the model represented by the USSR, or less perfectly by most of the countries of Eastern Europe. We think it highly unlikely here, for reasons we have already argued, except in the event of an economic catastrophe for which there is so far no evidence.

There is at least one further scenario that is perhaps of more interest: a *liberal socialist, decentralised* scenario on the models of Cuba and Yugoslavia, based on decentralisation of power to a large number of relatively small cooperative units. At present, this solution is fairly utopian for Europe – both eastern and western: there are few indications of any movement in the economy that would make it plausible. But, as we shall now try to argue, the present degree of concentration of economic power explicit in the dominant surprise-free scenario may soon provoke its own reaction.

The dynamics of history: towards a new rationality

The situation described in this chapter, it must now be stressed, is an emerging one. Europe did not pass at one point of time from an economic to a political rationality: certain individuals, groups, institutions and countries may be predominantly working within the framework of one rationality, while others use a different one. As with previous historical transitions, it is difficult for those caught up in the process to recognise clearly the outlines of what is emerging.

What does seem clear is that the process of historical change has been violently speeded up. Though historians would disagree about dates, perhaps all could agree that there was a period called feudal,

Table 3.1 Rationalities – social formation

Social Formation	Feudal	Early Capitalism	Complex Capitalism	Neo-Capitalism	2000+
	700/1200-1500/1850	1500/1850-1900/1950	1900/1950-1973	1973-?	
Rationality	Theocratic/(Divine Right) Hierarchical	Economic	Scientized (political-economic)	Political	a) [ethnic (regionalist)] b) [religious]
Social Organisation	Estates	Classes	Class/State	State	a) [regions] b) [hierarchical]
Territory of Operation	Local	National	Supranational	National	a) [regional?] b) [national?]
Ideological Appeal	Religious	Class struggle	Consumerism	Political self interest	a) [ethnic] b) [charisma]
Method of Political Control	Coercion/consent	Coercion	Consent/Manipulation	Manipulation	a) [consent/manipulation] b) [manipulation]
Types of Domination	Personal	Personal/Organisational	Organisational (fragmented)	Organisational (centralised though not spatially)	a) [small-scale organisational] b) [personal]
Political Organisation	Aristocrat	Party boss/Ideological mass party	Ideological mass party/Interest groups	Non-ideological mass party/Interest groups	a) [regionalist parties (ideological?)] b) [leader/boss]

which began some time between 700 and 1200 AD and died between 1500 and 1850 AD, having had a life of perhaps six centuries. Most would also accept that this was followed by a period of capitalism (or early capitalism) which lasted, according to country and also according to interpretation, between one hundred and four hundred years. Almost all observers would accept the existence of a modified form of capitalism, or welfare statism, which up to now has lasted only about thirty years, and which we have argued is now in process of transformation into something else. Each of these periods is associated with a specific form of rationality: the feudal period with spiritual rationality, the early capitalist with economic, the welfare state with a transitional economic-political form (Table 3.1). Thus rationalities succeeded each other at increasing speed.

The present time, in our analysis, marks the evolution of yet another stage, which we provisionally label neo-capitalist for want of a better title: its distinguishing feature is the dominance of political rationality. But one evident fact about this society is its instability: the political centre mediates between differing interests, and because of its power base it can do so only in a passive and highly conservative or non-innovatory way. It must respond particularly to the demands both of corporate managers and of trade unions in the large-scale manufacturing industry which grew during the period of economic-political rationality and is now threatened by competition. Because such industry – both in the private and the public sector – is geared largely to the demands of the mass-consumption society, there is little chance of a rapid restructuring of the economy in the direction of serving social needs. And because of the challenge of competition, there is likely to be increasing conflict in the political arena on at least two levels: between different industries which are candidates for state aid (aircraft versus vehicles, for instance) and between different plants in the same industry where closures are threatened. What is most significant here is that the traditional capital-versus-labour struggle becomes irrelevant: both find themselves on the same side in the battle for state favours and state resources.

Perhaps the most significant conflict, however, may concern the basic question of access to work. General recession plus international competition begins to create a condition of structural unemployment of marginal groups, including the immigrants, the poorly educated and poorly skilled, the older workers whose skills are no longer relevant, and the young school leavers. Together these may make up a group almost permanently without a job – and in the case of the young unskilled worker increasingly uninterested in getting one. The social consequences could be serious, involving the development of client systems based on official handouts and the development of disaffected sub-cultures. But because of the features we have already noted for this group – their general lack of organisation and their divorce from the means of production – a Marcusian revolution of the Lumpenproletariat seems increasingly unlikely. Far more probably is a gradual breakdown of public order, especially in the cities, associated with a spread of violence and crime of an apolitical kind and terrorism born of frustration among extremist groups.

The decay of the consensus culture will also affect those in work – through an alienation* of the factory worker who cannot identify with the product he had some minimal part in making, of the office worker who writes a small section of a report to be passed up the hierarchy, of the teacher who sees a class three times a week and makes no real human contact. Here, perhaps, rather than in the deeper and more hopeless alienation of the unemployed and unemployable, will be the point where a creative response – and thus a challenge to the spiritual deprivation of the depoliticised political society – may arise.

One of the main tasks of this book will be to suggest the forms this challenge might take. It could take the form of a religious revival, bringing a return to the theocratic rationality of the middle ages. Equally it could take the form of adherence to a messianic political regeneration, involving even a return to the fanatical nationalism of Fascist Italy or Nazi Germany. Alternatively, it could lead to a reaction against the principles of the nation state and such an assertion of regional or ethnic consciousness as is already evident in Scotland, Corsica and Vizcaya: such a regionalism, however, is likely to encounter bitter resistance on the part of the centralised state and its associated institutions and pressure groups.

In Chapter 11 we explore this problem at greater depth – and hypothesise the emergence of a new rationality – *cultural rationality* – which puts most stress on individual self-fulfilment and human self-esteem and emphasises the distinctiveness of different human needs. It would be based on people's own articulation of those needs through participative and representative democracy, and bring home to members of society much more fundamentally how they interact – thus reducing the alienation and social stress so evident today. These are principles rather than postulates for action – though in our final chapter we try to spell out some of the implications.

---

* Here we use the word 'alienation' in its strictest sociological sense. Later it will be used in a more general way; see page 71.

Meanwhile, we want to keep these principles in the back of our mind. The prevailing rationality, we have argued, is the economic-political, and that will bring with it certain acute problems for society in the medium-term future – in the remainder of the 1970s and the 1980s. These in turn will help to shape the development of the new rationality that will, we think, be the reaction to them. So our next task, in Chapter 4, is to look at these problems in overview: the problem landscape of the future Europe.

CHAPTER 4

Problem Landscape of the Future Europe

'What if ... ?' That is the fundamental question of this book, of the last chapter and of this one. We ask what may happen in the European future as a result of trends – some visible, some hidden – in the European present. We think that these trends represent strong historical forces with which European society and European polity must grapple. They are strong, but not immutable: they offer choices for action. That is the basic philosophical-historical attitude behind this book, and it explains our central objective, which is an educational one: to illuminate now the problems which may arise in the fairly near future, so as better to understand them before they overwhelm us, thus to arrive at considered and well-articulated solutions. To repeat: we do not present these pictures as firm predictions, but as the best ideas we can form about the future. They are intended to serve as a stimulus for debate, for alternative propositions, for new syntheses as further facts and interpretations come to light. That is central to our own view of our educative role.

Our objective in this chapter follows directly out of the analysis in the last. It is to isolate the deeper, underlying problems of the Europe of the late 1970s and 1980s, as perceived by various sections of European society at that time. These are the problems that will require solutions by the policy-makers of that time – producing the world of *Europe 2000*. We must be concerned not to over-stress the temporary, short-term problems that sometimes loom so large in the mass media; our concern is with the deeper structural questions that form the true agenda for society in any one age. Our view is that if this process of sifting can be done, then the public concerns of any period – as reflected in the content of newspaper articles and television features, in the results of public opinion polls, in the voting behaviour of people at elections and their market behaviour in spending their incomes – do truly reflect the basic priorities of individuals. Of course, there is plenty of evidence that the process gets distorted: advertisers create wants, media men create news, television crews rent a crowd, public opinion polls suggest their own answers, individuals and societies change views as experience shows them to be wrong. But much of this distortion affects the ephemeral short-run concerns, which we are trying to filter out. The longer-run, more deeply felt concerns surely do reflect the problems of an age – if language is to have meaning at all.

We are asserting that certain themes or concerns are the problems of an era. For past history seems to show this to be the case. In the 1930s people in the western world were obsessed by economic depression, in the early 1940s with survival. Then, in the 1950s and early 1960s, during the depth of the Cold War, thoughtful people everywhere were concerned at one or another level with the fear of mass nuclear annihilation. For virtually the whole period since the end of World War Two, people have been obsessed by fear of a recurrence of the mass depression and unemployment of the 1930s. In the 1950s and early 1960s this led to a belief in sustained and regular economic growth: but by the late 1960s many people were beginning to reflect on some of the negative consequences of the mass consumption society. The 1970s have seen the appearance of new mass spectres: shortages of basic raw materials, hyper-inflation and growing recession, or stagflation.

Some of the shifts in world view, during the 1950s and 1960s and early 1970s, are almost classic case studies of the process. The sudden concern with the negative consequences of material growth, around 1969 and 1970, is a case in point. A relatively few professional people – biologists, chemists, economists of an iconoclastic kind – became concerned with certain evidence: growing pollution, accelerating consumption of irreplaceable raw material assets. But as soon as they began to make their fears known, it was seen that they had touched a sensitive mass nerve. Millions of other people were feeling the same ideas, intuitively, without being able to establish chapter and verse. Very quickly, through the mass media, quite new ideas were proposed and were widely accepted: Small is Beautiful, Limits to Growth, Development without Growth, Conservation, Recycling, Intermediate Technology, became part of every language. Yet those who made this intellectual revolution had been aware of the situation years before: it just took a long time to get people to listen. Their ideas, to quote Donald Schon's phrase, were not yet an Idea in Good Currency (Schon 1971). In this chapter we are concerned to isolate those themes which may perhaps become Ideas in Good Currency during the 1980s and 1990s.

Values interact with facts. In developing our scenarios with variations in Chapter 3, we assumed that material socio-economic conditions would provide the fundamental driving force of political and cultural change. But we also assume that these conditions affect people's value systems, and that these value systems may – through a process of conscious political choice, in which men have freedom of action – become positive agents which affect the actions of critical decision-makers. The late 1960s and early 1970s provide an apt instance: the shift in values away from consumerism and towards conservation was in an important sense a reaction of thinking people to the material circumstances of the American-style mass consumer society that had evolved in the Europe of the late 1950s and early 1960s. Yet it was also an anticipation of new forces in the outside world: the growing scarcity and expense of raw material supplies, the competing claims of the Third World, the growing problem of large-scale pollution. In any event, once in existence, the new movement itself began to play a part in shaping the future, through its impact on political thought and practical decision making. In the short run, people can only react against events by reorientating their value systems; in the longer run, translated into political action, these systems in turn become an active factor in shaping events. And this is not to deny that value systems may embody an element of self-interested hypocrisy: it is *your* car that is the polluter, whereas mine was satisfactory until yours came on the scene; we now want durable, non-polluting articles that give good and reliable use for years – provided that they cost no more than the old examples of built-in obsolescence. What we are now witnessing, in one European controversy after another, is a clash between private self-interest and the claims of a wider community, in which the same person may shift roles according to his precise interests. And such controversy is unlikely to be resolved in any simple, tidy way.

Thus, one strong possibility for the future is that fairly conventional, consumer-oriented value systems – those characterising the 1950s and 1960s, and formed in the economic conditions of those years – will survive for a large part of the population, particularly for those less affluent classes who have fewer material goods and think they have a right to them like everyone else. There could then be a clash between the material aims of a large part – perhaps a majority – of the population and the concerns of an intellectual minority, especially if economic growth did not continue at the rate of the 1950s and 1960s. Another possibility is that value systems would in fact adjust quite rapidly to changed circumstances – as we know is possible from the experience of the United States, where anti-consumerist attitudes have spread very rapidly from college-educated to blue-collar youth (Yankelovich 1974). But much of this transformation occurred in the late 1960s and early 1970s, against a background of high economic growth rates; we do not know what reactions could arise to a failure of growth produced by external constraints rather than conscious choice. This is one of the major themes we must explore now.

It is probably over-sanguine to assume that neat, automatic adjustments could ever occur between material facts and human values. What is more likely is some disjuncture. Therefore, in what follows we prefer to trace out what seem to be the logical consequences of current trends – the trends already outlined in Chapters 2 and 3. These, we think, will constitute the immediate problem landscape of the late 1970s and much of the 1980s. We try to isolate about a dozen major groups of problems, which we term mega-problems. We try to classify them and to present them in terms of their impacts on people. They are the problems which we shall then discuss in greater detail in Chapters 5-10.

Admittedly, there is a disadvantage of this method: it could fail to isolate the apparently new problem that takes the world by surprise. But in our view such problems are rarely, if ever, new; they are problems which have been lying buried just beneath the surface of mass consciousness. The· whole pollution-energy-conservation debate, already discussed, is an example. We think that our basic working method, based on the scenarios in Chapters 2 and 3, should be fully adequate to isolate them.

Defining mega-problems: needs and their satisfaction

We start with a proposition: the criterion for a problem area is thwarted or frustrated human need. True, the concept of need is an elusive one; in Chapter 11 we shall want to define it more closely. Meanwhile, we can say that some human needs – we can call them ethological – are permanent and invariable for all mankind at all times; they include not merely obvious physical needs like food and shelter, but also psychological needs like communication, without which a human being will decay and finally atrophy. Some others – we can call them culture-based – are essentially also invariant, but their expression is affected by the prevalent culture. Generally in history, material needs have been adjusted upwards, following available supplies: we now need bathrooms, motor cars, television and universal education in a way that our ancestors clearly did not.

Thus definitions of poverty, and of minimum living standards, reflect the material conditions of a society and the resulting social values. And these values may be illuminated – or obscured – by the amount and type of information that the society makes available to its members. The only meaningful way in which we can define the needs of Europeans in the 1980s and 1990s, therefore, is in terms of the likely material situation then and in terms of the prevailing values that result – the kind of analysis we have already been developing.

We think one useful way of looking at broad groups of problems – or mega-problems, as we call them – is in terms of scale, or level, of effect. A need may be felt by the individual, by the same individual as a member of a group defined in terms of age or social class or region or other criterion, or by all individuals constituting a nation, or Europe, or the world. To some extent this distinction is artificial: a group does not feel a problem, only its members do. But the distinction is useful, in terms of the way individuals perceive their own problems. One problem – that of economic growth or stagnation, for instance – is felt by the individual as part of a total society and a total economy; while another – that of alienation at the workplace, for example – is felt primarily by the individual in his own capacity. Even then, admittedly, there are other aspects: the individual feels economic problems in his own life, and conversely he perceives that alienation is a problem affecting others than himself. But in terms of the primary impact, we maintain that the distinction is a useful one.

Accordingly, in the rest of this chapter we start by looking at the macro-organisational problems that may be faced by European society as a whole in the late 1970s and 1980s (some of these have already been treated in Chapters 2 and 3; here we summarise them). Then we turn to problems that may be experienced by particular groups of the population. And lastly, we consider a wide range of problems that are likely to be experienced by people as individuals.

Macro-problems: (1) Peace, war and security

First and outstanding among these is the one reflecting perhaps the most basic human need: security. Since the holocaust of World War Two, and the arrival of the possibility of mass world destruction, the world has seen the creation of an uneasy peace. The great world powers have staked out spheres of influence which have changed only marginally (Cuba, Vietnam) since shortly after the end of World War Two. Thus Europe has been divided; but progressively, culminating in the East-West German agreements of 1972, tensions between the two Europes have eased; and they even now exist in some kind of symbiotic relationship through trade and tourist links. There have been tacit agreements, and latterly more firm undertakings, to reject the use of weapons of mass annihilation. But instead, there has been a series of local conventional wars, fought at the margins of the great powers' spheres of influence, with unprecedented ferocity – particularly for the innocent civilian bystanders. None of these has taken place in Europe, and in 1975 the prospect seems remote: but it is not impossible – particularly if civil war developed in a politically unstable country due to a collision course between rival political blocs, supported by outside arms.

More likely is the escalation of guerilla warfare and terrorism, which we already discussed in Chapter 2. Though it has been a factor in world affairs throughout modern history, and indeed before that, it has recently increased at a speed without precedent: it is a force that is very difficult to de-escalate, for a violent response is likely to provoke ever more ferocious reaction. The multiplication of terrorist groups is a phenomenon with many possible explanations: the general sense of alienation, which we discuss later in this chapter; increasing disillusionment on the part of a minority with the possibility of a mass working-class revolution; the reaction of part of a generation to the prevalent materialistic, bourgeois society of its parents. At present, there seems no reason to suppose any weakening of the movement; the threat is rather one of intensification. Certainly, the general economic recession of the mid-1970s seems to have produced little change, suggesting that the roots are deeper. And in a strictly technical sense, there is an unhappy prospect of escalation. Just as tactical nuclear weapons have spread from the major powers to the medium and now the small ones, so they could come into the hands of dissident groups within one country. It is not improbable that by the late 1980s, a European nation could be faced with the threat of nuclear destruction in this way. The almost certain result is a massive escalation in the financial burden, and the social nuisance, of elaborate security control systems.

Just as great a potential threat to peace, in the medium term, is the clear risk of economic conflict between the First and the Third World – as we saw in Chapter 2. Except for those fortunate developing nations that possess monopoly supplies of oil or some other essential industrial raw material, Third World countries face a rapidly rising population, inadequate food supplies and increasing prices for industrial raw materials. The threat is that these countries may become politically unstable and resort to desperate measures – including nuclear blackmail – to avert mass starvation. Isolated examples in the 1970s show that, just as with internal terrorism, western governments find it very difficult in practice to deal effectively with violent threats. There is a kind of Gresham's Law of international behaviour, in which blackmail and the threat of force may drive out civilised relationships.

The threat could easily come the other way. As more primary producers emulate the oil producers of the early 1970s by exploiting their monopoly or oligopoly power, the developed industrial nations are likely to respond by moving back towards neo-colonialism and economic autarky. It would be done through the maintenance of friendly regimes and the elimination of threatening ones – as was admittedly done by the CIA when American interests were threatened in Chile. But, coupled with chronic political instability and the existence of guerilla groups, it does pose the constant threat of violent upheaval – which could spread back, via terrorist groups, into Europe itself. Thus, while the risk of major world war is perhaps minimal, the risk of small-scale war, and, still more, near-war, is likely to be far greater in the 1980s and 1990s than it is today. But the forces making this likely are also rooted in social development within Europe, and we shall need to return to them later in this chapter.

Macro-problems: (2) Growth, stagnation and scarcity

The second major theme concerns a hardly less basic human need: material security. Since the end of World War Two, a central concern of every government – whatever its political label – has been to try to achieve rapid and steady economic growth, unmarred by the oscillations of the trade cycle which scarred the life of the western world in the early 1920s. In this, nearly every government has enjoyed remarkable success. Whether committed to indicative planning, as in France, or to a fairly untrammelled social market economy, as in Germany, European economies have typically attained rates of growth apparently without historical parallel. A doubling of material living standards within two decades became normal. By the mid-1970s, however, one fact is apparent to all: that this growth is accompanied by galloping and continuing inflation. Whether or not the phenomenon of exponential growth could be applied to pollution or resource depletion, it began by 1975 to look uncannily like an ideal model for inflation. No-one was prepared to accept this as an inevitable effect of growth: and everyone had a different remedy. Some argued for a purely monetary solution, but a comprehensive monetary theory was lacking. Others – following a perceptive lead brilliantly given by the British economist Barbara Wootton as long ago as 1955 (Wootton 1955) – argue that the problem is caused by expectations of rising wages, and that it can be solved only by a general social contract as to the right distribution of gains in the social product. Broadly, during the mid-1970s, countries such as the United States and Germany were following monetarist policies, buying relative price stability by high unemployment; Britain was following the Wootton prescription with no general agreement and no conspicuous success.

There is and will be no general answer to the problem. One way – echoing experiments such as Roosevelt's New Deal and early Nazi economic policy under the direction of the master inflation-controller Schacht – may be to encourage employment in capital-producing industries and to keep down the resulting consumption by a variety of forced saving devices. Schacht did this by encouraging rearmament; the question still remains whether it can be done through peaceful investment, such as Roosevelt achieved in his Tennessee Valley scheme, since despite this the American economy still suffered from high unemployment to the eve of World War Two. What can be said is that the search for such a policy is likely to persist through the late 1970s and early 1980s – unless some crisis in world affairs causes the western economy to be put on a war footing.

Part and parcel of the stagflationary phenomenon of the 1970s is, however, a disturbing reversal of the deflation of the 1930s. Whereas then, primary material prices reached a record low, now they become both a reflection and a driving engine of the whole inflationary process. This seems to reflect the much greater dependence now of the western industrialised economies on imported raw material and energy supplies, plus the fact that some of these supplies are highly concentrated in a few producing nations. The oil crisis of 1973-4 can perhaps be seen as the first expression, but almost certainly not the last, of a resulting confrontation between the industrial nations and their suppliers. One major theme of the 1980s and 1990s could be a drive towards self-sufficiency on the part of western Europe in food, energy and major industrial raw materials – so far as this is feasible through intensive development of home supplies and substitutes. Insofar as it proves unsuccessful, it could lead to a movement towards special relationships with the primary producers – relationships that involved some degree of economic and cultural hegemony.

The raw material suppliers are bound to resist this. They are likely to defend their own interests by automatic indexing of their prices in step with general inflation. They may well also reach agreements to limit total world supplies, on the lines of the OPEC agreements. Some may try to engage in reciprocal imperialism through investment of their trade surpluses in western industry, commerce or land, as the Arab countries were already doing in the mid-1970s. But this in turn could bring them into ever-closer economic relationships with the industrial powers.

Whatever the outcome, within Europe by the final two decades of the century major industrial firms will almost certainly face shortages of raw materials and energy, and supplies will become difficult and erratic to coordinate. There will be a risk of 'material blackmail' in negotiating with suppliers, specially the nations of the Third World. Supplies will be obtainable only at rising cost, causing progressive inflation in the prices of consumer goods. This must in turn cause consumer resistance, particularly since in some areas – for instance durable consumer goods – the western European market may by then be approaching saturation. And, as we later suggest, there may be an increasing demand on the part of the public for goods built to last. But this should lead to an actual reduction in output and employment in mass-consumption, mass-production industries, which could be compounded by competition in those same industries from the more technologically-sophisticated countries of the Second and Third Worlds. By the 1980s, for instance, cars from Eastern Europe, Brazil and Korea should be competing vigorously in western European markets; but competition may also be felt in a wide range of products such as calculators, computers and control instruments; indeed, one of the drastic questions for European manufacturing industry at that time may be to find any area at all where it can compete.

We already suggested in Chapter 2 that the immediate response on the part of European producers may well be a demand for economic autarky, with strong support for European agriculture and a tariff wall against manufactured imports from the Second and Third Worlds. But this will be a highly controversial policy, opposed by some humanitarian and socialist groups. And in any event, there is likely to be large-scale unemployment in mass-production industries. After an initial period of shock, it is likely to be followed by adaptations: a programme of retraining and redevelopment in the tertiary and quarternary sectors of the economy, a development of craft industry, and an increasing emphasis on repair. There will be a much greater stress on the development of non-material services like education, which could be exported to the rest of the world. Within the manufacturing sector, there will be a move towards very well-built goods, involving much craftsmanship. And, related to this, there will be a dramatic increase in small-scale craft production, using relatively small quantities of material and relatively large inputs of skilled labour. Such developments could not only go some way to meeting materials shortages and competition from the rest of the world; additionally, they could provide an answer to the increasing dissatisfaction on the part of many people with the consumerist society we created in the Europe of the 1950s and 1960s. This is a subject we must now discuss. But it must be said immediately that such a shift in policy is not without difficulties. It might well lead to an increase in the real costs of consumer goods – and so engender opposition from wide classes of society which had not yet abandoned consumerist objectives. And it would almost certainly mean large changes in the productive structure – with resultant shifts in the distribution of income and wealth.

Macro-problems: (3) Complexity, social responsiveness and rationality

Our third major theme concerns the organisation of society. At the end of World War Two, a substantial minority of the population in most European countries – and in a few, an actual majority – still lived on the land and drew their living from it. They lived on ancestral farms in villages that might have changed little since the abolition of feudalism. Many more, though nominally urbanites, actually lived in villages in this same countryside, drawing their livelihood from small artisan workshops or family stores. A minority lived in great cities or agglomerations, where they were involved in the mass production economy that had been forged first in Britain, then in Belgium, Germany, France and the United States. But in the thirty years after World War Two an upheaval occurred in European social and economic life: millions poured off the countryside and into cities: in France, Germany and Italy, many made this transition within their own land, moving in great waves from southern and western France to the Paris region, from the villages of Bavaria and Württemberg to the agglomerations of Rhine-Main and Rhine-Ruhr, from Sicily and the Mezzogiorno to the cities of Piedmont and Lombardy; then they were followed by streams of migrants from the Caribbean and the Indian subcontinent to London, Birmingham and Leicester, from Portugal to the bidonvilles of Paris, from Greece, Turkey and Yugoslavia to Dortmund and Duisburg.

It was these great national and international movements which made possible the transformation of Europe into the mass-production, mass-consumption industrial society of the 1960s and early 1970s: but a high price had to be paid in social terms: alienation from work, boredom, separation of families and break-up of well-articulated traditional societies, psychological stress manifesting itself in medical and crime statistics. And this alienation, coupled with inflation, was already producing crises in urban public services by the mid-1970s as strikes in transport, refuse collection, and power supplies hit one city after another. By the middle 1970s the great migratory streams seemed at least to have been halted and even been reversed – at any rate temporarily. From Germany, reports emerged of migrants returning home to southern Europe; British newspapers found cases of disconsolate West Indians going back to their islands. The question posed itself: what would be the effect, both on the exporting and the receiving country, if such a trickle became a flood?

The keynote of the new industrialised and urbanised European society is complexity of organisation, requiring massive public intervention: what is still unclear is its scope. Society as a whole does not understand when it should intervene, and for what precise ends, and in what ways.

One point is evident: the whole organisation of production, whether of goods or of services, is still not responsive enough to human needs. This may sound like a standard socialist criticism of capitalist society, yet it applies to all modern societies whatever their ideological label. In western societies we have a division between a private and a state sector: but the state sector consists in large part of bureaucratic corporations which in practice behave like large corporations in the private sector – they defend their own interests and their own right to survive, by whatever means. They are in fact unions of producers, whose interests may not at all correspond to the wider needs of society as consumers. The point, however, goes wider than that: in a sense, all producing organisations can be regarded as potential conspirators against the interests of society as consumers. Schoolteachers are concerned not so much with education as with teaching in schools; hospital consultants are concerned not so much with health as with providing hospital care; musicians are concerned not so much with culture as with playing music. If society questions the claims of any such groups – asking, for instance, whether education is best provided by yet more years of compulsory education in conventional schools, or health care through yet more hospital buildings, or music through yet more live performances by professionals – it is likely to provoke a similar hostility as if it had challenged the right of General Motors to go on producing more cars. The permanent tendency of all producers' organisations is to confuse the *ends* of human welfare – education, health, culture, mobility – with their own particular *means* of producing them. Such organisations cannot be fully and flexibly responsive to human needs. But consumers' organisations are fragmentary and ill-organised in comparison with the producers' interests, and this is particularly so when the consumer interest is latent: adults who could benefit from continuing education but do not know it, sufferers from low-grade neurosis who do not complain, old people who put up with low mobility because life has always been that way – these are poor candidates for militant consumerism. So the power of the productive organisations is only weakly restrained by state regulation; and as more and more of them enter what Galbraith has called the 'planning system' they find themselves in actual alliance with the state to guard their interests and those of their workers.

This failure already manifests itself in all kinds of ways. At the most general level, there is what we have called the failure of economic rationality. The balance of production of goods and services is distorted by the institutional or organisational structure of production. Thus we have the paradox, in most advanced western countries, of scarce natural resources being employed in production of material goods destined for early obsolescence, while there is a shortage of goods – and above all services – which could use fewer material resources, which could utilise under-employed or unemployed labour, and which would serve more elementary social needs. (Housing and health care, in most countries, are obvious cases.) The mid-1970s crisis of stagflation, which results from a combination of increasing scarcity of natural resources plus the institutional power of producer corporations and trade unions, is a classic manifestation of this syndrome. The failure to consider the ecological effects of production – because of lack of knowledge and lack of ability, or will, to use the knowledge that is available – is another example. Yet another case in point is the extraordinary failure, in almost every country in both western and eastern Europe, to create a human built environment for the millions of new arrivals in the cities. The growth of the great urban agglomerations may or may not have been an inevitable result of industrialisation: what was surely not inevitable was the creation of millions of standardised housing units apparently without regard for human needs or the existence of communities. Lastly, there has been an equal failure in the educational systems of virtually all countries: a failure to coordinate the development of the child as he or she proceeded from one arbitrarily defined level of education to another, and a failure to coordinate the output of the schools and colleges with the needs either of the economy or of the community.

These problems are already well-known, and there is no lack of explanations: technology out of control, blind pursuit of the profit motive, failure of management, lack of sufficient resources are all quoted as causes. As to remedy, some look to ever more sophisticated systems of management by objectives; some to a simpler society where decisions are broken down to small and intimate groups, using a simpler human-scale technology. Maybe the answer lies in some combination of the two, whereby producers and consumers work in small units but within some overall hierarchy of social goals. Some see the answer in a more innovative society, whereby the social goals and the means to reach them are more frequently questioned; yet others would see in this the danger of an unstable, disoriented, nervous society. These questions need further discussion – in Chapter 7 and the concluding section of this book, Chapters 11 and 12.

But meanwhile, it needs to be emphasised that the necessary change would go very deep, involving not merely institutional attitudes but mass individual attitudes. Post-war Europe, and indeed the post-war western world, have been characterised by very general shared values transcending the ideological barrier down the middle of Europe: they make up what Herman Kahn has called the sensate culture (Kahn and Bruce-Briggs 1972), which is highly materialistic, concerned with satisfaction in this world rather than the next, liberal with regard to personal behaviour and tolerant of large-scale organisations that appear to deliver the material goods. This is an age, archetypally, where great social control in the public sphere is balanced by extreme privacy in the individual or family sphere; where the bread-winner leaves the giant factory or office for the anonymity of a suburban home. It is not an age where the sense of community counts for much, either at work or at home. It is an age where people, when they stop to think at all, often resent the fact that they seem to have become small cogs in a giant wheel: the car worker on the assembly line, the paper processor in the giant *Bürolandschaft* office, the suburban wife-chauffeur shuttling between school and shop and railway station. It is also an age where information sometimes seems to have got out of control: where the nightly information coming through the TV set may exceed the lifetime information received by a medieval (or early twentieth-century) peasant, where the professional worker is faced by a growing mountain of literature that cannot ever be read, let alone digested or used; where the ordinary citizen sometimes cannot cope with the multiple demands of a tentacular bureaucracy. Finally, faced with mounting evidence of minor disorder – petty crime, and sometimes major crime too, worsening labour relations, apparent chaos in the schools and increasing civil disorder in the streets – many citizens begin to wonder whether the apparent *purposelessness* of this society may not bring about its destruction.

All this, social critics suggest, indicates the failure of economic rationality and the need for its replacement by a higher form of cultural rationality. But such a change will hardly come overnight: as we earlier noticed, the move away from consumerism has been spearheaded by the more affluent, and the less affluent may well regard it as a shabby trick.

Macro-problems: (4) The unknown hazards

There is one other area in which economic rationality may prove deficient – and fatally so. Isolated cases, both proven (thalidomide) and non-proven (cyclamates, aerosols), suggest that chemical advances may have long-run side-effects which are extremely difficult to identify until it is too late. There is already a strong suspicion that less spectacular side-effects – in the form of chemical allergies, for example – may be growing in frequency and intensity. But the effects on general health and mortality patterns may take decades to prove. For instance, long distance commercial jet travel developed only from the late 1950s onwards; in the mid-1970s, a whole generation of regular jet travellers is approaching late middle age, a time of emerging health hazard: suppose it were then demonstrated that jet lag takes a long-term toll? This is a purely hypothetical example, without any empirical evidence: but it is easy to conceive of the panic that would result if evidence were to emerge. Demand would surely grow that all technological innovations should be tested for their longer-term effects before they were generally introduced; and this would present an acute moral conflict in calculating the trade-off between more or less certain short-term benefits and highly speculative long-term risks. These trade-offs may well become a major European concern of the 1970s and 1980s.

There exists, moreover, a more general failure to appreciate the longer-term consequences of decisions. When several aircraft manufacturers developed wide-bodied jets, that fact reacted on the decisions of others, making Concorde even less viable than before and several planned European airports more or less redundant. When Governor Reagan became embroiled with the students at Berkeley in 1967 and 1968, few saw that this presaged widespread confrontation that would weaken the whole image of universities in the western world and finally cause their plans for expansion to be drastically scaled down. This means simply that we need better mechanisms for linking cause and effect – or at least that we should use more often the mechanisms we have. One modest argument for the present sort of futures study is that it tries to do just that.

Problems of groups in society

Under this second main heading we are concerned primarily with questions of social equity. We want to look at the access of different groups or classes to what Harvey (1973) has called real income in its widest sense: not merely wages or salaries or dividends, but access to goods and services of all kinds – including environment, education, recreation and employment. Planners in Europe are only now coming to appreciate just how unequal is the distribution of these goods.

Historically, every society has faced the problem of distribution. Modern dynamic societies have periodically changed the ground rules in various ways, obvious and direct (taxation and welfare) and less direct (education, housing, employment services). But almost without exception the new rules create anomalies in some other area, requiring a new adjustment in turn. Groups campaigning for changes often conveniently forget that this will be the case: but in considering some of the inequities that we think will loom large in the 1980s and 1990s we should not overlook it.

Group problems: (5) Urban and regional disparities

In the first place, the Europe of the immediate future is likely to witness quite striking regional inequities. Migrations noted earlier have done little to equalise regional disparaties, and may have exacerbated them. Typically, major industrial agglomerations such as Paris, Milan, Madrid or Lisbon have per capita incomes which may be double those of the peasant countryside only 200 kilometers distant. A polarisation occurs, whereby industry, enterprise, innovation are concentrated in the cities, and the rural periphery is deprived of any possibility of spontaneous advance. Thus, though the peasant-turned-industrial worker may remit a large part of his income to his family in the village, this merely fortifies the dependence of the countryside on the city: and eventually the family will join him there, hastening the depopulation of the countryside and intensifying the problems of urban growth. In Latin America and elsewhere, regional development experts such as Albert Hirschman, Gunnar Myrdal and John Friedmann have developed a theory concerning the problem of diffusing innovative impulses from the primate city into the rural hinterland: they conclude that at some stage the centre-periphery contrast may become so stark that it produces its own political counter-movement. We seem to be seeing the beginnings of such a movement in many European countries at the present time – in Scotland and Wales, in northern Spain, in Brittany. This may prove to be one of the major problem areas of the immediate future for the governments of many European countries.

A further polarisation is taking place through desertion of the cities by the rich. Traditionally, in Mediterranean countries, rich and poor lived cheek by jowl in the densely populated inner city; suburbia had no attractions. In northern European countries, especially those with an Anglo-Saxon tradition, the preferences were different: there the richer and more knowledgable members of the community often led a flight to the suburbs which continued over many decades. Now there is evidence that this tradition is spreading: Paris, for instance, is decentralising on a vast scale, with the historic city losing people and suburbia spreading up to 70 kilometers in most directions. In countries with a purer Mediterranean tradition, the rich still for the most part choose to live in apartments close to the centre – though often with a second home in the hills or at the seaside, up to 200 kilometers away. In southern Europe, as in the developing world, it is the poor who seem to be banished to the edge of the city since they cannot afford the high rents near the centre. But everywhere there seems to be an accelerating process of social polarisation, whereby the city is differentiated into rich and poor rings or sectors. Within these, the poor are likely to find conspicuously inferior physical environments, access to services or transportation, and a general atmosphere of neglect and decay. The areas they inhabit may come to resemble islands of rural poverty in a sea of relative urban prosperity.

The spatial structure of the city clearly has a profound effect on access to the opportunities it offers: people migrate to cities for the sake of this access – to a bigger range of better-paid jobs, to a richer supply of retail goods at lower prices, to a greater array of services of all kinds. But the form of the city may either aid this access or frustrate it. If working-class housing schemes are provided at the periphery of a sprawling metropolitan area, or even way beyond it, if transportation facilities are poor or expensive, then the jobs and services may be either unreachable or reachable only at unreasonable cost in time or money. Swedish geographers have introduced the notion of a time-space budget, whereby people are compelled to make use of their most scarce common resource – time – in the most economical way. If the 'friction of distance' can be readily overcome by fast and cheap travel, or by substituting telecommunication for physical movement, they can make more effective use of their waking hours. This is easier for people who can use their own cars than for those dependent on public transport – which is often ill-coordinated and inconvenient. But all people in some degree, and some groups to an exceptional degree, suffer constraints in their time-space budgets. Women in particular may find a conflict between their career demands and the demands of rearing children. And there is no single easy answer: even good public transport cannot provide the flexibility of the car. Higher-density living has its own drawbacks. Telecommunications can substitute for bodily movement only to a degree.

Finally, there is the special consideration that the city is largely the custodian of Europe's cultural patrimony, and its integrity has to this extent to be safeguarded. The model instance is, of course, Venice: but hundreds of cities throughout the continent, though not so obviously of value in and for themselves, are none the less repositories of an irreplaceable past – and of a past, moreover, peculiar to themselves. The continued cultural diversity of Europe can be guaranteed – if it is to be guaranteed at all – only by the preservation of cities: the wholesale reconstruction possible without much loss in the United States, for instance, is hardly a viable alternative for Europe.

Group problems: (6) The female dilemma

The nature of discrimination against women is often misunderstood. Women share with the poor the legacy of under-education, whereby those who fail to obtain the right formal educational qualifications in childhood or adolescence will invariably find themselves barred from advance in their careers. The means for overcoming this handicap – day release and sandwich courses, Open Universities and night schools – are at present quite inadequate. Sexual differentiation starts early in the educational system of many countries, reserving certain kinds of training for boys and others for girls. Thus, with conspicuous exceptions (such as certain east European countries), women will find it relatively hard to become engineers or industrial managers; in some countries they may find it difficult to train as doctors or dentists. Hardly any European country, on the other hand, trains men as secretaries, while the traditionally female occupations, such as typing and nursing, tend in many cases to be conspicuously low-paid, partly at least because trade union organisation is weak. Nearly all western countries under-value women's work by failing to include it in the national income accounts.

Perhaps the most obvious form of discrimination against women, however, arises from their biological role. Giving birth to children, and then nurturing them through their early years, is notoriously difficult to combine with higher education or a professional career. The problem has been exacerbated by the decline of the three-generation extended family typical of agrarian society, where the grandparents could tend children while the parents laboured in the fields. Some radical commentators see an answer in the commune; others see it in the development of more effective nursery and day care facilities (but others would deplore the invasion of paid professionalism in this field). Meanwhile, women are faced with acute logistical problems of spanning time and space. Even if they have nursery facilities, to transport children to them, get to and from work and perform other household obligations may prove virtually impossible – especially in the giant metropolis where home, nursery, work and shops may be scattered. There are many obvious answers: decentralisation to small communities where distances are shorter, local day care facilities, work from home or from local offices or workshops, flexitime (*Gleitzeit*), longer shopping hours or deliveries from stores, labour-saving equipment in the home, convenience foods or take-home foods, more equal sharing of household burdens. But meanwhile, in this regard, women have no true equality.

Group problems: (7) Revolt of the old

Another major group suffering discrimination is the old. And this group is growing in number, due to Europe's demographic evolution. The late 1970s and the 1980s will see continuing large numbers of people passing firstly into the retirement bracket, then, at about 75, into the stage of increasing inactivity and dependence. Many have only simple skills and few resources. They will constitute as much as 30 per cent of the population in many west European countries by the 1980s. Up to now, perhaps because their early upbringing tended towards deference, they have not been a very vocal or active political force: but this could change, and the revolt of the old could release a political instrument of great strength. In the 1950s and 1960s, there was a heavy accent on youth – both in the private market for goods and services, and in public sector policies on matters like education. That corresponded to the political realities of a society with exceptionally large numbers of young child-rearing adults and their offspring. But one certain fact about the Europe of the 1980s and 1990s is the shift towards a society dominated by the old and the middle-aged: their needs and demands must weigh ever more heavily with political decision-makers.

These demands are likely to take at least two forms. The first will be for a new look at the whole phenomenon of retirement. The notion of retirement is quite recent: in agricultural and early industrial society men and women worked till they could work no more: and even then they still had a social role in minding the home and the children. All that has quite suddenly disappeared with the replacement of the peasant extended family by the modern primary nuclear unit, and it did so just as compulsory fixed-age retirement became usual throughout manufacturing and whitecollar occupations. Thus there has developed – first in the United States, then on a smaller scale in Europe – the notion of retirement colonies for 'senior citizens' where still active people vegetate for twenty years or more. Sooner or later, there is bound to be a protest at this kind of arbitrary prison sentence: it may take the form of a reaction against official retirement ages, or of a demand for new careers for the old, or even of a movement for the return of the extended family – which could have striking effects on living patterns, migration movements and urban forms.

A second demand will be for more systematic study of gerontology, of the physical and psychological needs of the aged; and for more resources to be spent on care for those who can no longer help themselves. This is likely to be a controversial demand, for such care is necessarily intensive, expensive in its use of resources, and difficult in human terms. There is bound to be renewed debate over the rights of the old to voluntary euthanasia, which could be to the European society of the 1980s what the abortion debate was to the 1960s.

Group problems: (8) The marginal groups

Overlapping with migrant workers, women and the very old is one last very large sector of the population demanding special mention: it consists of all the marginal groups who are divorced from real control over their personal environment. An important element in it is the dysfunctionals, or those who cannot fulfil the norms which society places upon them: the physically or mentally disabled, the chronically sick and the psychotic, all whose neuroses substantially impair their functioning in the adult world, and the senile. There is some evidence, admittedly inconclusive, that the proportion of such groups in the total population may be rising; and changes in the composition of the population – for instance, the proportion of old people who survive to very advanced ages – make it highly likely. It implies a growing burden of dependence on that part of the population that must continue to produce the goods and services which the whole of society needs – even though other changes, such as the fall in the birth rate, may work to reduce the burden.

Perhaps the most obvious fact about nearly all the marginals is that they are poorer than the average for their countries. The old subsist on pensions; guest workers are paid substantially less than native workers because they do less skilled jobs; young people earn relatively poorly, if they succeed in earning at all; the disabled tend again to subsist on state pensions. But the poverty is not just in money income: many lack educational qualifications; they may have language barriers in comprehension and speaking; few understand their way around the tentacular central and local government bureaucracies, to which many must go to help resolve their problems. They readily tend to apathy and powerlessness: they are classic candidates for alienation.*

The problems of these groups present a formidable challenge: within a fundamentally affluent and enlightened society, there could be a substantial minority of poor, alienated, frustrated, and dysfunctional people who could present a source of grave social malaise. The signs of such a delinquent sub-culture have up to now been much stronger in the United States than in Europe: some of the key indicators, such as crime (particularly juvenile crime), drug-taking, marital and family breakdown, school absenteeism and drop-out rates, have all been evident there for two or more decades. But there are isolated signs of the development of similar

* Here the word 'alienation' is used in a general sense. Cf. page 50.

subcultures in European urban areas, though as yet inconsistent and far from general. They form part of the wider phenomenon of alienation.

A word of warning is in order here. Putting pejorative labels on groups of people – especially labels which seem to be scientific – can be dangerous. Who defines what is dysfunctional, what deviates from the social norm? The tendency in European society has recently been to leave this question more and more to the individual conscience: that is the essence of what is loosely called the permissive society. Thus the phenomenon of 'dropping out' of society has come to be widely regarded as of no concern to that wider society – so long as the fabric of society itself is not endangered. But conservatives argue that before long this danger will occur, and indeed has already occurred; the ethos of doing one's own thing, if widely applied, leads to a breakdown of the informal codes of social relationships which permit a society to function without excessive regimentation (Buchanan 1975). Our guess is that this problem will come to loom larger in European society of the 1980s and 1990s, as a new generation comes to react against some of the consequences of the permissive society of the 1960s. And particularly problematic will be the existence of a lumpenproletarian sub-culture totally at variance with the prevailing middle-class norms, and originating in the impact of permissive values on individuals who lack the discriminatory capacity to cope with them.

Problems of the individual in society:
  (9) Alienation in industry
  (10) Alienation in education

This leads us to the most fundamental of the problems likely to face the individual, which in our view can be summed up in one evocative word: alienation. Given the complexity of social and economic organisation, and the lack of any evident guiding ethical or social principles, individuals feel they lack any meaningful relationship to the wider society or to any particular part of it; they are divorced from other people and objects to such a degree that they feel incapable of free action – or they behave self-destructively. They feel they are used by organisations rather than exercising creative autonomy within them. In education, this manifests itself in apathy, boredom and cynicism in the classroom; in absenteeism and a high drop-out rate; in occasional violence and vandalism; in the presence of large numbers of docile but weakly motivated students at the higher levels of the system. In industry, alienation expresses itself in similar ways: absenteeism, high labour turnover, poor quality control, bad industrial relations at the shop-floor level (including the prevalence of wildcat strikes), low productivity, and general reluctance to undertake industrial work for any sustained period of time – leading to the formation of a heterogenous, ill-assorted labour force. In society as a whole, it manifests itself in the form of non-material poverty: the empty lives of large groups which have achieved substantial material resources but have all too little idea of how to use them. In the body politic, it manifests itself in general political cynicism especially with regard to the formal processes of democratic election, and to a proliferation of political fringe groups. At a more psychotic level, political alienation demonstrates itself in the violence of the terrorist gang or the urban guerilla, and, though these groups appear as yet to be numerically small, they can exercise a disproportionately disruptive effect on social life as a whole.

For the most part, though, the reaction to alienation so far has been one of passive boredom rather than violent aggression – a passivity maintained by massive consumption of tranquillisers and other forms of treatment for minor neurosis. One strong possibility is that medical advance will continue to cope with most manifestations of the problem, and indeed to make further inroads on it. In penal institutions, for instance, there is much experimentation already in the use of drugs and other personality-modifying treatments for anti-social and aggressive behaviour. But as they are extended such methods are likely to excite increasing mass controversy – as indeed is already occurring in the United States (Hydèn 1972, Cohen 1974).

Less dramatically, answers may be found by adapting institutions better to cope with human needs. In education, there may be an end to traditional school categories (primary, secondary, tertiary) and their replacement by a life-long, voluntary learning system in which traditional barriers between education, work and retirement would be broken down. In such a system, it would not seem odd that a child of ten worked for part of the time in a factory, or an adult of seventy years returned to school. Such a change would entail also a transformation in the *content* of education, away from the old encyclopaedic tradition and towards a freer structure based on personal needs. In industry, the first experiments can already be seen in small-scale group organisation of work, whereby the group sets its own norms and its own pace and methods of work: to some degree, this represents a return within the framework of modern mass production to the small-master system typical of much eighteenth and nineteenth century industry, and still usual in craft workshops everywhere. This system would employ automation in its proper place – for the soul-destroying, degrading processes still too often left to humans. In penology, it is seen in the rejection – especially striking in some north European nations – of penal institutions as such, and their replacement by various forms of community involvement. These are among the most interesting first answers to one of the largest problems of the last quarter of the twentieth century.

But one must not be too sanguine. Recall for a moment the macro-organisational problems of society: existing bureaucratic institutions, with their prejudice in favour of the *status quo*, are everywhere likely to oppose innovation. School managers and teachers are not likely to look kindly on proposals for their abolition. Industrial managers reared in the present system of mass production will hardly view with favour the proposed break-up of an apparently disciplined, hierarchical flow structure into a possibly anarchic set of small craft units. In the service industries – particularly in the public services, such as education, welfare and penology, where much of the advance would need to come – the necessary technologies barely exist, except to a limited degree in education. Yet, through communications technologies such as the sound and video cassette, through teaching machines and laboratories, through cable TV, the necessary technologies already exist for self-education of a flexible kind, for learning about how to cope with complex problems of life in society, for linking small-scale units effectively into the organisation of mass production. What is needed is a change of attitude on the part of the institutions; and that could demand their total restructuring, either from inside or by external pressure for change.

Problems of the individual: (11) Alienation in the city

A third set of personal scale problems, overlapping considerably with the other two, concerns the individual in his environment. As Europeans have poured into the exploding cities during the past thirty years, they have too often found an environment that is sterile and inhuman. Urban planners notoriously seem unable to find a way of replicating the natural, unconscious built forms of earlier generations, which – unsatisfactory as they may have been from an elementary hygenic point of view – provided for the natural satisfaction of basic human needs. One aspect of this is the failure to think through the whole problem of what Chermayev and Alexander

(1964) have called Community and Privacy: the critical and delicate balance between the individual's need for privacy and solitude on the one hand, for gregariousness and a variety of both structured and unstructured human contacts on the other. Thus the new housing blocks often contain an inflexible division of interior space, adapted to the needs of some theoretical average household rather than to those of a real family: they do not provide adequate work-space for the housewife, play-space for the young children, study-space for school students, party-space for teenagers. Nor do they always provide adequate privacy, either visually or in terms of noise insulation, between one household and another. At a large scale, they present the problem of what the American architect Oscar Newman calls 'indefensible space': the public spaces around and between buildings that belong to no-one, are overseen by no-one, and become a logical opportunity for vandalism or crime (Wilsher and Righter 1975, ch.8). Coupled with this, there is too often a glaring lack of opportunity for informal social contact, for surprise and visual delight in the streets of the city, such as was provided by almost any medieval village street or town square. The new areas of the cities, in other words, lack a certain vital quality which cities previously had: the affective dimension, glamour, charisma, excitement.

Yet even while this is widely recognised and incessantly publicised, cities all over Europe are destroying the buildings and urban quarters that had these attributes, replacing them by modern blocks of offices or apartments that conspicuously fail to provide a human environment. The irony is that all the efforts of countless schools of architecture and planning cannot achieve what was regularly – and, so far as we can see, effortlessly – done by unlettered masons and carpenters and plasterers over many previous centuries. There are as many explanations as there are critics: the profit motive, or accountant's architecture; the high prices and high rents of urban land, brought about by speculation in an inflation-ridden world; modern building technology, which by rigid modules constrains human expression; insensitive and outmoded building, public health and planning regulations; crass assertiveness on the part of architectural bureaucracies which vent their fantasies on defenceless public housing tenants while their own members prefer to live in human housing from an earlier era. At the same time, experts in the developing countries of Latin America and Africa are suggesting one answer: that it is actually cheaper in real resources to let people return to their old ancestral ways and build with their own hands using the simplest of tools. In such self-help housing projects – which are seen also on the fringes of European cities such as Athens and Lisbon, where they are stigmatised as illegal – a new urban form is already arising: apparently anarchic, rambling, idiosyncratic, anathema to the professional architect, but above all highly personal. It may be the harbinger of a revolution in the way we build cities.

Problems of the individual: (12) Information – overload and starvation

A different problem, but one peculiarly associated with urban life in contemporary Europe, is access to information. It is a paradoxical fact that large numbers of people may be simultaneously suffering from information overload and information starvation: they have too much information they do not want and too little on what they really need. Information in this sense is a very heterogenous commodity: it includes personal contacts, the mass media, professional information. The modern European urbanite is bombarded from morning till night by a variety of information that may exceed by a factor of several times the information reaching a villager in the countryside a few kilometers away – and may indeed equal in one day what the medieval peasant received in a lifetime: information from the morning radio and newspaper, from talk overheard or advertisements on the journey to work, from contacts in factory or office, from reading papers and memoranda and reports, from lunchtime shopping, from the evening's television programmes. Children reared in such an environment begin to run the risk that they can no longer concentrate for long on anything that needs sustained attention: reading, save for the momentary perusal of a comic book, may become a lost art. The adult experiences a similar syndrome, but in addition he or she may suffer neurotic manifestations from the sheer inability to digest, process and act on a variety of signals that bombard the senses on every side. Yet at the same time, this adult may find at critical moments that there is a virtually total lack of information on subjects of critical concern: on the choice between different brands of consumer goods, for instance, or on planning proposals in the immediate neighbourhood. Such information becomes monopolised by private corporations or by bureaucrats in central or local government, who defend their possession by appeals to the public interest.

Information threatens the individual in another way – a way that has already occasioned much alarm in all advanced industrial countries. Not only is a surfeit of unstructured information directed at the individual; a surfeit is obtained from him and about him, often without his knowledge or conscious agreement. The use of interlinked information systems, related through unique personal identifiers, has very large-scale applications in both public sector and private sector corporate planning, which are already apparent in such varied practices as credit-worthiness ratings, 'junk mail' distributions and criminal investigation. But all these create the risk that organisations progressively amass – and exchange – a great amount of data about individuals, some of it having a potentially damaging character, without those individuals' knowledge. This is an invasion of individual privacy hardly conceivable in any previous age, and in several European countries it has led to legislation specifically designed to protect the individual. But to maintain this protection in the face of technological advance and of lack of scruple on the part of organisations will be increasingly difficult – as the American experience of the CIA so clearly shows. Central to these issues is the individual's access to information: not merely the theoretical availability of that information, but also the individual's capacity to find and use it. At present, access to information is easier for the relatively wealthy, the well-connected and above all the well-educated: they understand how to penetrate the bureaucratic jungle, how to use political representatives, how to organise information to a purpose. As the complexity of organisations constantly tends to increase, as the amount of necessary information tends also to grow, this disparity between the information-rich groups and the information-poor groups will also tend to widen – unless positive contrary action is taken. For the future, quite revolutionary possibilities open up with the widespread use of new devices such as two-way cable television or televised factual information. But, as with conventional libraries, the problem is that this new resource may be exploited first by the well-educated and the well-organised – unless the television networks can initiate a national (or a European) campaign for Equal Access to Information.

Summary and prospect: Mega-problems of the future Europe

Our review is complete. In the chapters up to now and those that follow we group related problems together, to understand their ramifications and possible solutions at greater length. Here is a review of some key questions that need to be asked under these groupings.

(1) Peace, war and security

In a world with insufficient supplies of energy, food and raw materials to meet the demands of the developed world and the rising aspirations of the developing world, on what principles should resources be shared out? By blackmail on either side or by new modes of international agreement? Are we condemned to the risk of terrorism in our daily lives – and what would be the popular reaction? These topics have already been discussed in Chapter 2.

(2) Growth, stagnation and scarcity

Can industrial Europe take a lead in developing styles of production and consumption that will stress quality rather than quantity? Will it be possible to enjoy the same real living standard – or even a better one – with a smaller volume of real resources? How far can Europe devise energy-efficient heating and transportation systems, truly durable consumer goods, and a stress on crafts and services with modest claim on resources? How will European industry react to the challenge from the developing world? These topics have been principal themes of Chapters 2 and 3.

(3) Farming, rural life and the natural environment

Will the social geography of Europe be polarised, with continued urban growth consuming irreplaceable agricultural areas while the remoter rural regions are gradually depopulated? Is there a prospect of a more rational pattern of population growth? What do the young people of rural Europe think about their future? What is the future of European farming within a pattern of world food crisis – that is, does protection of the rural habitat have to take second place to efficient farming? These are some of the questions raised in Chapter 5.

(4) Urban life and urban environment

Can Europe's mobile urban society assimilate its minorities, or will plural cultures and societies persist in its cities? Will urban society polarise as the middle class flee to the suburbs? In a generally affluent, informed and civilised society, is there a permanent prospect of a disillusioned and desperate urban under-class? Can architects and city planners find a way of building cities that use modern technology for modern social and economic needs, and yet preserve the visual, social and emotional quality of the great historic cities of Europe? If not, should the job be taken away from them? Could ordinary people do the job better, as for many centuries they appear to have done? What are the real obstacles to building liveable cities? These questions are examined in Chapter 6.

(5) Industry for human ends

Can the assembly line and the paper factory be replaced by new forms of organisation that give meaning to work and respect to the worker? Will automation – in service industry as in manufacturing – take over repetitive and tedious work, liberating workers for responsible decision-making or creative craftsmanship? Will these new forms involve workers more fundamentally in determining the social ends of their own production? This is examined in Chapter 7.

(6) Access to information

Will technological changes just ahead allow individuals to control the kind of information reaching them, or will this control pass altogether out of their hands? Conversely, what is the likely development in obtaining information about the individual by electronic surveillance and the like? How does the new information technology effect our thinking about education? This is the major theme of Chapter 8.

(7) The family – divided and reunited?

How can society work towards full equality of life opportunities for women, while recognising the biological imperative? How should women's domestic work be restructured – or, alternatively, recognised and rewarded? Is the equalisation of the roles of husband and wife a likely development? Will the old people of Europe rise in protest against their subjection in retirement and poverty? Will formal retirement processes be challenged, or might the old develop their own rival productive organisations? These are some of the themes of Chapter 9.

(8) Class and inequality

What different kinds of inequality exist and how are they diminishing – if at all? What is the relationship between distribution of income, distribution of wealth and distribution of opportunity and power – in the recent past, now and possibly in the future? These are the kind of questions addressed in Chapter 10.

(9) Alienation and a new rationality

Finally: how far are many of the problems so far discussed the reflection of a deeper phenomenon – the alienation of man from the society he lives in? How far could – or should – society go in enforcing social norms? Are social norms themselves changing? And will a new rationality to replace the prevailing rationality offer an amelioration of our present ills? This is the central set of questions discussed in Chapter 11.

This is not the place to discuss possible solutions; insofar as that is possible at all, it will be the theme of the last chapter. Clearly, some problems might be met by changes in organisation – in industry or education for instance. But none is purely a matter of organisation, and some problems seem incapable of being solved at all in these terms. George Orwell once said that the fundamental dilemma of political action was the clash between two viewpoints: that you could not change the system until you had improved human nature, but that you could not improve human nature until you had changed the system (Orwell 1951, p.18). That is as likely to be so in the future as it was in the past.

In this chapter we have, therefore, largely ignored the political dimension; and that goes in general also for the detailed chapters that follow. Our view of politics is that it deals with problems as they arise, and that these problems are created by underlying social and economic forces. Of course, the nature of political systems is likely to form a constraint on the range of solutions that can be found – but we can deal with this point best by looking at the impact of the problems on the political process itself.

That raises a last point. Chapters 2 and 3 were concerned to establish the dynamics of change in the world and in Europe. In contrast, the present chapter has sought to freeze change in a moment of future time; to establish a landscape of problems as it might appear to Europeans of, say, the mid-1980s. That also will be the approach of Chapters 5-11 which follow, as they examine some of these problems in more detail. Yet, of course, no landscape is ever completely static, and that fully applies to the mega-problems we have just listed. They will emerge at different points of time, alternative solutions will be debated and a preferred political solution will emerge. It will be tried and will probably prove to work not quite as well as was expected. In particular, there will be side-effects that were not predicted, perhaps on quite other areas of life or parts of society. Modifications will be needed, and the character of the debate will once again change. Though we can surmise that something will very probably appear as a problem within the coming one or two decades, we may not be able to establish with any certainty when it will appear, or in what form. The interaction of problems and solutions is particularly difficult to establish. But it must be attempted – and that is the final aim of the final chapter of this book.

CHAPTER 5

People and Land: the Regional and Rural Dimension

We start with the people and where they will live. After World War Two, Europe experienced a population increase barely equalled even in the Industrial Revolution. Following decades of decline birth rates bounded up again, giving a rate of natural increase which alone needed a vast building programme for new houses and apartments. At the same time population flooded from Europe's farms, propelled by agricultural reorganisation and drawn by the prospect of job opportunities in the cities. As urban areas grew, so they began to decentralise, impinging on areas of farmland many kilometers from the cities, and creating the prospect of a European Megalopolis stretching from Manchester to Milan. Now, in the mid-1970s, another reversal seems to be taking place: birth rates have been dropping in most European countries for a decade, and have reached their lowest ever point in some; the movement from the land may be in course of being stemmed, while some thinkers see a mass return to the land in response to the threat of world food shortages. Which way, in fact, will Europe's population go?

In 1898, in his path-breaking book on Garden Cities (Howard 1946, 1898), the English writer Ebenezer Howard asked this same question. His famous diagram of the Three Magnets showed the very different pulls of town and country. The town was the place of opportunities, both economic and social: it had a wide range of jobs catering for many different kinds of levels of skill, entertainment and cultural facilities, and the attraction of new friends and bright lights. But it was scarred by pollution, overcrowding and bad housing conditions. The countryside on the contrary offered pure air and water and the presence of nature. But it conspicuously lacked the opportunities of the town. That contrast still holds today, though electrification and the private car have diminished much of the starkness of the contrast. And Howard's third magnet – town-country, or the creation of garden cities – remains an ideal, realised in Britain's new towns and a few similar experiments across Europe, but far from having been achieved by the great majority.

In this chapter, therefore, we consider the central question of Europe's population and its distribution. In 'Chapter 4 we already looked briefly at the course of population growth in the recent past and in the near future. That logically leads us now to look at recent trends in the spatial distribution of the people – especially the division between town and country. That in turn will cause us to look at the future of Europe's agriculture in relation to the world crisis of population growth and limited food supply. And this will allow us to speculate on some alternative futures for Europe's agriculture and the rural areas of Europe – alternatives which in some cases embody a sharp reversal of recent trends. That, in turn, will provide the setting for Chapter 6, where we consider alternative futures for Europe's cities.

Urban growth and urban spread

Everywhere in Europe since 1945, the dominant population trend has been from the countryside to the cities. In most European countries by the 1970s, 70 per cent or more of the population was officially classed as urban – even though this uniformity concealed alarming variations in the methods of classification used by the census takers. In Britain over 77 per cent of the population of England and Wales lived in so-called Standard Metropolitan Labour Areas; in Holland, 52 per cent lived in socio-economic agglomerations; in West Germany, 54 per cent lived in city regions at the 1961 census, and this proportion would undoubtedly be higher today (Hall 1973, p.108). Further, in parts of north-western and central Europe, these agglomerations were tending to grow together into a Megalopolis stretching down the Rhine from Mannheim to Rotterdam and then across the North Sea from the Sussex coast to Lancashire and Yorkshire (Hall 1973, p.133) – a vast concentration of urban humanity numbering well over 63 million at the census of 1961, and probably close on 70 million today.

In contrast, the population map of Europe showed vast areas of rural decline or stagnation. Much of northern Scandinavia, the Highlands of Scotland, most of Eire, southern and western France, the upland borders of West Germany, the Italian Mezzogiorno all fall into this group. While the European Megalopolis – sometimes dubbed the Golden Triangle – occupies the heartland of Europe, these areas of stagnation and low incomes are all on the periphery. The reason is clear enough: the prosperity of Megalopolis is based on manufacturing and, increasingly, tertiary industry which locate near concentrated markets and labour supplies, specialised transportation and marketing services; they also seek to concentrate together in order to exploit economies of agglomeration and scale. And, because there are powerful forces of inertia working here, these activities tend to grow where they have long been concentrated: Megalopolis defines fairly accurately some of the great European trading routes of the middle ages.

But the process has its drawbacks as well as its economic advantages. Emigration of young people from the countryside – for it is they who principally leave – will lead to a rapid ageing of the population and eventually to natural decline. Over large areas, the population may become too thin and scattered to support modern services, in turn reinforcing the attraction of the great cities for the young people. And in the cities themselves, the new immigrants – especially those who have crossed international frontiers, and arrive ignorant of the language or of urban know-how – pay another heavy price in terms of poor housing, high rents, long and costly journeys to work, restricted job opportunities, and even hostility from the indigenous population. In the longer term, uprooted from a well-articulated rural culture, the second generation of such immigrants may well come to exhibit classic symptoms of alienation* from their new urban society.

At the same time as urban populations have grown, so logically they have decentralised. Especially has this been the case in northern and western Europe, where most of the large cities – London, Paris, Hamburg, Frankfurt, Copenhagen, Stockholm, Oslo, Amsterdam, Rotterdam – lost population during the 1960s. Of course, this was not a real loss: all around these cities were wide rings of suburban growth. While Paris lost, the entire Paris region grew; and similarly with London. Higher car ownership, motorway construction, the pressure to own housing as a hedge against inflation, and the basic search for more space all helped; the trend towards the periphery, once a virtual monopoly of the Anglo-Saxon countries, began to affect almost the whole of northern Europe and even gripped the French. In southern and eastern Europe, where the habit of living at high densities in apartments died harder, the trend was not yet evident: the cities still grew. Yet even there, the trend to second home ownership began to affect rural areas as much as two or three hundred kilometers from Paris or Madrid.

Some of this last movement has even begun to affect the stagnant

---

* 'Alienation' is here used in a general sense. Cf. page 50.

rural upland areas. But in general, the outward push of urban areas mainly influenced the lowland rural zones immediately around them; and these, in many cases, are still among Europe's most important agricultural areas: the London Basin, the Ile de France, the Rhein-Main-Gebiet, the Kölner Bucht, the Mediterranean coast around Barcelona and Valencia, the Po Valley. The irony, then, is that urbanisation may help destroy some of Europe's most precious food-producing areas, while the far less valuable uplands may come to be virtually depopulated.

These complex processes are a classic expression of the predominant economic rationality of the post-World-War-Two era, as we shall argue in Chapter 6. Everywhere, Europeans moved in search of higher economic opportunities, a higher material standard of life. This same motive dominated the Italian peasant migrating from Sicily or the Mezzogiorno to the factories of Milan, the worker from the small Greek town seeking a living in Essen or Dortmund, the London professional finding a new house in rural Berkshire or Surrey, or his Parisian counterpart looking for a weekend house in the Dordogne. Forgotten, in the whole process, were the longer-term consequences and the effects of developments on the rest of the world. To some of these wider relationships we must now turn.

Towards agriculture in the year 2000

In the course of the last quarter-century, agrarian Europe has been profoundly transformed. What new changes must be expected in the coming quarter-century? The prospects lie, without doubt, in the area between several extreme hypotheses which may be posed.

The situation now

European agriculture is very heterogeneous. Consider the differences between Britain, with its large-scale commercial farming; France, with its great agricultural potential; the Netherlands, with their highly developed technical level; and Spain, distinguished by technical backwardness. But on a world scale, the differences blur and the main features of western European agriculture appear more clearly. European farmers, mostly still working family farms, practice an agriculture which is both intensive and technically advanced. Thus western European agriculture distinguishes itself from eastern Europe, North America and Australasia and the less developed countries.

Most of the family farms of Europe are small – more precisely, very small. Their area and livestock totals are not large enough to give full employment to their occupants if they were to use the best techniques and the most modern equipment. If current techniques allow a two-person farm to cultivate 50 hectares and keep 50 dairy cows, a farm of two persons with only 20 hectares and 20 cows is clearly too small.

The evolution of this agriculture has, however, been very rapid since the beginning of the 1950s. Production has increased notably, though the active agricultural population has fallen rapidly: at certain periods there has been a 3 per cent growth per annum in production with a 4 per cent fall in farm workers. These figures indicate a growth in labour productivity of 7 per cent per year – that is, a doubling every 10 years and a quadrupling every 20 years – which is a more rapid rate of growth than in industry.

The number of farms has fallen less rapidly than the active population, for it is the wage earners and the family helpers who have left the farms. The average area per farm has, however, notably increased. The problem of too many farms has not been resolved as rapidly. The farmer who 20 years ago was cultivating a farm of only 15 hectares still feels his 25-hectare farm of today is too small; at the same time as his farm area grew, so at least as rapidly did his capacity to cultivate a bigger area with the best techniques.

Another aspect of change is the growing integration of agriculture in what one now calls the 'agribusiness complex'. Here agriculture becomes only one link in a chain which runs from the manufacture of the means of production right through to the retail distribution of the products created by the food industries. Many farms are thus linked by contract to the supply sector (manufacture of means of production) or the demand sector (merchants or industrialists).

If cooperation for purchase of the means of production and the sale of products now occupies an important place in many countries, this is far from being the case with cooperation at the level of cultivation itself. Even in France, where it is better developed than elsewhere, group (cooperative) agriculture still occupies only a minuscule proportion of the total cultivated area.

At the political level, the reduction in the numbers of farmers has reduced their influence hardly at all: in many countries majorities at elections are obtained with very small swings, and here the peasant vote can be decisive.

Since European agriculture is both intensive and technically developed, and since it cannot bring new land into cultivation (indeed, the likelihood is that certain poor land will be retired from agriculture), one might imagine that its potential to increase production was limited. But studies in several countries show that there are important differences between the best and the worst farmers, or between the average and the best. This is so in France and, to a less degree, in the United Kingdom and the Netherlands. Certain regions, often considered rather mediocre, thus possess great potential: in France, for instance, Limousin – a region of middle altitude – has a potential for fodder production comparable to that of the Netherlands.

If one strikes a balance, one is driven to the conclusion that European agricultural production could be greatly increased, especially in France, both by the remedying of backward techniques and the appearance of new ones. Every year, new varieties of grain appear with better yields than the older varieties: and one can in particular envisage a big growth in cereal production. The area in cereals can be increased at the expense of pasture and fodder crops, and the reduction in the latter can be compensated for by intensification of fodder production. On the level of possible techniques, the Europe of the Nine could together become a net exporter of cereals.

One view of the future: technical optimism

Among the forecasts made for the future of European agriculture, some stress the prospects of progress through new techniques. In particular, that is the view of Günther Thiede in his book *Europe's Green Future* (Thiede 1975). Thiede enumerates an impressive list of technical advances of all kinds which are transforming conditions of production in European farming. Yields can be increased to a considerable extent: Thiede speaks of cows yielding 8,000 or 9,000 litres (1,800-2,000 gallons) of milk a year. New equipment allows a reduction in the labour force. The future is one of big mechanised units.

In face of this tremendous potential for production, the demand – in particular that of the less developed countries – will not be very great. It will thus be necessary to limit production by taking large areas of land out of agriculture.

Certainly, Thiede puts no date on the progress he envisages: but if the situation he describes were to occur well after 2000, one certainly need not fear a shortage of outlets for the produce of European agriculture.

The hypothesis of heavy demand

It is not at all inconceivable that between 1976 and 2000 the growth in demand for agricultural products in world markets will substantially exceed supply. World population continues to grow at a rate exceeding 2 per cent per year. In certain less developed countries the national product per head is increasing rapidly, thanks to the progress of industry, which is creating a demand for foodstuffs that cannot be met by the farms of the countries concerned. For it is often easier to create modern industry, with big plants, than to achieve progress in an agriculture dominated by a large number of small family farms. Some observers even think that the developed countries will maintain a relative advantage in agricultural production. The developing countries would thus pay for food imports by exporting industrial products.

On the other hand, for the poorest countries which make up one-fifth or a quarter of the world population it will be necessary for the rich countries to provide aid in the form of food – first to relieve actual hunger, then to permit economic development, particularly in agriculture so as to overcome what is called the vicious circle of hunger.

Certainly, today's reality is very far from the situation described above: in particular, there is nothing to suggest that in the near future there could be a massive increase in aid in the form of food, as is claimed by an increasing number of experts. But many things may change between now and the year 2000. On the hypothesis of rapidly increasing demand for foodstuffs on world markets, Europe's agricultural potential must be used to the full. It will be necessary to introduce technical developments of all kinds as quickly as possible after they have been proved in agricultural research establishments. There will be no question of retiring large areas from agriculture, with the exception of certain poor areas; in mountain regions, instead of abandoning agriculture completely to forest one should develop extensive forms of stock rearing.

On the other hand, consideration of ecological risks may transform certain systems of production – in particular through a return to the systems of mixed farming, which allow fertilisation of the soil through organic fertiliser, thus reducing the need for artifical fertiliser, and the need for pesticides.

For many reasons, such an evolution (growth in production and a return to complex systems of production) would affect labour requirements in agriculture. One could in this case imagine a slowing-down in the loss of agricultural population: it is even possible that, by the end of the century, numbers in agriculture might again start to increase.

Of these two possibilities for the future, which has the greater chance of realisation: huge ultra-modern enterprises working on a greatly reduced total agricultural area, or a massive growth in production from farms remaining in family hands?

It is difficult to imagine that the next quarter-century will pass without a more vigorous attempt than in the previous quarter to solve the problem of world hunger. And as certain obstacles to the development of agriculture in the poor countries are difficult to overcome in one or two decades, they will necessarily depend on agricultural surpluses from the advanced countries. Whatever may be the potential contribution from North America and Australasia, it is possible that these countries will need European surpluses – in particular of cereals and dairy products.

A middle hypothesis: continuation of present trends

Analysis of the factors for change leads to elimination of the hypothesis of major change. In all areas, one can define the trends, all creating obstacles to very rapid change. It is certain that new techniques will be introduced in the coming decades: but experience shows that a long period elapses between the first announcement of a technique and its general adoption. To quote only one example, for a long time there has been talk of inducing twin births in cattle. Research continues, but so far without practical result.

In the field of dissemination of knowledge, efforts are being made to reduce still further the differences in technical level to bring the poorest farmers up to the level of the best: but if important differences are still visible in the Netherlands, there is no reason to think that these efforts will be any more successful elsewhere. Progress will occur, to be sure, but major differences will still exist at the end of the century.

All the same, the intensification of fodder production, technically possible in many regions, poses problems. Even where it is possible, to obtain yields comparable to those of the pastures of Holland demands very wide technical knowledge (growth methods, conservation, methods of feeding animals), major financial resources (fertiliser, fencing, storage of fodder crops) and even extra labour, which may be difficult to find. Yet intensification of fodder production is a necessity if one is to extend the cereal area without reducing animal production.

Developments will thus probably continue, but with important limitations.

The great stimulant of agricultural production is demand. As already noted, the hypothesis of poor outlets for European agricultural production seems pessimistic: demand will rise in all the less developed countries, and aid in the form of food will in the end greatly increase. And the possibilities of North America and Australasia, considerable as they may be, are perhaps more limited than one may think.

In the United States particularly, intensification of cereal production in the zones where it is technically possible may pose problems of labour supply that are difficult to resolve. Outlets thus exist for European production. But European farmers continue to see production costs rise, which does not make matters any easier on the world markets; on the other hand, it is not impossible that certain less developed countries with rapid population growth may prove successful in starting up their own agriculture, and thus be able to meet more completely their own demands by their own production.

It is probable, finally, that a stimulus of demand exists, but only to a moderate degree. For all the reasons mentioned, one can foresee continued growth of European agricultural production – notably in cereals – but remaining well below its full potential for growth, which appears very large.

Growth in demand will simplify matters somewhat for family farmers whose units are not too small. People may be again attracted back to the land: certainly the numbers returning to the land remain extremely small, but it is not impossible that more young people in the rural areas will wish to remain farmers, and the loss of agricultural population could thus become a little less rapid. And the creation of very large farms will be hindered by the difficulty of finding enough land. One may thus predict for Europe the same evolution as in the United States: an evolution towards larger family farms rather than towards big units employing many wage earners.

But it must be remembered that the hypotheses of 25 years ago have been contradicted by the facts. What French expert at that time would have dared to predict that cereal yields would approach five tons per hectare? And who could have imagined a France with barely 10 per cent of the population farmers? On the other hand, if far-reaching changes are rare, they are not altogether impossible: one can imagine, for instance, that a period of 25 years could be long enough for Europeans to realise the dangers of over-eating and modify their diet accordingly. Ecological risks could also have unforeseeable consequences. So the most reasonable prediction is that of continued steady evolution, but with the possibility of major changes not excluded.

The major problems of today and tomorrow

European agriculture is confronted now, and will be confronted even more urgently in the future, with problems some of which are world-wide, some specific to Europe.

(1) World problems

European agriculture is feeling the consequences of higher energy costs. Whether one makes a strict economic calculation of the costs of production or a wider review of saving limited natural resources, the organisation of agricultural production must aim at limiting energy consumption. The example *not* to follow is that of the American agribusiness which, at every stage including manufacture and distribution, is an enormous consumer of energy. The object must be to reduce the consumption of energy per unit of production, not merely at the farm gate but also at the point of arrival on the consumer's table.

A second world problem is that of the environment. It is often said that the farmer is the guardian of nature, but conflicts do exist between farming and the environment, in particular regarding pollution of agricultural origin. On the other hand, it is necessary to underline the acute nature of the competition between agriculture and the other sectors of production for the use of land – particularly in countries and regions with dense populations.

European agriculture equally will experience the changes that will occur in food demand. One may envisage a more systematic orientation of production towards the satisfaction of physiological needs. In this regard, one important point must be stressed: the production of animal foodstuffs through cereals or through the products of land capable of growing cereals is very wasteful; but this is not the case for stock farming on land where other uses are economically impossible – mountain regions in particular.

(2) Problems specific to Europe

Among the problems peculiar to Europe, the first is the high cost of production. Even technically advanced agriculture will be costly if it is practised intensively on a small area, as opposed to the methods used in North America and in Australasia. These high costs will be further increased in the future by the prices of basic inputs (such as phosphates and nitrates) and the necessity of returning to those kinds of agriculture that require more labour (for both ecological and energy-saving reasons). These high costs will make it difficult to export European agricultural surpluses.

Every major world region has its own internal diversity, but it is particularly evident in the case of Europe, where natural conditions and levels of development show very great differences between north and south. It will be vital in the future to work towards a reduction in these regional disparities. The policies for development of the mountain regions are important in this context.

Thus, the transformation of the rural areas is both a reality and a necessity. Evolution does not always happen in the most favourable way. It is necessary to aim to maintain life in the countryside by developing industrial activities – in particular food industries – and in planning villages and rural centres in a way that will create an attractive framework of life for rural dwellers.

The challenge of environmental quality

One particular problem must be stressed: the real threat that exists now and will perhaps grow in the future to the natural habitats of rural Europe. Europeans are highly conscious of this problem: they appreciate the concepts of ecology and ecosystem, they fear environmental deterioration and a possible ecological crisis, they increasingly understand that the biosphere is limited as population increases and that it may already have been damaged by human actions. But so far they have assimilated only the negative or perturbing aspects of this interdependence of natural systems, and the results of this bias are pernicious: exaggeration and even hysteria, lack of proper scientific judgment, and a failure to consider the distributional impact of 'no growth' policies. Ecological movements are in danger of being labelled elitist – a charge we must avoid at all costs here.

Yet the bases for a more sober, objective appraisal are uniquely present in Europe, through the range and quality of the available scientific information. This allows us immediately to appreciate one point: at first sight highly heterogeneous, Europe is nevertheless ecologically speaking a relatively uniform continent because human influence is everywhere so completely dominant. Without humans, Europe would almost be a monotonous forest rather than the rich mosaic of fields, forests, heaths and grasslands we see. Except for a few rocky and inaccessible mountain slopes, no part of Europe is today free of human influence. This mosaic was produced by millennia of human occupation, giving a uniquely balanced and self-sustaining system of exploitation of the soil, in which intense cultivation alternated with periods of rest or less intensive exploitation (Firbas 1949/1952, Hilf 1938, Krzymowski 1939). But during the present century, this balance has been threatened by social and technical change – above all by pollution, chemical and biocidal agriculture, urban growth, recreation and transportation. Europe today is threatened by an unprecedented increase in human interference with ecology, especially through the intensification and extension of industrial agriculture; the transformation of natural and urbanised ecosystems; chemical, organic and thermal pollution; and interference in sedimentological and hydrological patterns. (COPLACO 1973, 1975, Coomber and Biswas 1973, Seto 1973, Touring Club 1973, McHarg 1969, Detwyler 1971, Pack 1964, Whitman et al 1971, Icona 1974, Icona 1974-5, Bracey 1963, Farvar and Milton 1972, Gonzalez-Bernaldez et al 1976, Liapunov and Titlianova 1971). The forces threaten a regression, or simplification, of the ecosystem, affecting the fine structure of European landscape, and the quality and diversity of its animal population. Conservation and intensive exploitation cannot co-exist; the solution must lie in a radical transformation of the landscape, to bring it into line with today's social and economic needs. But this certainly does not mean the conversion of vast areas into nature reserves free of agriculture, which – as in Donaña National Park in Spain or the Lüneburger Heide in Germany – perversely makes it impossible to preserve the very species and landscapes it is intended to keep. The European natural environment needs more subtle, more detailed protection than this; and National Parks, far from being wilderness areas, should include areas of specialised agricultural use in need of protection.

This suggests an alternative approach; not obsession with pure conservation, but rather the use of the biosphere according to rules based on a rational survey of environmental resources and the ways in which they are being lost or eroded. Such a survey will show that the most important human actions which lead to environmental decay include: loss of space suitable for cultural, educational or scientific use; growth of outdoor recreation; improvement of agricultural productivity; alteration of the hydrological cycle through interference with catchment areas or inland waters; and negative influences on marine ecosystems or air masses. All these systems can be mapped to make an inventory; then they can be graded in importance according to the proximity to major population masses or transportation corridors, their rareness or uniqueness or fragility (McHarg 1969, COPLACO 1973, Grupo de Analisis Ambiental 1973, Leopold et al 1971, Isard 1972, Whitman et al 1971).

The survey will undoubtedly also show that many environmental problems are typically European. For instance, one of the most frequent causes of environmental degradation world-wide is increased pressure on the environment to obtain food: in Europe, by contrast, many imbalances are due to the abandonment of marginal land. The general use of gas throughout the rural Mediterranean lands has led to the disuse of wood: at first conservationists were delighted at the reduction of pressure on the scarce and scruffy Mediterranean woodland and scrub, but the resulting disorderly invasion of woody vegetation soon produced inpenetrable forests, destroying the habitats of interesting plants and animals. This vegetation is in any case so highly combustible that forest fires now destroy enormous surfaces of semi-natural and reforested vegetation. The almost complete disappearance of the goat from these areas has had similar effects (Brahtz 1972, Naveh 1974).

Consider another example. As small farmers and farm labourers have left the Mediterranean upland pastures and woodlands, there has been a tremendous reduction of extensive grazing by sheep and cattle. The result in many areas has been the loss of plant communities, which are replaced by unstable, highly combustible vegetation of no value (Naveh 1968, Naveh 1974). In the Pyrenees, where villages and large agricultural areas have been abandoned, a rich landscape texture has been erased; numerous animal habitats have disappeared; and some omnivorous animals (the wild bear and the fox) have increased prodigiously. In the foothills, chemical agriculture – the only feasible alternative – has destroyed the landscape texture. Large areas of European upland have thus been converted from a variegated scene into unpopulated areas of poor, monotonous forest (Elton 1966, Tuxen 1950, Patrimonio Forestal Del Estado 1973). In Britain, unrelieved Forestry Commission plantings of exotic conifers – again without any animal life – have replaced landscapes that were structured and rich in wild life (Elton 1966).

Other problems derive – or apparently derive – from the intensification and industrialisation of European agriculture. Mechanisation, biocides, genetic perfecting of plant varieties and domestic animals and intensive fertilisation all lead to a simplification, a 'trivialisation' of the landscape and the agricultural environment (Margalef 1975, Ucko 1969, Klapp 1958). With this there goes the great increase in the rate and the physical impact of urbanisation, with increasing demand for homes and associated buildings in a 'natural' setting, especially in the highest quality environments, with tremendous resulting effects on ecology. (From an ecological viewpoint, indeed, it would seem logical to do the opposite and choose the least interesting areas – as is done, much of the time, under the rather strict British planning system.) Often, for reasons of economy, developers will uproot the natural vegetation, leaving a treeless suburban desert.

One of the most dramatic examples of a threat to scarce ecological resources is the occupation of Europe's coastlines. Countries such as France and Spain, which have a great deal of shoreline, now contain only 10 centimeters of coast (both developed and undeveloped) per person. Yet there has been an anarchic urbanisation of the southern European littoral: the concrete wall extending along the southern European coast from Yugoslavia to Cadiz represents an almost irreversible fact. Equally selective and equally disastrous is the siting of industry on the most productive soil. In the semi-arid parts of Europe, where irrigation is important, the large urban and industrial agglomerations tend to follow the river terraces, which often have the only fertile soil and which carried the first agricultural occupation. Thus, almost by definition, within a few years the most fertile areas are paved over, removing them from agriculture and from weekend recreational use. To make matters even worse, these valley areas cannot easily disperse atmospheric pollution because of air stratification and the predominating air flux patterns; they seem destined to become European analogues of Los Angeles (Detwyler 1971, Pack 1964, Sellers 1965).

Europeans also have a prodigious appetite for recreational land – at least as compared with much of the rest of the world. But, though agricultural and recreational uses may be developed together, often they will necessarily be in conflict. And there is a limit set by the recreational carrying capacity of the land; it has been calculated that this is 50 persons per hectare in more humid areas and considerably fewer in some semi-arid zones (Seto 1973, Blondel 1969, Icona 1974). The cost of equipping and maintaining natural recreation areas can be high: 37 million guilders (£5 million) in Holland alone, for instance (Touring Club de France 1973). Maintaining and managing green zones near urban areas may be particularly costly due to ecological instability; multiple use may be necessary, as in the Mediterranean, where recreation can be combined with wild life preservation, landscaping, lumbering, and sheep grazing.

Hunting and shooting, if uncontrolled, can have a disastrous effect on the wildlife habitat. Add to these the very varied aesthetic, technical and safety aspects of locating such major structures as power stations (including nuclear ones) and power lines, especially when they need to be close to existing agglomerations of people, and the prospect for Europe seems daunting.

Solutions to these problems can be found only through planning: planning on a European scale, which takes into account not merely the location of buildings but also the movement and the preferences of population and the availability of resources. The need for an international dimension is particularly obvious in Europe's inland and quasi-inland seas, such as the Baltic, the North Sea, the Mediterranean and the Black Sea, where there is exceptionally high concentration of transport pollutants (such as oil), coupled with rapacious exploitation of marine resources. Inland waterways which cross frontiers are related examples, as is the movement of atmospheric pollutions from one country to another. As a minimal first step, one attack on this problem requires a Europe-wide network of continuous measuring and monitoring of air, water, soil, agricultural and marine products. On this basis, Europe should move to supra-national norms, coordinating public interventions in such areas as maritime transport, industrial location and transport links. They should be based on environmental cost-benefit analyses, environmental design, and impact minimisation by careful location of new investments. But it would be a mistake simply to hand over the job to technocrats, for experience shows that some of the most important defences of environmental quality have come from lay people.

To these problems there are four broad strategic solutions – though the first is, in truth, no solution at all. The first, *extrapolative*, assumes that the ecological dangers will be ignored and that mankind will try to muddle through, so that war, epidemics and famine will decimate the population and devastate whole areas. The second, *realistic*, recognises the problem in part and tries to deal with it by means of technical measures, such as industrialisation of the Third World (which will help reduce population growth there), and development of substitute materials (such as desalinated sea water and nuclear energy). Agriculture remains dependent on technology and the present structure of urbanisation and transport remains largely as it is now. The third, *back-to-nature*, represents a sharp break with present trends, including a reduction of population, an end to the use of artificial materials based on synthetics, the use of natural agricultural methods, a depopulation of the cities and a minimisation of travel. and a return to small self-sufficient communities. The fourth, *breakthrough*, also assumes that a real ecological crisis will be recognised but will be met by a development of new technologies for the production of energy: recycling on a large scale and new biological and biocybernetic rules for urban, agricultural and transport systems. Economic growth will not be limited (as in the back-to-nature strategy) but redirected; and frontiers will disappear as people become citizens of a single world.

A balanced and realistic solution would involve a mixture of the last three of these models. The nature of the ecological crisis will be recognised, but above all its different *intensity* in different areas must be quantified as a basis for a solution. Certain ecological crisis areas will need to be defined – in southern Europe more than in northern or western Europe. The realistic strategy could suffice for the less severely endangered areas of the north and west; the back-to-nature strategy must be applied to the crisis areas of the south, and the breakthrough strategy for the more limited crisis of the north and central Europe (including above all the sinking coastal areas, such as the North Sea Littoral or the Venice region, which may demand international action, together with the polluted North and Baltic Seas and their associated river systems). But it is above all in Mediterranean Europe – the polluted coastal areas further threatened by the development of tourism – that radical answers are needed. In general, across the whole of Europe the most seriously threatened areas are the densely settled coastal areas, especially on the inland seas such as the Mediterranean and Baltic; the industrialised river basins; and the larger urban agglomerations. Between these are less seriously-affected areas. So the answer must be to develop appropriate strategies in each case.

The retreat from mountain Europe

One problem specifically mentioned in previous sections – because of its importance both to Europe's agricultural productivity and to its ecological stability – has been the long-continued loss of population by its more remote mountain and upland zones. Logically, throughout Europe's history these have been barrier zones which repelled settlement, so that many of them lie astride national frontiers: the Ardennes-Eifel between Belgium, Germany and France, the Pyrenees between France and Spain, the Alps between France, Germany, Switzerland, Italy and Austria. Even where they are within one nation state, as in the case of the Scottish Highlands or the Massif Central or the mountains of Corsica, these regions are often very remote from the central metropolitan region or from main axes of communication, which intensifies their problem of attracting new economic growth. Such areas are among the most sensitive regions of Europe.

The facts are partly in line with the popular stereotype, partly not. True, most of these regions have experienced large-scale losses of farm populations, especially since World War Two: but this has been counter-balanced, in some regions, by a development of service industries – above all tourism – and even manufacturing. Generally it can be said that (as in France, for instance) the bigger the proportion of farmers to total population, the more rapid the decline. Conversely, the wider the range of non-farm employment, either in the area itself or within commuting range, the greater the possibility of an actual increase in population. Some of these regions, having experienced overall population loss for up to a century, have seen increases since World War Two – despite population pyramids that are very top-heavy, with a high proportion of old people. In such cases, the births are exceeding – or at least just balancing – the continuing out-migration of younger farmers and their families. But even so, the great majority of individual communities are losing people while the compensating gains are concentrated in a few favoured places. In other words, there is a strong out-movement from the mountain areas, which are gradually becoming depopulated; the choice is whether this movement can be kept within the region by selective development, or whether it must migrate over long distances outside the region, to metropolitan areas either in the same country or abroad.

Our inquiry in depth into the problem areas suggests some key lines of a new approach. If the mountain areas are worth keeping for their value as recreational areas or landscapes or green lungs for Europe, their basic agricultural populations must be maintained at a level of life comparable to that of other Europeans. Certainly, agriculture in these areas must be made viable, and that may require no more than a revision of the laws of inheritance. But in addition, the forests must be protected as a vital element in the maintenance of the natural environment. And other elements of the mountain economy must be developed in some kind of harmonious balance. Stock-rearing can be aided by measures to help the transportation of animals, to protect local breeds and improve the health of the stock. The rural economy needs to be diversified by development of small local industries that can compete in remote locations, such as electronics, wood products, tourist industries and food production. Tourism must be one of the most important economic bases, though it is not the panacea; it includes winter sports, but there can be a clash here with farming and with ecological considerations. Lower down the slopes, a diverse kind of tourism seems best. Critical for the development of the tourist industry is, however, a programme of training for the local population. It may be necessary to extend the special aid given to mountain agriculture, particularly to encourage young farmers to settle there – principally through aids to construction. At the same time this kind of aid should perhaps be extended to new groups of people. There is also a need for an adequate and an accessible level of basic services such as education, health and transport. These will be costlier than elsewhere, and one critical question is whether a supplementary charge should be levied for their use on those who are not permanently resident. One way to reduce these costs is to rationalise the settlement and communal structure, grouping communes where necessary. Such a new structure could be based on village centres providing the necessary local services and infrastructure.

Four futures for European agriculture: an inquiry among the youth of Europe

Thus European agriculture at the present time poses a curious set of contradictions. On the one hand, large-scale industrialised agriculture – especially in the more economically advanced regions or northern Europe, such as the Netherlands or southern England – presents a possible threat to the stability of the environment, especially where it is joined to the challenges of urban growth and of recreational demand. On the other hand, there is a problem of the actual depopulation of some mountain regions, with an equally serious but different threat to ecological balance. And these, of course, are essentially two sides of the same coin, resulting from the continued strength of economic rationality in Europe during the thirty years since World War Two. It is this rationality that has placed economic efficiency and economic growth – both in terms of personal income and in terms of national income – above all other possible objectives, and has led to the most profound changes European agriculture has seen in centuries. But from many quarters, not merely in Europe but perhaps much more strongly from the United States, come hints of a radical change in attitudes. A different kind of rationality, a different set of resulting values, is causing many young people to abandon settled careers in the urban-industrial economy and to return to the land, where they deliberately eschew large-scale industrialised farming methods and instead cultivate with due concern for ecological principles. And since the available farmland is precisely that which was abandoned by an earlier generation of migrants to the city, these new farmers find themselves reoccupying the marginal zones – especially the mountain and desert and hill areas.

Could the same processes occur in Europe, fundamentally altering the direction of its recent history? *Plan Europe 2000* investigated the responses of 1500 students aged 17-19 in schools in both urban and rural areas in 16 countries of western Europe, to different priorities for social and economic development, with special reference to agriculture. The first alternative, *increase the national wealth*, reflected the economic rationality that has dominated the three decades since 1945. The second, *improve the quality of life*, reflected one major facet of a policy arising from cultural rationality, as did the third, *aid developing countries*; but these two objectives could well be regarded as in some sense competitive. The last, *assure the national security*, simply reflected the concern over food and raw material supplies arising from the energy crisis of the mid-1970s. All students were asked to judge each of these policies as to *personal preference* (or what they wanted to happen) and according to *probability* (what they thought would actually happen).

Improving the quality of life proved to be the top preference everywhere, and by a comfortable margin. But in discussion it became clear that different students define 'quality of life' in different ways. In Scandinavia and Germany it means reducing pollution and noise; in Spain and Portugal it includes low-cost housing for the poor and better working conditions. Bottom priority in four regions was national defence; but the group comprising Germany, Switzerland and Benelux put national wealth last. Here Belgium and Luxembourg put defence last, but were outweighed by Holland, Germany and Switzerland. Greece dissented from the rest in Mediterranean Europe, giving aid to the Third World last priority.

But there was a very interesting divergence between what students want to happen and what they believe actually will happen. They gave top priority to quality of life and a low (in some cases bottom) priority to national wealth: but they believed the increase of national wealth would get top priority in fact. They expressed considerable concern for the Third World, not only in their questionnaire choices but in discussion: yet they believed that society would give this bottom priority.

On socio-economic systems, the results were sometimes unexpected. Students in Scandinavia, the British Isles, Germany,

Switzerland and Benelux chose a regulated free market economy as first preference; France and Italy split between this solution and a 'cradle-to-grave' welfare state. Students in most countries – Scandinavia, Germany, Switzerland, Benelux, France, Italy – also felt that a free market economy was the most likely dominant form of the future; in the British Isles and the Mediterranean, the welfare state was thought slightly more probable. Wide open capitalism and full state control were very unpopular and were also thought least likely in practice.

On the future of cities, there were wide divergencies. Although decentralisation was supported by a significant minority group, the first preferences in all regions were either remodelled cities or medium-sized towns of around 100,000 people. Present-day cities were least liked everywhere; yet they were thought to be far the most probable in the future, except in France and Italy, where students gave remodelled cities the highest probability. Decentralisation was everywhere felt to be quite improbable – oddly, perhaps, in view of the fact that it is the present trend in much of Europe.

The answers on agriculture were perhaps surprising. Highly mechanised farming emerged as clear favourite in all regions except Scandinavia, where a return to small farms and a rural life-style was preferred. Mechanised farming was also seen as the most likely outcome except in the Mediterranean, where factory food was thought more probable. A liberal farm policy was thought unlikely; it vied as least probable solution with a return to small farms.

Some of these choices, it might be thought, are almost schizophrenic. Many students voted for quality of life as first preference, but also for a regulated free market economy and a mechanised system of agriculture; few saw the possibility of basing an improved life-style on a return to the country and to traditional agrarian forms. But overall, perhaps the most significant finding is the divergence on so many issues between what young people want to see happen and what they think will actually happen. They expect the world of economic rationality to continue its domination, giving them material economic growth and the kind of large cities they already know. But overall, they prefer a different style, based on quality of life and a stress on medium-sized towns. If they prove consistent in their views and act on them when they reach adulthood, then the consequences for European life could be profound – especially if one accepts the concept (Yankelovich 1974) of the diffusion of ideals from the more highly educated young groups to the rest of the population. Here, as in the following discussion on the future of Europe's cities, the critical question is whether the evident negative consequences of current trends will bring a kind of dialectical counter-response in the values of the European population.

CHAPTER 6

Urbanisation: Towards a Human Environment in Europe

Urbanisation in Europe has a long history; its expression is correspondingly diverse.

This is true in many senses. Geographically, it is possible to distinguish between highly urbanised countries (Britain, the Netherlands, Belgium, Federal Germany) and those that are weakly urbanised (Spain, France, Yugoslavia, Greece, the Scandinavian countries). Considering the type of urbanisation, we can distinguish between countries with a dispersed urbanisation spread evenly throughout the country (England, the Netherlands, Northern Italy) and those where urbanisation is concentrated in certain cities (France, Spain, Hungary, Rumania).

The origins of urbanisation are equally diverse and have given rise to differing forms: traditional governing and cultural centres (Paris, Vienna); trading centres (Hamburg, Amsterdam); foundations or developments that were entirely industrial (Manchester, the Ruhr, Lódź); new towns and satellite towns; tourist strips (Barcelona-Alicante, Trieste-Split-Dubrovnik, Venice-Rimini-Pescara). We can speak of countries that are predominantly (or to an appreciable degree) 'urbanised' (such as England, the Netherlands, Belgium) and those where there is still a dichotomy between town and country (France, Spain, the Scandinavian countries, Rumania, Greece). In between we find countries which are fairly evenly and generally urbanised but where both urban conurbations and intensely rural areas stand out as polarised islands (Federal Germany, Denmark, Italy, Switzerland, Poland, the DDR).

So it would appear foolhardy to treat this geographical, historical developmental, cultural and economic diversity of Europe in terms of one uniform concept: urbanisation. By contrast with the growth of urbanisation in the United States or with the rapid developments in the former colonial cities of the Third World, where there is growth on a relatively uniform pattern, the unique feature of

European urbanisation is its diversity. The characteristic features of this diversity can be attributed to socio-economic development processes which led to an overlapping of historical city types: thus we find elements of the burgher town of the feudal Middle Ages overlapping with the aristocratic and residential city of the Age of Absolutism, the industrial town of the Liberal Era, and the new town of the Social Welfare State or the Socialist System (Lichtenberger 1970, p.47). Beside these we find towns that did not experience this process of repeated superimposition and which today are particularly threatened by the problems arising from the mass society. These 'one-period' towns occur in backward rural regions (France, Italy) and in static or declining industrial areas (South Wales).

Despite this diversity we can list some characteristic features of the European city 'image'. Non-economic factors were as a rule responsible for the city core and its symbols (cathedrals, churches, monasteries, town halls, parliaments and palaces; more recently, palaces of culture or sports grounds – Oslo, Helsinki). The road network did not follow a uniform pattern but grew historically and is now often marked by radial axes leading from the centre to the medieval city gates. Urban growth took place as a rule by incorporating village communities with a tremendously fragmented mosaic of sometimes thousands of tiny blocks and strips (Lichtenberger 1970, p.46), a process whereby the distinct socio-economic features, the individual landmarks and shopping streets were often maintained and reflected the local spirit of the inhabitants. Squares often determine the centres of urban activity; the most impressive visual distinctness of European cities is the quiet skyline, since skyscrapers initially were confined to restricted zones. A relatively high built density and intensive land use is typical even in the more recent suburbs – a heritage of the built density of the walled medieval city. A clear division between centre and suburbs, which derived from the social segregation of the Middle Ages when privileged groups could live inside the fortified places and town walls, and which survived even the expansion of the capital cities during the nineteenth century, finds expression today in the radial or tangential boulevards which became the axes of planned suburbs (Berlin, Budapest, Munich, Marseilles, Madrid) or in boulevard-rings along the old fortifications (Paris).

Nor are the social patterns of the cities as uniform as in the United States or the Latin American countries. The traditional social gradation from the centre (privileged sections with high incomes) to the edge is still frequently observable, except for some

Mediterranean cities. Numerous sectoral divisions occur (the great contrast between East End and West End in London and Paris); and there is a correspondingly irregular slum distribution in European cities (which means that crude definitions linking slums with criminality and unemployment are not possible), with slum-like areas often recurring throughout the city. The development of central business districts is also often marked by traditional associations: the functional mix of historic city centres was generally not abandoned as thoroughly as in the United States; cultural features (universities, museums, theatres) often remained in the centres, as did social provisions such as hospitals (Vienna, Munich); courtyards were used by small crafts (Berlin and notably Mediterranean cities); small businesses were often able to survive in the central business districts (partly with government subvention). This unity-in-diversity derives from the fact that apart from occasional pure industrial foundations European cities have grown historically and are as much a structural expression of political and cultural forces as a reflection of social diversity.

Problem symptoms of modern urbanisation in Europe: unification of development trends

In the last 150 years, the urbanisation process has accelerated enormously in Europe. The traditional processes of urban development were rapidly overthrown. The cities grew by leaps and bounds and new urban agglomerations were created by the extensive industrialisation following the Industrial Revolution. Two features are characteristic of this industrialisation in the heroic age of capitalism: the rapidity and magnitude of its quantitative growth, and the consistent application of the basic principle of economic rationality. With this the process of modern urbanisation, starting in Britain, took on forms and dimensions which progressively threaten the cultural foundations of European city life.

Thus economic rationality has failed – and increasing numbers of Europeans are coming to see that it has failed – to meet human needs. That is a central thesis, perhaps *the* central thesis, of this book; nowhere is it better illustrated than in the area of the physical environment. But at the same time, there is a need for realism. A better physical environment may find itself conflicting with objectives of economic growth; and the case for economic growth does not automatically disappear when economic rationality is replaced by cultural rationality. Rather, as we stress more than once in this book, cultural rationality emphasises quality rather than quantity of growth. In doing so, it must by definition include the environment as a vital element in qualitative growth. But there is another critical element in quality: the question of the distribution of the fruits of growth, not merely in the form of money income, but also in the form of all kinds of collective goods and services, among different sections of the population.

This is nowhere better seen than in Europe's fast-growing urban regions, where, it may be remarked, the pursuit of economic rationality has caused a breakdown in man's relationship to his environment. But here the environment is an even more complex concept than the one we considered in Chapter 5, because it includes not merely the natural environment which urban growth profoundly transforms, but also the artificial, or built, environment which man creates himself, as well as man's environmental perception. The balance between man and environment – in both senses – is particularly subtle and rich in Europe because of the great concentration of population and the long tradition of urbanisation which, by a process of trial and error, led to some of the greatest triumphs of high quality urban environment. It was a basic thesis of Project 3 of *Plan Europe 2000* that in recent decades this quality has fundamentally declined.

We must first sketch the growth of European urbanisation since the start of industrialisation, so as then to indicate future trends and the basic problems they will bring. Again we shall have to work in broad categories, which cannot do complete justice to the diversity of the European city.

It is possible to distinguish two development phases in modern urbanisation. The first is marked by a strong concentration of population in the cities. The new industrial concerns found a labour reservoir in great human masses, drawn from the rural areas. Where industry depended on mining, many new cities arose in the coal and iron regions. Industrialisation and technological development also created the condition for the second phase of urbanisation: with the growth of material welfare and the development in transport technology in the present century a trend away from the city centres to the suburbs and rural fringes has taken place. This deconcentration process is becoming progressively more marked; since the 1950s it has been the dominant trend of European urbanisation. Various causes led both the people of the cities and (at any rate in part) productive concerns to move increasingly into the area around the city. Problems in the centres (traffic bottlenecks, noise densities, air pollution, the lack of natural landscape) are increasing so rapidly that where income permits, people prefer to live in the suburbs and the rural fringes. Land values at the centre have increased so rapidly that according to the criteria of economic rationality 'unproductive' residential uses are no longer feasible, which in turn gives rise to the development of monostructural urban cores (offices, department stores, sometimes cultural provision). The smaller trades and medium-sized industrial concerns shift to the edge of the city. The principle of functional division (propagated by the Charter of Athens in 1933 as the solution of urban problems) leads to a one-sided relegation of certain functions (living, work, leisure activities, traffic) to particular quarters, so that the cities become distended. Today, then, we can talk of a general decentralisation trend towards the suburbs and the environs.

In some instances, urban sprawl grows into multi-centred agglomerations (the Ruhr, Upper Silesia, the West Midlands); in others, metropolitan regions emerge which are functionally dependent on a single core city but show a settlement pattern that continues to expand and sprawl into the environs (Paris, Madrid, Rome, Milan, Vienna, Belgrade, Athens, Warsaw); in yet others, large regions develop which are marked by urban settlement throughout, so that metropolitan core zones form a functional unity with the smaller and medium-sized communities, interconnected by means of strong commuter traffic and communication contacts. This new form of urbanisation, *megalopolis*, is becoming particularly prevalent above all in Britain and North-West Europe (Netherlands, Rhine-Ruhr Region, Rhine-Main-Neckar).

The problems of these kinds of urbanisation are sufficiently well known: density problems (traffic congestion, environmental pressures), functional isolation (dormitory sources, office deserts, industrial zones), high traffic volumes (with the population spending an excessive percentage of their time travelling), the building-over of the countryside and the destruction of important natural regulation systems (forests, rivers, lakes). Deconcentration into metropolitan and megalopolitan forms can only make these problems ever more difficult to handle by planning and control, since the physical reality almost everywhere outruns the competence of the political decision-making organs.

If we assume that present trends continue, the future of European urbanisation will emerge as an enlarged and intensified version of the present. A continuous megalopolis from Merseyside to Milan; the further proliferation of metropolitan regions (especially around the capitals and the traditional industrial towns (Lyons, Barcelona); the possibility of a second megalopolitan zone arising from the coalescence of the conurbanisation in Southern Belgium and the

Ruhr with the metropolitan regions of Hanover, Berlin and Warsaw and – via Leipzig, Dresden and Prague – as far as Cracow. Besides this, urbanisation will prevail above all in the cultural sense: as a definite way of living and thinking. The dichotomy between town and country, moulded by particular economic contexts and the attitudes these produced, is fast dissolving. Opportunities for technical mobility and communication, together with the demands of industrial distribution (the consumer society) and the physical process of deconcentration, explain why it is now possible to see the urban way of life as the norm for most Europeans.

The diversity of European urbanisation is thus threatened by the new trend. However much the intensity of the process may differ in individual instances, the general trend of future European urbanisation appears fairly uniform; historical, national and cultural distinctions appear in the long run unlikely to survive, so that the different stages of urbanisation in Europe are only a question of time-lag. If present trends continued, by the year 2000 some 80 per cent of Europeans would live in extended urban regions. But should the problems associated with urbanisation increase at the same rate as the urbanisation process, the question is whether the urban environment of most Europeans will be an environment worth living in. Because the most probable future European settlement structure will be that of an urbanised Europe, it would be a highly unrealistic policy, to start trying to solve the problems which were created by urbanisation by reversing the process of urbanisation itself.

Forgetting for the moment the variety of the European experience, we now present a simplified picture of the problems of urbanisation in Europe.

The basic problems of modern urbanisation in Europe: Disproportionate exploitation of the environment

Urbanisation, as a form of use of the environment, is concerned with three factors: space, artefacts (buildings, institutions, infrastructure) and man. According to the principle of economic rationality, these three factors until now have been treated almost entirely as economic production factors: 'Land', 'Capital' and 'Labour', which have been managed to guarantee maximum private profitability. Thus the three components of 'occupation' of the environment, which are: Space, Artefacts and Man, become economic production factors (Land, Capital, Labour) in the process of industrialisation and technological development.

Thus the factors of production become subject to efficient allocation in the sense that they are made calculable, i.e. only those factors are considered which can be quantitatively assessed. This proves easiest with capital; which explains why it was not only at the centre of the urbanisation process, but was also the primary factor determining the direction of urbanisation. To simplify, one could say that in European urbanisation since the Industrial Revolution the built environment (the artefacts) was treated as the comparatively stable factor, determinable on economic utility criteria, to which the supposedly 'flexible' factors, man and nature, had to adapt if not submit themselves. In locating and determining the 'stable' stock of built artefacts, the adaptability and capacity for self-regulation of the 'natural' components, man and the natural environment, was taken for granted. Since the natural environment and man as production factors were invariably seen and treated only in terms of their *direct* cost, the stock of artefacts came to assume a dominant and fixed role; as a man-made element, it could be entirely subjected to the objectives of production and the criteria that govern them. Yet ironically, in reality it is precisely this artificial, man-made environment which should be most readily susceptible to planning and technological innovation.

At the same time we find a parallel process of cultural urbanisation: the advance of the urban way of living and thinking. This aspect of urbanisation is also the outcome of industrialisation, in that its progress depends on the increase in material welfare and the organisational structure of the economy. For as long as urbanisation existed in the sense of a spatial concentration of people in permanent structures, a cultural dichotomy between the two ways of life existed, parallel to the physical contrast between country and town, and to the functional contrast between extensive production subject to natural rhythms and concentrated production independent of natural processes. This cultural dichotomy ascribed static attributes to the country (a sense of safety, neighbourliness, virtue) and dynamic attributes to the town (landlessness, mass society, vice). With rising living standards, with the increase of people living in towns as against those living in the country and with the artificial creation of wants characteristic of economic rationalists, value judgments have shifted in favour of the dynamic urban way of life. Psychological insights and their physical counterparts are mutual stimulants: the dynamic urban way of life requires geographical mobility; opportunities for mobility give rise to a more dynamic way of life which is characterised by the absence of any stable point of reference, such as the connection with the country and the dependence on natural rhythms.

The predominance of economic rationality gives rise to a total exploitation of the environment (in the physical and cultural-behavioural sense) governed exclusively by the laws of this principle:

> The main effort of finance capitalism today is directed at the total restructuring of space in its different dimensions and scales, from regional planning to the domestic habitat, because this form of colonisation is one of the means of sustaining the mechanisms of production: maintenance or growth of the rate of profit, augmentation of the total volume of profit due to the economies of agglomeration, so as to reduce the cost of reconstitution and reproduction of human capital, to acquire geographical monopolies, to industrialise housing, to encourage consumption, etc. (Vielle 1974, p.32).

The stock of artefacts, existing as a factor of production compared with fixed capital, dominates and makes excessive demands on the adaptability, capacity, and independence of the two other urban factors – the natural environment on the one hand, human territorial behaviour on the other – by treating these two spheres only as production factors, 'Land' and 'Labour', to be allocated.

The city that results from the principle of economic rationality – we can call it *Econopolis* – is thus marked by its neglect of the laws of human territorial behaviour and the natural environment. There is virtually no evidence that biologically or psychologically man is different now from what he was in the middle ages or at the beginning of history: he cannot simply adapt to changes in his physical environment within a short time without evident strain. The natural environment, as we are only now coming to realise, is an extremely complex and interrelated set of systems. If it is disturbed without understanding, it will not adapt; rather it will tend to break down. Similarly the built environment is, at least in the short run, fairly immutable: the great majority of built structures now will survive to the year 2000, and conversely the majority of structures that will exist in 2000 are already here. Purely technical or design solutions that ignore these constraints are doomed to failure because they assume too much adaptability on the part of man. Thus the only real variable or 'manipulatable' part of the relationship is man's perception of his environment and his consequent understanding; it is here that research has been lacking and should now be concentrated. The crisis is thus not one of lack of technical means, but one of lack of understanding.

The chief problem areas of modern urbanisation in Europe

The basic problems, we have seen, arise from neglect of the laws of the natural environment and of the demands of territorial behaviour necessary to human survival. Man's requirements from his built and natural environment have been largely neglected; the full extent of man's human territorial behaviour has not been acknowledged, least of all in urban construction (Malmberg 1977).

Social and communal needs, too, were only considered to a limited degree in urban building – where this seemed necessary for maintaining human reproductivity as a production factor. Too little account has been taken of the needs of members of different social, age, and other groups. Yet in a progressively urbanising Europe, where many more people live in cities than in the country, an urban policy that takes account both of human territorial behaviour and social needs is becoming daily more urgent.

As regards the natural environment, increasing urbanisation makes it more and more urgent to consider the effects on natural cycles – especially when the self-regulatory powers of these cycles are threatened or already destroyed, for this can mean the beginning of an irreversible destruction of the conditions that make human life possible. Here again, one-sided consideration of the natural environment from the viewpoint of economic rationality made an unquestioning assumption of the flexibility of nature, in the sense of its adaptability and ability to regulate itself. More detailed ecological investigations, which are only now beginning to be undertaken, show that natural cycles function as highly complex multi-hierarchical systems with a delicate, easily-disturbed equilibrium. The trend to dispersion, now characteristic of European urbanisation in many regions, threatens scenic beauties and unique natural areas: it also ignores ecological balance. Disregard of ecological factors causes a concentration of air, water and noise pollution in the urban atmosphere; water levels are altered, the operation of climatological factors is ignored, and valuable soil is lost to building.

Alternative solutions for a future urbanisation of Europe: the conflict between values and technologies

Our brief analysis of problems arising from the interaction of artefacts, man and nature gives rise to the question: how can we master future urbanisation in Europe?

Two extreme basic approaches are possible:

1. to give primacy to the urban factors of man and nature – the hitherto neglected factors of urban development – with a policy directed at changing values in order to make human behaviour and natural cycles the sole determinant factors in all developments;
2. to give full primacy to the urban factor of artefacts, notably construction techniques, telecommunications and transport, with policy directed at mastering existing problems and avoiding future ones by means of a massive and a single-minded deployment of these technical resources.

We could describe the two alternative solutions as *Humanopolis* and *Technopolis*. But are these realistic approaches?

It seems relevant to postulate alternative urban futures which are ideological in the sense that they represent the different value systems of different social groups. The most likely of these would result from an assertion of preferences by all those who find present trends unacceptable. This could be a wide spectrum of groups: the immigrants to the city who find there no substitute for the rural communities they have left behind, young people who find the newest, far-flung suburbs unattractive, older people who want to rediscover the lost virtues of an older city. It would be based on a central notion of community; in which people lived and worked and had their roots: *Humanopolis*. But it would not merely be a sentimental movement, an attempt to reassert the values of a past age; on the contrary it would be based on concepts of economic self-sufficiency and social balance that have proved themselves abundantly viable in such working communities as the British new towns.

Such urban communities might take various physical forms; indeed, it would be a serious mistake to try to equate physical form and social function in any simplistic way. But the most likely seems to be some variant of the bundled or clustered form, or 'concentrated deconcentration', in which communities of different size – ranging from the large village to the medium-sized town of about 100,000 to 200,000 people – are grouped around a larger central city, with lines of transportation and communication connecting them on a many-to-many basis rather than along the radial lines which at present dominate the urban regions of Europe. Different-sized communities offer different services, with the big central city taking care of the more specified functions such as recreation, culture and high-level services. This kind of settlement pattern offers many interesting possibilities for experiments in new forms of transportation and communication technology, such as park-and-ride at the edge of the major central city, para-transit and semi-metro systems (light railways) to connect the nodes, express buses on reserved tracks and broadband communication networks.

Within the central city, the appropriate technical developments are very similar to those that might be developed for a policy of high-density concentration. Indeed, implicit in the idea of the clustered urban region is that this central city offers the greatest possibilities of high-density, short-distance, face-to-face accessibility. Accordingly, this city would be the home of experiments in traffic-free zones, bicycle routes, personal public transport modes (para-transit), public transport priority and extension of the telephone network to carry voice, data and images, leading eventually to the development of broadband networks for two-way transmission of all kinds of information. Thus, people with a particularly high demand for information will naturally come to locate in cities where this special service is available.

In complete contrast, it could be argued that the reaction against Econopolis will take a different form. According to this model, many people will seek to rediscover a sense of community by migrating back to the countryside, where they can live in small place-bounded communities and combine an ecologically-conscious agriculture with the manufacture of industrial goods by craft methods. Thus Humanopolis, the urban form resulting from the arrival of cultural rationality, would take the form not of concentrated or clustered city regions, but rather of the urbanisation of the countryside. Such a settlement form would give interesting possibilities for using natural systems (earth, wind, sun, vegetation), would reduce heating and cooling loads, and would tend to develop self-contained utility systems (individual or group wells, sewage conversion, energy production). If such a model managed to provide employment opportunities locally, it could work without any heavy energy demands. But more likely the need for communication arising from specialisation and division of labour would lead in this model to an extensive use of the private car and virtual elimination of public transport, with the risk that in the long run neither system would prove viable. Buses and para-transit would form the only conceivable mode of public transport; cars might be locally banned within villages and small towns, to benefit the environment. The telephone network would be greatly expanded, and intensively used, despite its high infrastructure costs in such physical circumstances.

Given the general willingness in Europe to countenance public interference in the process of physical development, the choice between these alternatives (and their various combinations or permutations) can and clearly should be a matter of public debate. In practice, of course, there is unlikely to be a hard-and-fast choice for one system or the other. Much will depend on the existing development of the urban region, particularly its transportation and communication systems, and the resulting constraints. In practice, many large central cities are likely to continue to carry specialised jobs and services, and to support populations living at rather high (though perhaps decreasing) densities. An increasing proportion of all people, and all jobs, will, however, decentralise to smaller-sized settlements within the broader urban sphere of influence, which will thus become a polycentric or clustered urban region; and another group, perhaps the fastest-increasing of all in percentage terms, may settle for a dispersed life in urbanised villages, depending on local work in craft industries or services, or irregular commuting to the nearest big or medium-sized town. It perhaps goes without saying that the more people evolve from assembly-line manufacturing industry to the relative freedom of the professional or managerial or administrative job, the easier it will be to give freedom of working hours and working days – especially if telecommunications assist the process.

This leads to the extreme of dispersion: *Technopolis*, or the Nonplace Urban Realm of Melvin Webber (Webber et al 1964), in which community is achieved without propinquity, through the universal extension and cheapening of transportation and communication systems. In such a community, people would find affinity not with their next-door neighbours or the people in the next street, but with like-minded people half-way round the world, whom they frequently travelled to see and with whom they communicated regularly. The Nonplace Urban Realm thus supposes a constantly lower cost for transportation, especially over longer distances, as was true throughout the 1950s and 1960s and may yet be true of the 1970s. More fundamentally, it implies a rapid development both of improved conventional communications devices (world-wide direct telephone dialling, world television system linkage via satellite) and also the next generation of broadband devices, including multi-channel two-way television and computer systems. By such means – provided always that they could be supplied at reasonable cost – the home could become the usual office for a great array of professional and managerial workers, leaving conventional city centres for those rare occasions where face-to-face meetings were necessary. But it has to be said that in the energy-conserving 1970s the prospect of infinitely varied, infinitesimally cheap physical movement has somewhat receded. In any case, the theory tends to contradict a lot of empirical research which shows that most people, even high-level professionals, tend to interrelate most of the time over rather short distances. And it certainly ignores the fact that most men go home at night to wives and children, who tend to have a very restricted life space.

Nevertheless, the nonplace urban realm contains important insights which it would be foolish to ignore. The whole notion would greatly assist the dispersal of activities from traditional city centres into the country, allowing a combination of the nonplace realm with a highly place-bounded society for certain everyday services. And such a possible alternation may correspond to what many people want. When we look at some of the wider relationships, however, the margin of choice is further restricted. Technological changes will allow the development of alternative urban structures, as we have seen. Certain of today's problems, such as traffic congestion or pollution, could be eliminated or greatly reduced. But this would not at all change the main factor which now determines the process of urbanisation, which is economic rationality and the resulting obsession with efficiency. So it must be doubted whether it will be possible to effect a fundamental change in the form of the city, unless values are changed. Technology alone will not be able to achieve it: it will demand a change in society's fundamental objectives. Technological developments are likely to affect symptoms rather than eliminate causes; they are a palliative, merely suppressing deeper possibilities of self-realisation and political division. Technical decisions are finally political decisions, and technical projects are political projects. The risk is that technical advances may represent political retreats. So the right course is a cautious one, which respects the delicate relationships between man and nature. As Schumacher has put it:

> ... The battle of the future will be between two groups of innovators, whom we might name 'the people of the forward stampede' on the one side, and the 'homecomers' on the other. The former always talk about 'breakthroughs' – a breakthrough a day keeps the crisis at bay – and these breakthroughs almost invariably imply more violence to nature and a greater, more constant, more inescapable subjugation of man under the requirements of 'the system'. The latter are concerned with bringing things back to the human scale, to real human requirements, and to the organic harmonies of nature. The 'homecomers' will require more creativity. Any intelligent fool can make things bigger, more complex, and more violent. It takes a touch of genius – and a lot of courage – to move in the opposite direction. (Schumacher 1973b, p.9.)

If we summarise the findings so far of Project 3 of *Plan Europe 2000*, we see a profound dilemma in trying to deal with the problems of urbanisation in Europe in the future. Economic rationality has established the primacy of artefacts over human territorial behaviour and natural systems. A total reversal of this trend does not seem possible: technology offers no solution, because ultimately it merely reinforces the primacy of artefacts and cannot solve the basic problems. The city posited on a total change in values and social behaviour, Humanopolis, appears unrealistic and in the long run could not provide the material basis for European life. A realistic view of the future cannot reject industry and technology as the guarantors of material welfare. And if beyond this we consider the future potential for a change of economic structure within Europe, we may assume that an important function of the world economic role of Europe will lie in the progressive concentration on the highly specialised products of the secondary sector, the so-called science-based industry. We also assume that tertiarisation of the economy will continue (and develop into quarternisation). Industry, in particular the technological main branches and the service sectors, will continue to play the leading role in income generation in Europe. This in future is likely to imply the need for industry to rethink its relation to other sectors and spheres, i.e. its relation to agriculture, to the economically less-developed countries, and, not least, to urbanisation.

This greater concentration on science-based production areas requiring scientifically-based, technologically advanced and qualified human capital may well increase the significance of urban agglomerations in the future. This is because the conditions for this type of production, at all events in the middle-term future up to the year 2000 – such as educational capacity, communication density, and zones of face-to-face contact – exist to an adequate degree only in urban agglomerations. In the Europe of the year 2000 the role of urban areas will therefore be not merely quantitatively but also functionally more important than it has been so far.

The problem facing future urbanisation in Europe is therefore this: on the one hand urbanisation will assume increasing importance in terms both of quantitative distribution and of functional role, while on the other it will continue to be based on the principle of economic rationality, which fails to do justice to the autonomous requirements of the two factors: natural environment, and men as inhabitants of cities.

Coping with future urbanisation in Europe: equilibrium between the three components of environmental exploitation, or the rediscovery of the Centre

The answer to the problems of European urbanisation in the future cannot, therefore, lie in a rejection of urbanisation, but in learning to treat the man-made, built environment as a flexible field of operation, which has to be adapted to human behavioural demands and social needs, to global ecological interdependencies and to microecological conditions. The man-made, built environment should be shaped so as to provide justice for diverse social groups and allow for different expressions of environmental perception (territorial behaviour); it should also preserve the natural world as the basis for existence of future generations and make possible a closer direct contact between man and nature.

We can therefore distinguish two major points of departure for a future-oriented urbanisation policy which aims to create a human environment: a human and social scientifically-oriented sphere and an ecologically-oriented sphere, both of which can again be subdivided. In the human and social-scientifically oriented sphere, we must have regard for the environmental requirements which satisfy individuals' territorial behaviour and for the demands of different social groups on the environment to satisfy their needs. In the ecological sphere, we must bear in mind the global macro-ecological interfependencies, so as to avoid irreversible crises threatening human existence; the phenomenon of ecological cycles; and the incorporation of natural components serving as self-regulators of micro-ecological problems in urban planning.

Returning to the specific characteristics of European urbanisation as already outlined, we come to a further important sphere of action: the permanent integration of the cultural heritage as an essential feature of European evolution. From the geographical standpoint, Europe is a relatively small continent, with a dense population and many diverse nations and social systems: ecological considerations, therefore, require that the 'hard' trend of further deconcentration within agglomerating regions should be carefully monitored and controlled, and greater attention directed to what already exists. In certain European regions the insatiable consumption of land is already leading to problems, while the possibilities of reusing older, already urbanised regions have not always been fully examined.

Europe has created cultural institutions which are unique in their diversity and their reflection of human attitudes in urban terms. These are urban forms which have not yet been moulded by economic rationality: they respect the demands of human territorial behaviour. New towns, on the other hand, lack any cultural anchorage. That applies equally to the new towns of the Social Welfare State, as in Britain, and to the satellite towns of northern Europe, with emphasis on their development and the resettlement of the population to relieve the metropoles and to the new towns of those socialist states which are based on industrial capacity and the necessary labour force (Eisenhüttenstadt in the DDR, Dunaújváros in Hungary, Nowa-Huta in Poland, Dimitrovgrad in Bulgaria).

One result of the trends we have described is that social inequalities, social isolation and social marginal groupings manifest themselves spatially in the development of ghettos, slums and decaying quarters. Particularly in the older urban areas one can frequently observe the pull effects, drawing the population from overcrowded, impoverished or unifunctionally isolated urban centres to the periphery, and push effects, driving the lower income groups into urban quarters which offer housing facilities appropriate to their incomes. Urban regeneration, including the preservation of historic monuments and old quarters, will not be able to halt the trend towards deconcentration. It can, however, provide an important contribution towards the establishment of a more human environment, since it is concerned with both social and cultural values and since even ecological considerations demand the preservation of what already exists.

The three components of environmental occupation – Space, Artefacts and Man – can be brought into an equilibrium which allows for the balanced expression of their autonomous principles – Cultural Rationality in Urbanisation:

NATURAL ENVIRONMENT	BUILT ENVIRONMENT	HUMAN ENVIRONMENTAL PERCEPTION
Global system-interdependence (macro-ecological scale)		human biological, ethological, and psychological territorial demands (human scale)
local effects and direct contact with nature (micro-ecological scale)		social and groupspecific environmental needs (social scale)

Towards human environment in Europe: five spheres of action for future urbanisation

The problem in achieving these aims is that not enough is known so far about the mutual relations and interdependencies of the three urbanisation factors: nature-man-artefacts. The need is above all for scientific enquiry. Political, geographical and cultural diversity within Europe scarcely permits of a uniform ideal concept of urbanisation. Besides, even when we consider our insights into the interdependencies of the three factors, nature, artefacts and man, it seems hardly possible to come to any generally valid concept of European urbanisation that does justice to every aspect of the subject. The key to any future solutions must, therefore, be sought in a piecemeal process in which five spheres of activity seem to stand out:

1. a dynamic policy of urban conservation, urban regeneration and an integrated protection of historical monuments;
2. a consideration of global ecological interdependencies, so that the extent and direction of the entire European urbanisation process is treated as part of an ecological functional unity – Europe;
3. a consideration of the micro-ecological effects of urbanisation and the application of ecological principles to urban planning;
4. a greater consideration of the dimensions of human territorial behaviour in the planning of cities;
5. regard for the differing social needs of urban populations

Towards a dynamic policy of urban renewal

When we look at the different approaches to urban conservation, we find that the objective of improving conditions in old or decaying urban areas has failed because the causes of this decay have in most cases not been analysed.

The decline of these quarters, as already mentioned, is due to functional and/or technological changes which have outrun both the physical-spatial arrangements and the cultural and social norms which initially determined these cities. The exodus of the higher-income groups to the periphery and the excessive concentration of the tertiary sector in the city core, with its concomitant traffic generation, destroy the mix of functions that was characteristic of the older city. The residential areas, abandoned by those moving to the periphery, become a refuge for lower-income groups, and ultimately ghettos for foreign workers. This process did not occur evenly throughout Europe; particularly in southern Europe and in some traditional metropolises (such as Vienna), the centres are often still intact. Yet the same principles of deconcentration ultimately operate even here. Historical buildings become museum pieces as traffic makes them less easily accessible and mass communication techniques (television) make visiting them less appealing.

Priorities for urban renewal have shifted in the course of time. If hygienic considerations predominated once, today problems of mix and balance and 'efficient functioning' are the centre of concern: urban renewal is seen within a larger context of equalising the quality of life for all. Urban renewal is thus linked to three major problem complexes:

- *physical problems*: improvement of hygienic conditions, improvements in comfort and safety;
- *functional problems*: avoidance of monofunctional urban quarters and spatial concentration of social groups;
- *cultural problems*: preservation of historical buildings, streets, quarters and townscapes; finding functions for historical buildings and quarters.

The fundamental mistake in most urban renewal projects so far undertaken in Europe has been the disregard for the interaction between these problem areas, so that each particular problem was dealt with by a specific policy. The result has been three mistaken policies: one of demolition and rebuilding, resulting in the destruction of all functional and social ties of the inhabitants, and arising from the mistaken belief that new physical provisions must automatically create new social life forms; one of rehabilitation involving the provision of new residential quarters with the intention of attracting the inhabitants of the older quarters, thus freeing these quarters for gutting and rehabilitation; and one of conservation of historical buildings. Each of these policies, regarded in isolation, is open to criticism. The policy of destruction wipes out valuable social contacts and neighbourhood connections; it is negative in that the new homes are normally much more expensive than the old. Rehabilitation has similar drawbacks, while it often happens that the abandoned areas are occupied by other marginal or socially even worse-off groups. Conservation ignores the fact that historical buildings are ultimately valuable as part of the cultural heritage only when functionally integrated into modern city life.

The conservation of our urban cores must be based on the realisation that their decay results from a divergence between functional use and physical lay-out, resulting from economic rationality: those functions which depend most on spatial contacts (commerce, finance, service sectors) expel into the suburbs and the environs those functions that are less dependent on economic accessibility (housing) and those which are more dependent on external conditions (industry). To create a human urban environment we need a dynamic policy of urban renewal, which can overcome a pure economically rational exploitation of the urban region. Among its objectives would be the following: to avoid an undue concentration of given functions at the city core, by means of overlapping complementary facilities; to preserve especially those functions which determine the cultural bases of a vigorous urban life but which cannot compete economically for land (parks, cultural provisions, institutions); and to preserve historical structures which give the city centre its identity. A policy of urban renewal with these aims would not merely preserve the city core, but also ensure that this core itself would expand towards the periphery instead of merely moving the centre to uptown, as would occur under economic rationality.

A dynamic policy of urban renewal should combine the three fundamental policies (destruction, rehabilitation, conservation). In every instance it will be important to see that the multiple problems of urban conservation and renewal are not tackled by means of a closed 'ideal solution'. Urban cores have very different attractions, so that each city and within each city each sector calls for a detailed special study.

Existing policies, following the development of objectives towards human revitalisation in the urban areas, have not been based on an adequate body of doctrine. In fact, they have produced fundamental errors, rigidities or injustices of all types: social, economic, financial, spatial and aesthetic. Most developed countries now accept the need to elevate the urban renewal operation into a range of integral, continuous policies and programmes, but less developed countries imagine that their scarcity of resources obliges them to relegate renovation to a secondary position; they thus place a total priority on new urbanisation, abandoning, for the time being, the blighted areas.

After 25 years of experience, the policy of massive demolition now appears as misconceived: it is expensive, slow and ignorant of social and economic reality. The policy of abandonment and rehabilitation, by trying to get a surplus in the housing market, depends excessively on the capacity of the market to filter down houses; it neither recognises the authentic problems of renovation, nor does it attract private capital towards them to exploit their economic potentialities. A policy based on monumental conservation paralyses the natural evolution of these areas, impeding their solution or even adding new problems in the form of an accelerated exodus of activities from the action area.

As a result of these deficiencies and failures of experimental programmes, and of the impossibility of controlling the processes from a theoretical standpoint, all that is possible is an ambiguous incrementalist and disjointed policy. So traditional functional planning, with its unfulfilled desire for a comprehensive approach, should be either abandoned or supplemented by an effort at disjointed incrementalism (Hirschman and Lindblom 1962).

Towards an ecologically balanced urbanisation

In Chapter 5 we emphasised the need to see Europe as an ecologically functioning unity in order to prevent irreversible environmental damage, particularly in certain European crisis zones, where it is vital to restrict further industrialisation, traffic generation and urbanisation. The danger here is that systems of ecological self-regulation may be destroyed through entropy. Already parts of the Baltic have reached a dangerous degree of pollution, in the sense of exceeding self-regulating capacity; whole river systems have passed the danger-point of entropfication; large sections of the Mediterranean coastline have been extensively damaged by tourist-induced urbanisation as regards both their natural balance and their recreational value. There is no need to extend the list; nor do we wish to conjure up the threat of a planetary, ecological catastrophe. But as urbanisation inevitably continues we must have regard for the macro-ecological consequences if we are to ensure that coming generations will find not Technopolis but a natural environment as the essential constituent of a human environment.

This entails further research into macro-ecological inter-dependencies, but especially into the relations between urbanisation and the problems of the ecological crisis areas and pressure zones. This must be done on a European scale, and could become a major task for a European institution. The results could benefit not merely Europe but also the many countries of the Third World where urbanisation is occurring at a far more rapid pace and often on the basis of a far more brutal economic rationality than in present-day Europe, recalling the excesses of the industrial revolution. Thus it might enable us to avoid major and possibly irreversible errors in large areas of the world.

We also identified the micro-ecological sphere as a major field of action in controlling and directing urbanisation in the future; and in the last chapter we listed several strategies that will avoid the direct impairment of the natural environment through nearby urbanisation. Two of them seemed particularly realistic and germane: a strategy of 'back-to-nature' and a 'breakthrough' strategy.

The back-to-nature strategy suggests a complete alteration in the ecological cycle so that it becomes again self-regulating. Agriculture would depend on natural regeneration, not on artificial fertilisation. Urban agglomerations would be broken up, and sections would be displaced into the rural hinterland as new small towns, linked to existing small towns and villages through a public transport system which would relieve the need for private transport. Green belts would be established in urban areas to maintain heat balances and avoid pollution concentrations, and also (through air circulation) avoid overheating of cities. Part of the excess heat would be used as energy for intensive food production in nearby agricultural areas. Thus some of the displaced urban population would find homes in the countryside. Both the new and the existing rural towns would form intensive agricultural communities with new functions: they would have their own educational and communication systems, and they would be divided into small groups with responsibility for the care of the young, the old and the sick; production, living, education and leisure would be closely connected.

The breakthrough strategy is similar, but assumes that problems can be solved by applying science and technology. However, we do not think that this is possible without a corresponding change in human values. It would include 'bioacclimatisation' in the near vicinity of the city, which would allow heating of urban areas without heating the environment, thus saving energy; building materials could be lighter (thus being produced in smaller units) and building complexes containing both workplaces and residences could be developed. The development of new small towns would be similar to that envisaged in the back-to-nature strategy, but the application of technology would allow food to be produced on a smaller area, allowing large areas to be restored to areas of ecological protection; these would contain no population, so they would be established in the more sparsely-populated highland zones.

The future urban pattern in Europe, therefore, might consist of decentralised units organised along axial belts, with large numbers of small towns and villages using new kinds of 'soft technology' and intensive agricultural methods, thus creating a productive system based on recycling, and permitting a general rehabilitation of the degraded environment. Each unit would correspond to a natural ecological cycle-system, and ecological methods would be used in both land-based and city-based production. These systems would be autonomous and to a large degree autarchic. But there would be new connections and dependencies and, therefore, new cyclical systems to take account of. Each system will both exist in a larger system and consist of smaller sub-systems. Neither economic liberalism, nor the centrally-planned economy, will be appropriate to the management of such a new order. Each ecologically-conceived town-land system will consist of a relatively autonomous unit, which must be connected and communicate with other units in new ways. The system will be neither fully decentralised nor fully centralised. Urban areas will loosen up and reorganise themselves, but they will not disappear; their area could even increase. They will tend to be surrounded by special nature-protection areas, planned to reduce the negative effects of the city on the countryside; but this will be possible only if other areas (including some near the cities) intensify farm production, with the development of village agglomerations which will become more urban. Settlements will take the form of Living-Shells which will be self-determining communities.

Even if we do not go so far as to structure the entire urbanisation process around ecological requirements, ecology can offer important insights that will help us to improve the quality of urban life in the cities of today. Urban climatological factors are in many cases still not sufficiently regarded; building and land use allocation occurs in most cases irrespective of the character of land as an ecological factor; the relations between land use planning and air pollution are too often disregarded; the efficacy of plants to absorb noise and dust is generally still underrated, by comparison with costly and unsightly protective walls. The list could be easily lengthened.

Conscientious observation and recording of local data will be needed in order to allow the findings of urban ecology to become effective. In calculating research costs it should be remembered that ecological findings can lead to a strategy of urban planning which economises in resources and makes short-term palliative measures to protect the environment unnecessary.

A one-sided committal to any particular strategy appears to be wrong here as elsewhere. Policy should be dynamic and flexible, having regard to specific local conditions, the degree of urbanisation, existing ecological capacities and technological potential.

Towards a human-scale built environment

Such radical and all-embracing total solutions cannot satisfactorily deal with the problems of urbanisation. If we wish to make a more purposive analysis of the effects of the built environment on man in the future, a value system that is purely theoretical or based on an ideology will not serve us. We can only discover the 'dimensions of the humane' in the urban environment by a study of concrete cases, by observation of actual pictures of the city and its built environment, by judging its performance in terms of daily experience and behaviour. On this basis we can arrive at the classification of human dimensions which follows; it makes no claim to logical order and was found by analysis of the available European literature on urban planning, published mainly in the last twenty years.

First, *socially-oriented dimensions*. The first of these can be called *solidarity*: not the solidarity of the mass movement, but the feeling that comes from a common sense of belonging to a place and a home. It can include solidarity with marginal groups (the old, the weak, ethnic minorities), solidarity concerning the protection of general interests against outside attack, and solidarity in terms of readiness to offer mutual aid. Such solidarity is conspicuously lacking in many of our present cities, due to a number of factors: the loss of community in industrial society, the failure of civic spirit, the segregation of different groups, the dismemberment of traditional communal structures, the emphasis on private ownership and the development of official social security. The second, *communication*, is intimately related to questions of spatial distance, population density, urban form and social structure. Here the older urban forms offered opportunities, in the form of cafes and small shops, that are often lacking in their more salubrious replacements. This suggests protection of the individual character of a particular city quarter, the development of public events such as local festivals, the planned creation of communications centres and social spaces in and around buildings, and local newspapers or local sections in newspapers. Particularly important in planning the physical form of the city is the development of adequate pedestrian routes, with care that new highways do not sever existing communication links.

The third aspect, *accessibility*, is related to distance as well as socio-cultural barriers and economic assumptions. Transport systems here play a particular role. But accessibility means far more than that: it includes access to living space, to a social milieu, to the labour market, to leisure and culture. In general, a mixture of land uses makes accessibility easier; segregation of uses (as in most recent planning) leads to loss of urbanity. Closely associated is the fourth aspect, *tolerance* – a traditional quality of the city since earliest times, expressed towards other people, other values and expressions, but often associated with a certain lack of concern for others. The problem here is to develop an urban milieu that encourages human contact and understanding: qualities that the urban developments of the last quarter century, with their inhuman tower blocks and monotonous suburbs, have conspicuously failed to achieve.

The second group of the human dimensions could be called *individually oriented*. One of these is best called *living as an individual in society*. Different groups have different needs: consider children, the employed, the old. Thus the young may need an environment based on sport, leisure and social contact; the old may have a need for independence in their own home, separate from children and relatives but perhaps near them. Another quality is called *individuality*; another *freedom of movement*, a psychological feeling that can be disturbed by insensitive planning, such as alien underground subways. Yet another is *self-determination and personal development* (including the possibilities of work and of education). For instance, psychological research has shown how important it is that children have free opportunities to explore the world around them – something that is much easier in a home with garden than a high-rise flat. Finally in this group, there is *spontaneity*: a quality, especially important in children's play, that is restricted by population density and by too rigid structure of built forms; it is encouraged by openness, by places for the unexpected and extraordinary. In general, spontaneity seems easier in older urban areas, where casual meetings and contacts encourage a personally-oriented style of life.

The third group can be termed *emotional dimensions*. One of these, *intimacy and the feeling of being at home*, can attach itself to parts of cities or to whole cities. It is assisted by the number of local contacts and by their particular setting; a critical indicator is the local availability of shops and services, such as pubs or cafés. But also important is the spatial distinctiveness of a place, as marked by walls or towers or squares. Another quality, *comprehensibility*, is particularly associated with the vertical scale and the distance between activity areas in the city, which if too great can completely destroy the quality of the city. Thirdly in this group we can mention *livability*, which can depend on the size of the city, the distribution of functions and the built form. Two aspects are particularly important here: the specific quality of the areas of experience within the city and the range of possibilities of experience in a changing, functionally-mixed city. *Beauty and aesthetic factors* belong in this group, as does *socio-cultural continuity*, which is often threatened by urban renewal. To avoid this it is critical to maintain the social continuity of residential areas, the forms and expressions of traditional living arrangements, and the union of new and old buildings.

Lastly, in a group of its own, consisting of the *biological-physiological* dimension, there is the quality of *well-being* in the fullest physical, mental and social sense. It clearly depends very greatly on the degree to which physical planning has full regard for all aspects of public health – including not merely traditional aspects, such as pure water and adequate drainage and refuse clearance, but matters such as protection against noise, which are assuming more and more importance as the general level of industrial and traffic noise tends to increase. Here city planning can play a critical role, by developing zones with different noise levels, by developing noise barriers or green belts. But planning too is vital in its effect on psycho-neurotic disorders, which have been shown, for instance, to be much more frequent for dwellers in high-rise flats than for those living in houses.

Until now planners have tended to take a far too simplistic, physically-determinist view of such questions. It is now clear that no such simple connexion exists between the built environment and social relationships, and that to try to achieve a desired social structure through physical arrangements is misguided and counter-productive. What is now needed is a more flexible style of planning that gives scope for the needs of the people who live in the city. In this light the critical factors that planners have assumed to operate – density, social mix, kinds of architecture – are seen as far too narrow and even as wrong.

Towards a needs-oriented city planning

Thus we are suggesting that, in the future, the kind of urban environment people get will depend to a large degree on what they want. But this should not be understood in any simple-minded way. Human needs are not necessarily constant from one year or one era to another. They are certainly not autonomous; they are very open to outside influence. They therefore cannot readily be identified by any means such as a public opinion poll. They are not predictable, and some would argue that for political reasons one should not even try to predict them. We are sure that some of them (including those identified with large social groups) never get sufficiently identified in the decision-making process. The models we need to develop in this field are concerned with public participation in the planning process: with how views are formed and how then they are expressed – especially in conflict situations where a decision must be made.

The basic principle is that people should define their own needs. But planning has to be based, not on individual expressions of need, but on the needs of society. The necessity, therefore, is to define sufficiently large social groups. Then concepts must be developed which explain the political and social consequences of alternative policies. Alternatives must be based on different social goal-finding processes, oriented to the needs of the population. These will be model alternatives, intended as a learning aid, and developed in the form of scenarios.

They must each be based on a central city-planning concept. For simplicity we need to limit this to a particular type of urban area and to a particular planning objective. By way of example, we can consider the objective of communication. Two contrasted types of quarter can be considered: one 'self-contained' (with most kinds of jobs and services provided locally, and with a wide social mix) and one 'open' (dependent on other parts of the city for many goods and services, and with a narrower social mix). They can be evaluated under various functional headings – living, working, shopping, education – and from the viewpoints of major social groups, age groups and sex-marital status headings: examples are male workers, female workers, housewives without gainful employment, children at school, retired old people.

If one looks, for instance, at a family with a male worker and a wife who is not working, the male has needs quite different from those of his wife, who is at home bringing up small children. He may prefer the open quarter for its access to a wide range of jobs and services in the city as a whole; she may prefer the closed quarter for its easy local access to shops and other services. But each is likely to have contradictory needs that cannot be served by one model or the other; while some needs can be equally well served by both models.

There is thus no patent formula for needs-oriented planning. Some of these particular needs could be met by general improvements in communications which would apply equally well to both kinds of quarter. Some do depend on the choice between the two models. In general, the self-contained quarter performs better in orienting the individual as to his range of social opportunities, in obtaining agreement between reference networks, and in intensifying communication. The open quarter does better in offering possibilities of social contact, in supplying social interests, and in optimal use of skills. But there is no absolute distinction in the real world, and a mixed form is often likely to perform the best.

The need then is to develop lists of criteria on which a judgment can be made. Then the problem is how to aggregate the preferences of different groups. Some criteria will conflict even for a given group: thus parents would like easy access for goods delivery vehicles to their front doors, but also traffic-free streets for their children. What can be done is to produce constellations of needs and typical profiles for different types of quarter, so as to understand whether the needs of different groups are compatible. Only in this way is it rationally possible to discover whether a mixture of different groups in a certain part of a city – whether these groups are defined by age, by social class, or by any other criterion – is possible or desirable.

Towards a human environment in Europe through planning?

This is not the place to recommend direct solutions for concrete problem situations. Many areas of knowledge necessary to help us create a human environment in the extensively urbanised Europe of the future are not yet properly discovered: here are new tasks for science and research. We reject as unrealistic the notion of a complete transformation in values and objectives if we continue to see industrial and technological development as the basis of urbanisation. What then is the right planning policy to tackle the problems that crowd in on us?

Certainly, it is neither possible nor desirable to develop a closed concept of an urbanisation policy or 'human' urban planning. Cultural rationality calls for a recognition of differing conditions, needs, desires and objectives and seeks to find a compromise between them. This applies at the European level, where the unity of Europe amidst its national and cultural variety represents a major potential for use in the future. From this it follows that the main task of future urban planning will be to extend the scope of decision criteria by including findings from the arts, the social sciences and ecology and to harmonise these with findings from economics and technology. This also implies far greater consultation than hitherto with those affected by the planning process. Citizen participation which in the past has often operated only in cases of acute social conflict, should operate as a permanent element of planning.

If the urban environment of the future is to become a human environment, understanding and action will be the two decisive factors. Understanding depends primarily on intensification of research, and this research should be redirected towards the social-psychological perception of the environment, towards research into human needs, and towards ecological studies. Better insight demands above all an extension of the kinds of information used in decisions.

This demand may appear at first unrealistic, since in totality it would require a complete transformation of the system of values, with a corresponding change in the social system. Yet many untapped opportunities exist for widening the basis of decision-making even within present-day social systems. The need is above all for a major expansion of information on the complex and universal interconnections between the three basic urban factors: nature, artefacts and man. 'If the city is no longer to dominate man but man the city, he must understand what is happening around him.' (Arndt 1975, p.95.) That applies as much to the larger contexts, starting with the ecological unity of Europe, as to the lesser processes that directly affect the everyday life of city dwellers, for example the development of children's playgrounds.

Beyond that it is necessary to increase the scope of social action in helping to shape future urbanisation. More citizen participation in the development process, through better information and more consultation, is an essential further step towards achieving cultural rationality. Citizen participation calls for a substantial and qualitative improvement in information. The conditions in most areas can be recognised as extremely complex and diverse, with different interest groups in urban renewal; apparently irreconcilable conflicts in human attitudes towards the environment, which seem to have their basis in human nature; and irreconcilabilities between the differing needs of the different social groups. So total information would only lead to total perplexity among those affected, or information pollution. This points to an important field of action, scarcely touched upon in the past: the need to prepare in comprehensible form the information produced by science, research, and the decision makers, so that ordinary people – those affected by decisions, who are outside the circle of specialists – will be able to understand the laws and processes of urban communal living.

This is of course not the entire answer to the future problems of urbanised Europe. Most cities now suffer from acute financial crises; they lack real power over their own affairs, because of the *de facto* extension of the area of central government; housing problems are by no means solved, especially in towns with many old buildings and especially for the poorer of the community; land speculation is an unsolved problem, and the right to the free disposal of private property in land compromises most urban planning projects;

marginal groups such as children and the old are segregated as non-productive factors, and so on. Urbanisation policy is ultimately social policy. Future urban planning should be more than merely a technically-rational process in terms of set objectives. To achieve cultural rationality in town planning, we need planning in terms of goal-setting as an 'aid in coping with the whole social complexity and attaining individual self-determination and participation' (Hesse 1972, p.17). The planning process must include the process of discovering the objectives, it must embrace diverse values and interests in alternative strategic projects which will form the basis for action by political decision-makers after public discussion and attempts to obtain consensus (Hesse 1972, p.30). We must ensure that research findings and changes in our insights can immediately become part of our planning, so that we can balance the claims of environment and human environmental perception. The objective for these two realms must be to set certain limits to further urbanisation, which should not be transgressed ('marginal planning') and to set up and consider from the outset alternative models for certain types of pressure ('problem planning') (Greger 1973, p.16). Such attempts to isolate the mutual interdependencies between nature, artefacts and human behaviour could provide starting points for a policy to deal with the two planning constraints which currently operate in almost every European country: the right to the free disposal of private property in land (and, concomitant with it, land speculation) and the restrictions imposed on public planning by administrative boundaries and political barriers.

CHAPTER 7

A New Role for Europe's Industry

European industry must find a new set of roles if it is to face the challenges of the last quarter of the twentieth century. In doing so, it will be forced to reassess and redefine its nature and objectives. Without such a radical step, we will argue, other changes it may make will be of small value. This is the theme of the present chapter.

European industry: Its world role

Not long ago European industry, like industry anywhere, could be defined in a fairly simple way. It was involved in the production of goods and services according to principles of rationalisation and efficiency (Weber 1968). Even after World War Two, its rationale remained fundamentally unchanged: privately – and also publicly – owned enterprises still produce and distribute goods for the market; the producer's and supplier's primary motivation is to maximise profit or to achieve a maximum return for invested capital; the consumer's motivation is still his individual welfare; and the whole system is apparently self-optimising, since any discrepancy between output (whether in quantity or in quality) and wants (whether of individuals or other firms or the whole of society) cannot exist over any long period. Through increasing mechanisation and automation, industry has achieved an enormous increase in productivity; so that a constantly growing national product and individual income come to be regarded as normal.

In all this, the question of the *structure* of industrial output and its relation to human *needs* is regarded as of minor importance. Industry's primary goal is not to meet existing needs, but rather to create new needs through the phenomenon of 'psychological obsolescence' (Dupuy and Gerin 1974, pp. 156-91). Industrial producers not only determine the range of marketable goods from which consumers must make their choice; they also try to persuade customers 'to choose that which is being produced today and to "unchoose" that which was being produced yesterday' (Mishan 1968, pp. 148-9). The production process is treated as an end in itself; planning is applied to this end, but not to the greater end of serving social needs; and thus no yardstick has been developed for obtaining a rational mix of industrial output (Galbraith 1958, passim). Further, often industrial management solves its problems of adjustment without reference to the social problems that arise: for example, it does not see unemployment as its problem. Workers on their side may see their work simply as a means to income, rather than in the context of a social role. The development of social security systems can be seen as an attempt to ameliorate the worst results: while the state sector is left to fill the unprofitable gaps (public utilities, hospitals, education) that the private sector will not touch. Problem-solving in industry has thus come to consist of a series of partial tinkerings with individual aspects of the industrial process.

The only way out of this dilemma is by trying to understand the wider system of production, work, education, income, consumption and investment as a single interrelated complex; and then to develop suggestions for structural change within this complex. To that theme we return at the end of this chapter.

Before we do this, though, it is essential to understand the particular characteristics and special role which European industry has come to perform within the world industrial economy of the late twentieth century. The features we have described above apply to all industrial systems – including socialist – down to the present time; but they are particularly evident in advanced industrial countries entering a post-industrial age, such as those of contemporary Europe. This is precisely because such countries have reached the point where the output of goods and services almost achieves saturation of the market and want creation becomes increasingly vital to maintain output and sales. But at the same time, an increasingly affluent population becomes steadily more conscious of the failure of the system to satisfy other human needs; in particular, it appreciates the damage the system causes to the ecological environment and the human psyche, in a way that is not so evident in less developed countries.

This relates in turn to another feature: in the world industrial division of labour, Europe is forced increasingly to compete in products and in productive methods that require a high output of capital to labour. Not only has national and international competition led to a very considerable capital accumulation in

Europe; in addition, it has led to a differentiation in the capital structure, whereby the production of highly sophisticated machinery requires a labour force with high educational standards and specialisation. Thus European industry characteristically specialises in high-quality products. All this will remain true so long as economic rationality, applied through technological advance, remains the main driving force of economic growth. And this is unlikely to show any very rapid change. Therefore, Europe's future will remain in the production of sophisticated products such as goods with very high quality and reliability; goods which are particularly easy to service in an economy where labour costs rise and where 'do-it-yourself' becomes more and more important; products with a long lifespan; and non-polluting products which take account of the problem of social costs; and the plant which developing countries will need to build up production with an intermediate technological content. In addition, Europe can and should collaborate with the developing countries in the production of a technology suitable to their capacities and needs – for instance, easy-to-repair farm machinery. This will be necessary because the world outside Europe will not stand still. If European industry fails to adapt by concentrating on those products and those methods in which it has greatest competitive power, the result will be progressive failure vis-à-vis the newly developing countries.

In this, it will be critical for European industry to stress more and more the role of research and development. Indeed, much of its product in the future may consist, not in industrial goods, but in the export or the knowledge of what goods can be produced and how to produce them. Though most of industry's revenue will still come from sales of goods, more effort will go into provision of systems and services. Increasingly, the question will be not *how much* Research and Development, but *what kind* of R and D. As we saw, our past efforts have increased the efficiency of production but have not advanced human welfare as much as they ought. So in future Europe will need to stress the development of technology for end-products that better serve human needs: not the supersonic project, but rather technologies that grapple with themes like energy shortage, pollution, and congestion of transport and communication. One possibility is to develop 'soft' technologies allowing small-scale, decentralised production processes with perhaps a greater labour content. It will need also to concentrate on applications in the service sector – in hospitals, schools and the like. This demands a new and wider role for technology assessment – in which also Europe could and should take the lead. And this will pose new problems of the organisation and finance of R and D; government or independent agencies must increasingly take the lead in coordinating research and the exchange of its results.

One theme particularly stands out for a reoriented R and D industry: the need for industry generally, and European industry particularly, to adapt to an era of energy and raw material shortage. Though energy experts do not always agree on the size of world resources, and although new reserves may well appear in the future as they have in the past, it seems indisputable that energy and raw material resources will not allow us to continue production in the same wasteful way as we did in the recent past and are still doing today. And for Europe this is particularly germane, because most of the energy and raw materials providing the input to European industry do not originate in Europe. As the raw material producers exercise their power over their own resources, as they themselves begin to industrialise, we must expect that European dependence will increase; and European industry could find itself in a vicious circle, with high energy and material costs leading to high prices of industrial goods in primary producing countries, leading in turn to higher material costs.

In the long run, this would clearly be suicidal – for Europe if not for the world. So the alternatives need very close scrutiny. All of them presuppose the notion of *qualitative growth* involving selective extra demand on material resources, emphasising renewable resources, recycling of materials, and limiting use of non-renewable assets. One is to concentrate on those industries that use relatively small amounts of material and energy, relatively large amounts of skilled labour and specialised capital: for instance, fashion-based industry, and high-technology sectors, plus service industries, in which in part European industry already tends to specialise. Another alternative is to concentrate on production methods that substitute capital, especially in the form of new technology, for energy. A third is to develop a new inter-regional and international division of labour, whereby energy-intensive and material-intensive industry is located where production costs are lower – phosphate fertiliser production in North Africa, petrochemical production in the Near East – integrating at the production and/or marketing levels with resource-rich countries or regions. But this in turn raises the particular question of the relation of European industry to that of the developing world, and to this we must now turn.

European industry and the Third World

In the world-wide division of labour, highly-developed European industry has been governed by narrow principles of economic rationality: it has concentrated on those branches of production demanding sophisticated technology and a highly qualified workforce, while the simpler industrial processes, either based on processing of resources or involving a large labour content (textiles, leather, electronic assembly) went to the developing countries. This form of division of labour – promoted and conditioned by a strict monopoly and centralisation of capital and markets through the multi-national companies – has predictably led to the same results as can be seen within European countries: an enlargement of the development gap occurs between the European and the developing countries, with all the socio-economic and political consequences that follow. This has been modified in the case of the oil-producing countries and may well be further modified in future by other similar energy – or material-rich countries; but otherwise there is little present prospect of a radical change. Rather, as we already saw in Chapter 2, the likelihood is one of agreements between the EEC and certain developing countries, whereby EEC industry guarantees its supplies of raw materials by promising development aid.

If the developing countries try to break out of this vicious circle by developing substitution industries, especially the assembly of durable consumer goods such as cars – as is occurring in Latin America, South East Asia and Africa – problems arise due to the small domestic demand and the higher production costs, which demand protective tariffs. In some ways the best policy is one of compensating production, whereby such a plant uses imported components from Europe (such as engines, instrumentation or carburettors) while the European firm concerned also buys raw materials from the developing country (such as leather and other semi-finished products). In this way the developing country benefits twice, first because its industrial products become more competitive by reason of the imported components, and secondly because of the export of raw and semi-finished materials. On such a basis a new division of labour might arise, whereby Europe retires from certain industries or at least certain processes in given industries, in return for the supply of such processes to plants in Third World countries. These processes involving the use of indigenous natural materials or large amounts of cheap labour would progressively be taken over by the developing countries. This involves important policy decisions by European agencies, both private and public – export credit agencies, multinational firms, European consultancies – to steer the right kind of investment into the Third World, so as to aid the development of a new world division of labour.

Such a policy – expressed not only in capital investment on the part of Europe, but also in the supply of research and development knowledge – would clearly benefit the developing countries; but it also seems to be essential for the future competitive survival of European industry. Without it, the virtual certainty is a trade war leading to increased protectionism in both Europe and the developing world. With it, the possibility exists of a progressive increase of trade between Europe and the countries of the eastern and southern world. It requires not only trade agreements between the developing countries and Europe but above all plans for capital investment and the export from Europe of the appropriate technology which will often be manufactured in Europe and exported to the Third World.

The multinationals and European industrial policy

Above all, it means that the multinational companies will have to be harnessed as positive agents of development – a development that must be based on principles other than purely economic-rational ones based on profit maximisation by the individual firm. Whether the multinationals can be persuaded into such a role, which their past history and present structure in no way fits them to play, is one of the key questions for the future of European industry in the world.

Whether they are American-based (as more than half are) or European-based, the multinationals are firmly established in Europe – a product of the long period, in the 1950s and 1960s, when European currencies were underpriced in relation to the American dollar, and when European trade and customs policy favoured them. The multinationals have become very sophisticated in manipulating policy: they have split markets and manipulated prices and taxation. Their managements are considerably more sophisticated, flexible and knowledgeable than those of the unions – especially because of the failure so far to develop effective European union organisations. In a world of growing international trade and political relations, the multinationals are a dominating force in technological policy, social change and political influence. Their enormous and growing power has to be controlled, and this can occur only through the development of a European policy developed by European institutions on the basis of agreed European development goals.

The opportunity to do this exists because the structures of a European industrial system are still more open and flexible than those of the constituent national systems; so that conscious planning should be much easier on the European scale. But it is also a danger in that existing national policies may rush in to fill the gap; and these, as we have seen, are based on a quite inadequate understanding of the complexity of the problem. Thus, so far, no generally accepted objective exists for industrial planning within the EEC; rather, without any statement of the final objectives it is desired to achieve, plans of varying degrees of comprehensiveness are being framed on a European, national, regional and individual industry level. To replace this, Europe now needs a plan based on a clear understanding of the role of European industry within the world economic system, both as an agent of change and a recipient of it; the function, role of and conduct of the system in relation to European society and the individual; and the shaping of the organisation of the system, of conditions of life and work in the widest sense.

The first essential in this would be an' enhanced role for existing supra-national agencies, both in the EEC and elsewhere. One way towards this might be through interdisciplinary and multi-European organs of decision for definite problem areas such as inflation, unemployment, alienation at the workplace, and destruction of the environment; such bodies could have temporary and limited powers of decision and control over resources. Additionally, in relations with the world economic system, with economic blocs, or with the multinationals, European industry could be increasingly represented by central supra-national bodies. Though individual 'countries will undoubtedly want to negotiate separately on certain issues, the aim should be to treat these increasingly as exceptions to a general rule.

One problem that is likely to loom large for any such European supra-body will be that of differences in the strength of different countries and regions within Europe. With increasing integration of the European industrial system, it becomes increasingly difficult to rely on automatic compensating adjustments for weak economies – as the British example shows in the mid-1970s. As the pattern of trade within Europe moves away from complementary trade (of goods for which one country or region has a particular advantage) and towards exchange trade (in which all countries or regions exchange similar goods), there an increasing problem of differences in cost structures, wages and capital yields, and competitive strength generally. If structural crises emerge as we hinted in Chapters 2 and 3, then certain industries and certain countries may try to compensate by bilateral trade agreements with other industrial nations and the Third World – leading to a trend towards disintegration of the EEC industrial system. To compensate, it may be necessary to pay the price of increasing bureaucratic control and resulting loss of flexibility. This is one likely scenario for European industry in the 1970s and 1980s.

Regional equity and the role of European industry

The problem for European policy is perhaps even more pronounced at the regional than at the national level. As we already saw at the start of Chapter 5, since World War Two population has been concentrating at the regional scale. As a result industrial growth within the European industrial system is unequal: the essential characteristic of a European regional policy must, therefore, be decentralisation. The total economic growth of the EEC states has in recent years continually increased, but the citizens of the Community or of individual regions have not participated equally in this growth: the extent of regional disparities – measured in the differences in *per capita* income, in the level of production or in the rate of increase in production – has not been reduced by national or European regional policies framed within the process of economic integration: on the contrary, the existence and development of the EEC has led to an increase in regional disparities. European industry has assisted in increasing the wealth of those places which were already wealthy.

Underdeveloped regions are characterised by severe structural under-utilisation of resources and high long-term unemployment of manpower: possibilities of work in these regions often depend mainly or entirely on agriculture, or in part on antiquated branches of industry which are viable only if subsidised by governments. Passive amelioration in the shape of a high rate of emigration from these regions only increases regional and social disparities. These disparities will not be removed without the formulation of a clearly defined concept of a pan-European regional policy; and an equal apportionment of economic activities to the individual regions is indispensable for the integration process and for the further evolution of the EEC. It is not only fairness and justice which demands that less qualified work-forces should receive the same possibilities of economic and cultural expansion as their more favoured contemporaries; the economic potential of European industry does so too. New operational centres, chosen from the point of view of equal regional industrial growth, must be established at new poles of growth where work-forces are available: and care must be taken to project an optimal network of poles of growth – a policy of concentrating on a limited number of new centres would undoubtedly contain within it the danger of discrimination. If, for example, one were to choose the frontier zones of the EEC member states whose development has hitherto been neglected, other equally deserving regions would continue to suffer from neglect.

The EEC bodies and the national governments possess only limited possibilities of carrying out such a policy of decentralisation: so that, if a much larger number of private entrepreneurs do not decide of their own free will to transfer some of their production to the neglected regions, indirect incentives to do so must be augmented, especially in the field of tax concessions. A European development plan ought not to suppress the capacity of the capital and labour markets to direct their own operations, but it should seek to extend this to the neglected regions. The longer-term development potential of European industry will be able to expand in a meaningful way only if the quality of life of its people receives precedence over purely economic considerations.

Internalising industrial externalities

European industrial planning must be based on a wider rationality: that is the key message of this chapter. Centrally, it posits that the aim of industry should be to serve, not a narrow objective of more efficient production, or higher profits, or even higher wages for workers, but human welfare. One of the reasons for the existing gap between industrial output and decreasing welfare in the human sense is, we suggest, the 'nature of the accounting and costing system ... which has served to mask many of its deficiencies' (Bell 1974, p.280). On a regional or national level, the product is used as the main yardstick for measuring economic productivity and welfare in a society: but the GNP cannot serve as a yardstick for human welfare, for this concept includes only products and services which are exchanged over a market and have prices which are determined at these markets; it does not consider products and services which are not marketable, or which do not have a positive price. Side-effects of production and consumption are likewise not appropriately taken into account in the GNP concept. Thus, for example, an increase in car output means an increase in GNP value, but the additional resources used for building hospitals which are needed for the rehabilitation of people injured in car accidents are also added as new values to the GNP. In the private sphere, the GNP concept, with its method of adding up single products and services, fails to take into account the complexity and interdependence of modern industrial production, and the same is true for such spheres as defence and the school system. This means that the GNP concept of success indicators for private and public welfare is misleading the producer and consumer with regard to which products should be produced and consumed and in what quantity.

Economists recently proposed correcting the measurement of production output by the subtraction or addition of negative or positive external costs. Enlarged accounting concepts are being discussed which do not limit themselves to products and services with prices, but compare the 'goods' with the 'bads' of the production and consumption processes. Social costs evolving from the production and consumption of goods are subtracted from the national product in order to gain a more welfare-oriented picture of a national economy, a region, or a city (Hochwald 1961). The revision of the traditional accounting system thus leads us to an integration of negative side-effects of production and provides us with a more realistic basis for economic and political decisions.

Advocates of the concept of 'internalisation of external economies and diseconomies' – a concept which has been long discussed in economic theory and which regained attention recently in connection with environmental disruption – propose to take the 'social value' of a product as its real price for decisions about the output structure. The real price or 'social value' is the market price minus the estimated value of damage inflicted on others by producing it and/or using it (Mishan 1968, pp. 82-3). But there are serious theoretical deficiencies in this concept: it is difficult to measure the side-effects of industrial production in money terms, for these effects typically do not have market prices, and to find adequate shadow prices means to rely in one way or another on a subjective value system. And since the idea of the enlarged accounting system is to find a more welfare-orientated criterion for measuring economic activity, we cannot rely on the traditional value and price system, which is based on market forces which do not generate competitive prices. The most important deficiency lies in the fact that in some cases the analysis may come too late to reverse the process, as for example in the case of environmental disruption.

Recently, so-called social indicators have been used for measuring human welfare: the idea is to employ an individualistic approach in the form of material, quantitatively measurable output indices, such as cars per person, hospitals and public theatres per 10,000 persons, schools and universities per 10,000 persons. But again there are considerable difficulties which lead us to doubt very much whether the concept of social indicators can be a successful one – especially if our goal is political action. First of all, we do not know how people questioned about their ideas of personal welfare compare their standards, i.e. we do not know how far priority orderings in the list of quality of life indices of different groups correspond to the priority orderings in the list of other social groups. Secondly, and more important, it is not clear which body should have the task of drawing up a quality-of-life list of social indicators. After having found out what different social groups define as their quality-of-life standard, it should be easier for politicians to evaluate the trade-offs for their political decisions for those groups. If the public is informed about the quality-of-life standards of all different social groups, it can also measure political actions and decisions according to those lists: but only if political organisations such as Parliament or the parties had the power to influence or change the output structure of industry could the concept of social indicators fulfil its role. Since this is not the case in capitalist societies, social indicators should be used only as an instrument for demonstrating what preconditions must be established for creating opportunities for all social groups to participate equally in the same standard-of-living conditions.

These are not academic questions; they affect the choice of remedy. The more difficult an externality is to measure, the more difficult it is to assign a price to it, and conversely the more likely it is to be controlled by changes in maximising rules (for example, a company may create a higher quality work environment despite the fact that it is difficult to assign and index to the quality of environment). In some cases there may be indirect economic benefits derived from improving externalities – such as increases in productivity and decreases in absenteeism arising from improved work conditions. So one strategy for industry would be to seek out these indirect benefits from improving 'externalities'.

In general, public pressure and changes in social behaviour (not working for companies that pollute, for instance), will be the primary forces that change the maximisation rules within industry. The more measurable externalities are frequently controlled by assigning costs to the physical measure in the form of a penalty for violating the externality. This brings quick industrial change because it is more profitable not to incur the cost. Difficulty, however, then occurs in assigning the cost penalty because the damage for violation is often indirect and difficult to calculate.

In some few cases normal economic processes, such as major price increases, make previously considered 'free' or discarded factors valuable. For example, the recycling of certain materials, previously thrown away, becomes economic because of high prices.

In all cases of internalising externalities there is the problem of upsetting local competitivity: in an area that internalises as opposed to the one that does not (one area allowed to pollute, another not), where companies in both areas are operating in the same market. This calls for a uniform policy over the entire market areas. It poses difficult problems for Europe, where different regions are at different stages of economic development and so may take very different attitudes to problems like pollution.

Co-determination – a European model?

The new rationality we have described in Chapter 3 would affect not merely the relationship of industry to the community and society. It would also powerfully transform productive relations within the individual plant. At present economic rationality has evidently failed here also – sometimes to the extent of failing in its own terms. Though the unions in most European countries have secured adequate wages and minimal work conditions for their members, they have not made industrial work any more inherently satisfying. Absenteeism, low productivity, wildcat strikes are some of the manifestations of a general alienation from industrial work. In many countries, it is difficult to persuade young people to undertake the long and arduous apprenticeships that are still necessary to become a skilled worker; and existing skilled workers may disappear from the factory into occupations they now find more congenial. The workforce, including the factory floor workers, is steadily becoming more educated and consequently less willing to accept tedium or low status; workers are questioning both salary and status differentials. As plants increasingly depend on part-time, temporary or women workers, they find it necessary to make new kinds of working arrangements. Safety, health and environmental legislation all have their impact. And, at least in some countries, trades unions are turning from the old concentration on wages towards questions like working conditions, participation in management, and share in the profits of the enterprise.

Already, at least in some European countries, managements have begun to react. They have realised that, even in terms of traditional economic rationality, to achieve higher productivity and more effective work it will be necessary to reduce absenteeism, turnover, and poor product quality. New forms of work organisation have already been developed to improve industrial relations: job rotation, job enrichment, autonomous groups. All tend to delegate tasks and responsibilities to those at the medium and lower levels of the hierarchy, with more autonomy for each individual. There is discussion of continuous education in industry and of fuller integration of work and education, including work sabbaticals, educational credits, and postgraduate training in industry.

All this tends to centre on the possibility of creating a new, non-bureaucratic way of taking decisions within industry. European industry for the most part is not as advanced here as in Japanese industry, for instance. But one must realise the magnitude of the change that will be needed: real participation means decentralisation to the level of the shop floor and the office, whereby each employee has an opportunity of influencing his work environment. Budget control too would need to be further delegated. This goes a great deal further than the basic German notion of *Mitbestimmung*, where workers have a role on supervisory boards; for here the power is still effectively centralised. And it is in fact unlikely that the concept of *Mitbestimmung* will be accepted by the majority of European trades unions, since their practices vary considerably. It may be more realistic to concentrate on a more human environment and a greater sense of autonomy in the local plant, which could enhance the attitude of the average worker to his job and to his life.

Does this mean a fundamental reversal in the trends towards increasing scale in European industry, observable for many decades? Will the future lie in small-scale units, perhaps scattered in rural areas where people can combine industrial work with farming? Will the tendency be to return to craft production? Caution is necessary here. It is clear that 'big' industry has economy-of-scale advantages compared to 'small' industry, both on the input and output side. Big industry has better possibilities to collect information necessary for industrial production, to undertake R and D, to gain access to the capital market and the qualified labour market. Basically small enterprises have these possibilities too, but their size and mentality impede them. On the output side, big industry can build up a systematic marketing strategy and sales organisation, especially in international markets. As a result of these advantages, big industry produces more efficiently than small industry. This conclusion cannot however be generalised; its validity depends on the specific industrial branch or even product in question. Recently there has been a tendency for small industry to take over production areas and activities lost to big industry. These are areas in which the costs of collection and distribution from the big plant are relatively high in relation to the low cost of mass production in big industry, so that the smallness and flexibility of small industry give lower costs and overall efficiency. And it is clear that management complexity increases more than proportionally with respect to size; there is an increased vulnerability to strikes and other forms of disorganisation.

Thus there will probably be a need for balance in industrial size and location: the decentralised large firm, or medium-sized company, will combine many advantages of small- and large-scale organisation. It can obtain the advantages of locating industry in rural areas – cheaper labour supply, lower real estate costs, lower crime rates and social tension, and indirect benefits of less pollution, less traffic, cheaper housing for employees. (This also would permit the revamping of culturally and historically famous towns of which Europe has such a wealth.) But one should not forget the typical problems of locating in rural areas: higher transport costs, lack of infrastructure, lack of support services, lack of educational institutions (difficulty in hiring and keeping a highly educated workforce). Thus there will be a need for integrated industrial rural development, as we already saw in Chapter 5.

Beyond indicative planning

Since private industry often fails to provide society with goods and services which the state apparatus conceives to be socially necessary, the state and its agencies participate in the market process; it is understood that the state has the right and duty to assume private business functions whenever its representatives think it wise to do so. Until recently the state's economic function was to provide collective goods and services such as education, health services, defence, basic research, regional and international policy and social security systems, goods and services which the market typically did not provide sufficiently, or which were thought to be too important to be left to the market alone. Now, with the increasing complexity of modern industrial societies, governments try to influence by direct measures, laws and administrative rules, or indirect economic incentives, the levels of employment and structures of employment in the case of specific types of employees, such as women, the handicapped, the young and the elderly. In the field of economic development the state does not limit its activities to supporting a general overall growth strategy; it also promotes the economic growth of certain industries at the expense of others by subsidies (Lindbeck 1975).

Increased demand for public services – which rose especially as a consequence of centralised planning in World War Two – gives the state an even greater influence over the control of economic processes. Through purchases of goods and services, building highways, directing migration through agricultural policy, contracting with private business in the field of technology, fiscal policy, defence policy, foreign trade regulations, and the banking system, the state exercises more influence on the shape and development of input and output structures in industry than is normally expected in market economies (Durgin 1974).

Yet these state economic activities are still thought of only as support for or correction of market processes: investments are indicative and indirect rather than direct and imperative as they are in socialist societies. Indicative plans are best known and were applied partly successfully in the French planning attempt to supplement the information supplied by the market and the price system, so that private firms can plan investments more rationally. It is in this sense that, in the words of P. Masse: 'French planning ... is essentially the extension to the national level of the kind of planning effort made by any private business with thought for the future' (Cohen 1969). It tries to influence economic behaviour, but without recourse to power and on a purely informational basis. Thus the argument for indicative planning is that it improves, through better information, the performance of private industry, of the whole economy, and of government activities as well. None of the economic actors has reason not to follow the guidelines of indicative plans – especially since all important socio-economic groups are involved in their preparation and compilation – as long as the information they provide seems to be accurate. This fact is of importance for a future reorientation of industry, in which indicative planning will have a vital role to play. But indicative planning has its limits. The final demand is not estimated during the planning process; it is assumed as 'given' outside the planning process. This has the consequence that though indicative plans can influence the direction of economic development they cannot stear it in a direction quite radically different from that which would have prevailed in the absence of the plan (Cohen 1969, p.15).

Thus the corporation remains independent – and finally the key agent: in highly industrialised countries the 'critical instrument of transformation is not the state or the individual but the modern corporation' (Galbraith 1974, p.38). The economic process of capitalist development has led to the concentration of capital and power in relatively few firms and trusts, and consequently in the hands of relatively few people; at the same time, this power is often used to influence socio-economic factors of relevance outside the single firm: invested capital at stake is too large to leave uncontrolled the economic processes having direct or indirect effects on its profit rate. This means that within the corporate industry system 'things that need to go right must be made to go right' (Galbraith 1974, p.39). Industry has to try to influence the state's action for the benefit of its private economic goals: big corporations not only plan their own activities, and as far as possible influence the course of actions not under their direct control, they also develop defence strategies with which they are able to counteract and offset uncontrollable activities. This is simply a question of economic survival: and the greater the concentration of capital, and thus the greater the economic and political power, the more successful the corporation will be in its efforts to influence the course of economic development. Since the most important criterion of success in private business is economic growth, economic power enhances growth, and this in turn leads to more economic power. The political concept of pluralism in western democracies vastly underestimates the economic and political power of private corporations and tends to assume that it can be neutralised. This, however, is not the case: since private corporations have a much more effective apparatus for economic management at their disposal than do the state or its agencies they are the more successful side in bargaining with the state, and this is especially the case where the state bureaucracy lacks the necessary knowledge about economic activities involved in contracts between state agencies and private corporations. As we have seen in the example of capitalist indicative planning, it is the corporation which uses the information provided by the state in pursuit of its own economic, social and political goals, rather than the state which imposes its own goals on private industry. The deep 'symbiotic relationship', as Galbraith (1974) calls it, between public and private organisations thus tends to be one in which the state follows the economic development path of private industry: and the fact that the activities of corporate industry are primarily analysed according to economic rationality (return on investment, profits) makes it even easier for industry to impose its political goals on the state. It is here that it becomes most obvious that this overriding rationality in highly industrialised societies should be extended to include other criteria. It might be argued that any participant in economic activities tries to influence as much as he can the socio-economic conditions under which he is acting. While this is true, the difference lies not in interest but in ability. Small participants have to act collectively or get legislative support if they want to avoid some of the consequences of the competitive market: even then they are often not very successful and critical public attention is drawn to them immediately. The big corporations, by contrast, deal primarily with the bureaucracy of the state so as to modify the economic environment to suit their own purposes, and since bureaucracy is more powerful and more effective than legislative market regulations the large corporations accomplish much more without receiving the same critical public attention. The necessity for the state to regulate and control the economic process for the benefit of society thus becomes more urgent but its chance of success in doing so diminishes: the state will thus be forced to act more and more as an active participant in economic production and the solution of distribution problems.

Strategies for improvement

The question, therefore, forces itself on our attention: what strategy or strategies should be pursued by European industry – and European society – if they are to plan the industrial future on the basis of a wider social or cultural rationality?

A first alternative could be to improve the existing instruments of socio-èconomic policy, with the hope that an increased rationalisation and articulation of decision-making processes in both the public and private spheres would lead to a qualitatively better functioning of the industrial system. Yet it is not very likely that improved instruments alone in the sphere of the production and consumption process will result in a better assessment of the interrelation between 'industry' and 'society in general': more elaborate steering systems and more sophisticated organisational forms in industry will complicate an industrial production that is already highly complex. The most characteristic feature of society's present reaction to problems caused by dysfunctions of the industrial system is that the applied instruments do not solve them but only cure them superficially. Even if science and new information provide us with new knowledge about the basic reasons for industry's malfunctioning, they will 'very seldom be transferred to the decision-making process' in public sphere (Menke-Glückert 1970, p.16).

A second alternative is that the key aggregated determinants of socio-economic developments are controlled and planned directly by society, and the crux of this lies in procedural method and organisation. One method would be though nationalisation of all or the most important industrial branches: in nationalised industries, the state can direct and control investment, output structure, prices, in such a way that they correspond to society's general welfare. The positive aspects are obvious: society has, through its elected bodies, a chance of steering socio-economic development in a planned way that may differ considerably from the development generated by the market process; but it must be stressed that this is only a chance, not an automatic improvement in allocation of resources, distribution of income, or higher employment. Experience with nationalised industries is not very encouraging: nor should we overlook that, with few exceptions, industries have been nationalised after they have been mismanaged for many years. Nationalised industries must of course worry about economic efficiency, not less than private industry does, but more, if nationalisation is to be an acceptable instrument of socio-economic policy: only if the nationalised industries work more effectively from society's point of view can they be seen as such an instrument. But in practice many nationalised undertakings prove neither very efficient nor very socially responsive.

Another, less rigorous method of acquiring greater control over industrial output and the consequences of industrial performance is to control and direct private business investment. While there is no generally accepted definition of 'investment control', private business investment decisions in market-oriented societies have always been 'guided' by various instruments: economic and administrative stimuli have been used, and recently other, more direct investment planning has been discussed. One possible method would be as follows: on the basis of a long-range plan for socio-economic development regional and structural components would be defined, outlined and plans for individual sectors or regions would be disaggregated; private business would compete for the implementation of investments necessary for fulfilling society's development plans, and the agencies responsible for setting up plans for socio-economic development would have the right to cancel private investments if they were not in accordance with them, or to insist on certain minimum investments that were socially desirable. After that, the actual private business performance would, as before, only be guided by general performance rules and indirect methods. The advantage of such a combined method of investment control can be seen in directing socio-economic development *ex-ante* from society's point of view with the help of private business.

But who would be responsible for false economic decisions, i.e. wrong investments resulting from bad development plans, and who would bear the negative consequences? The answer lies in viewing industrial investment in a social rather than a purely industrial context. Alienation from the industrial system on the part of the great majority is caused by the fact that they are not playing an adequate part in discussing society's social goals and industry's instrumental role, output and performance. Only at the enterprise or plant level are we yet experimenting with the first methods of co-determination in the production process: at the branch or even the overall industrial level we have failed to find reliable mechanisms for interesting the whole workforce (as distinct from management and unions) in participating in discussion of the general output structure. 'What is missing is a political technology for system-wide participatory planning (future oriented decision-making mechanisms)' (Menke-Glückert 1970, p.16). It is often said that participatory planning and democratic discussion of highly important socio-economic processes is futile, because the industrial process is so complex it is impossible for a large participatory community to understand it and so take the correct decisions: and while this is true, it is also true that private business taking decisions affecting society's socio-economic development is in no better situation so far as the understanding and analysis of the complex socio-economic process is concerned. 'Conscious calculation of social direction must, therefore, partly replace the automatic and semi-spontaneous adjustment of society to new knowledge that generally sufficed in the past' (Dror 1968, p.5). And this calculation should be made and discussed by all relevant social groups whose interests are affected: the consumer, the labour force represented by the trade unions, private entrepreneurs, various minority groups and state representatives should be responsible for setting up socio-economic development plans.

Against this approach, it may well be argued that in conditions of risk and uncertainty, social representatives or the state and its agencies are no better equipped to avoid wrong investment decisions than private business working on a market basis. Public councils will be largely bureaucratic and administrative, and it is the nature of such bodies to avoid risks. So only the investment size and structure in industry should be fixed in development plans; private firms would then compete for their implementation, with the chance of profits and the risk of losses; unjustifiably high profits could be taxed away, unmerited losses could be made good. This does not mean that highly industrialised societies could afford to produce inefficiently over a long period; it means regulating the consequences of wrong decisions, with more consideration for the individual.

Our conclusion, then, is that the planning methods employed hitherto – in the West European systems indicative planning with a system of incentives and directives, in the East European imperative planning – have been only partially successful if measured against the objectives they have set themselves: both planning concepts are clearly oriented by socio-economic theories which correspond only imperfectly with reality. A system of 'piecemeal engineering' is, to be sure, better than passivity, but if the socio-political system is to be made more amenable to direction, we shall not be spared the necessity of creating instruments for this purpose embracing the whole of society. The resistance of political bodies and of economic management will at first be as it was before planning at the level of undertakings and companies gave way to the indicative planning of entire branches of industry or of the whole economy; and the danger cannot be minimised that, so long as there exists no generally accepted system of values, the socially strongest groups may make their values and objectives prevail over those of weaker groups. A more socially-oriented and better-controlled planning process for industry must, therefore, go along with an improvement in the possibilities of active participation on the part of all groups involved.

Within such a framework, how would the industrial manager or entrepreneur fit? Undoubtedly, a new kind of entrepreneur would be needed: one who was socially-oriented and socially-conscious, whose task would not be limited to providing goods and services, but would be concerned with total social responsibilities. Such a person could function only within a new management and auditing system, corresponding to these additional tasks. There might then be three spheres in which society required responsibility from the industrial enterprise:

- an inner circle, corresponding to industry's traditional task of providing goods and services;
- a central circle, where the fulfilment of industry's traditional economic function still dominated but only within constraints (environment, psychological security of the worker, job satisfaction);
- and an outer circle, where enterprises were required to use their productive resources for solving central and general problems in a changing society.

The aim would thus be to break down the general term 'social responsibility of industry' into identifiable components and to develop scales by which these components can be measured and compared. Such new responsibilities might include: investment in existing production units for eliminating negative or destructive environmental effects; location planning as a measure for structural improvement; improvement of the infrastructure in a given region; measures for humanising work conditions; profit-sharing with employees; economic employment of natural resources; and consumer information beyond conventional publicity.

European industry in a post-industrial age

It has often been said that Europe, like most other advanced industrial societies, is passing into a post-industrial age in which the great majority of the working population will find their living not by making goods but by producing services. But it would be a fundamental mistake to conclude from this that the future of European industry is of no importance. In the post-industrial society, in fact, it will be the high productivity of the industrial sector that makes the other developments possible. But paradoxically, as we have seen, this very productivity has too often been obtained at the expense of other costs which have nowhere been allowed for. Services, as far as we can see, have far fewer obvious negative exernalities such as physical pollution or resource depletion.

The service industries could also provide another vital role. Even in a period when quantitative growth has been replaced by qualitative growth, it is very likely that manufacturing industry will continue to rationalise its productive methods; and consumption likewise will be rationalised (with less waste). Consequently, the prospect is that industry will be able to produce a constant volume of product with a steadily diminishing labour force. This would permit – and would indeed demand – the development of a wide variety of new service industries in order to provide full employment. But it has to be faced that a service economy poses all kinds of new social problems, due to the inequalities of status that will probably result. This may indeed be one of the main problems of the Europe of 2000. Related to it is the point that the total number of senior managerial jobs, in both manufacturing and service industry, will not rise very rapidly if population stagnates and economic growth slows down. This could lead to acute social tensions if the output from universities, colleges and high schools continued to increase. One way out of the dilemma might be a new kind of flexible life cycle with alternating periods of study, service and manufacturing work, more responsible and less responsible jobs. It would fit well with the notion of permanent education which we outline in the next chapter.

In any case, in a service-dominated society industry will have new roles. In the first place, there is the development of services directly supporting industry: for example postal services, transportation services, data processing services, business consulting services, maintenance services. There are considerable problems for industry when the efficiency of such services is low – forcing industry to provide its own mail services for example. Then there is the development of services not directly supporting industry: social services primarily in the form of health, education and public administration. Further, there is the potential market for industrial products in the social service sector, for example constructing hospitals, providing electronic instrumentation,or data processing.

Finally, the service-dominated economy already poses one question that will loom increasingly large. Many public services, such as schools and hospitals, have been organised on the principle, not of economic efficiency, but on a multiplicity of welfare criteria, which often are more difficult to measure and to agree. Many people are now asking whether this does not lead to inefficiency and misuse – for instance, to the deliberate creation of surplus employment with inevitable inflationary effects. Some of the same criticisms have arisen of state purchase and planning in the manufacturing sector – for instance Concorde, or nuclear plants or telephone equipment in many countries. If in future a wider spectrum of manufacturing industry is to be organised on such principles, then these accusations must become the centre of a serious debate.

It is now time to sum up our argument, and then pose some basic questions for the development of European industry – questions that we expect to dominate European discussion in the 1980s and 1990s.

First: until now the European system of industry has been geared purely toward the efficient production of goods and services; a social security system has been set up to compensate for some of the grosser abuses which have arisen; but almost completely ignored have been the wider performance aspects, both internally and externally.

Internally, the primary goals have been profit and sales, leading to the deliberate creation of new wants, and thus to a waste of resources and energy on products and services which do not necessarily contribute to welfare. For example, work satisfaction, or health at work, have been relegated to a secondary importance. This problem of priorities cannot be tackled by small-scale adaptations: it will require new production technologies or new methods of production, oriented towards the human constitution (both physical and psychical) making production processes understandable and controllable by ordinary people. This may require a small-scale, decentralised structure for production. The stress will move away from purely economic efficiency, and towards a multiplicity of different socio-economic goals.

Externally, the sub-system 'industry' today determines the development of the system 'society'. This order will need to be reversed, so as to take account of the negative effects of industry on the natural and on the human environment. This means stressing again that industry is merely instrumental in serving wider social goals. These goals need to be debated by the European public and expressed by European institutions. The international character of production and consumption will eventually need to be reflected in an international system of planning and coordination. Above all, there will be a need for the active and continuous participation of all groups – workers, consumers, the general public, employers, trades unions, federations of industry and the like. Techniques of forecasting can contribute a great deal here, by sensitising different groups to forthcoming problems – at least so long as they are simple enough to be understood by all groups and if they also take into account the divergent interests of different groups. But actual decisions will need to be taken on the balance of what may often be conflicts of interest.

Finally, we pose the problems that may dominate the European industrial debate in the coming decades.

First: what shall be the *international strategy* of European industry. Should it attempt to integrate more deeply its production and marketing with the energy-rich, materials-rich countries of the developing world (North Africa, the Middle East)? What would be the alternative?

Secondly: should European industry seek to develop a distinctive international character based on a very high investment on *research and development*? What form should such a strategy take? Should it be basic or applied? Traditional or advanced? For manufacturing or for the increasingly dominant service sector?

Thirdly: what should be the attitude of European industry towards the movement for greater *participation and decentralisation* of decision-making? Should it break down its present decision structures and stress more democratic procedures? Should it encourage the participation of workers at the centre or on the shop floor?

Fourthly: how far should the *pattern of industrial development* within Europe be extended from the traditional industrial areas to the rural periphery? How far should it be encouraged to remain in older industrial areas – including the older central cities – where it is now rapidly declining?

Fifthly: what should be the relationship to *national or international planning systems*? Should the present degree of relationship, or non-relationship, with national governments continue? Or should there be a move towards industrial cooperation inside a European system of industrial planning, superceding many of the national powers?

Sixthly: should the present system of *financing of industry* – mainly through private funding, partly through direct state funding – continue? Or should a conscious effort be made to tap new sources, either by extended equity markets or by more direct participation on the part of workers?

We give no answers here because we do not know them. Nor do we think that European societies will necessarily know them. But our strong presumption is that, around the year 2000, European industry will be moving into new institutional relations with state and international organisations, new modes of finance, new patterns of internal organisation – and, above all, a new basic rationality.

CHAPTER 8

Information, Education and Power

The communication of information – of 'knowledge' in the widest meaning of the word – will represent a problem to the European of the twenty-first century; and this will be due paradoxically to the enormously enhanced capability he will possess in this field. And this problem will not only be paradoxical: it will be novel, and will, therefore, have to be faced without the possibility of reliance on precedents in the formation of policies. What will be at stake will be on one hand the distribution of power within society, on the other the rights and psychological integrity of the individual.

The technology which will be essentially responsible for raising the communication of information to the status of an unprecedented problem already exists – we shall describe some of it in a moment – but for the most part it has not yet been pressed into service: the way in which we at present employ television as a tool of education, for example, compares with the way in which we could employ it if we used all the technology available to us much as a sixteenth-century printing press compares with the presses of a national daily newspaper. So that, while the communication of information is already to some degree a problem – its more obvious aspects have been exposed in Chapter 4 and need not be repeated here – we are really only at the beginning of the 'information era'.

None the less, our experience so far has been sufficient for us to be able to make fairly confident predictions in this sphere, for plainly, unless something altogether unforeseen occurs, the technology we possess but have as yet not fully employed will become more and more active and produce a greater and greater impression on the life of society and of the individual. In this chapter, then, we propose to discuss, first, some of the details of this new communications technology and the probable continuing role of the current, by now almost 'traditional' media; the problems this technology will raise for the individual in the form of increased psychological risk; its effect in the field of education – a form of communication of information which could well be revolutionised; finally the twofold implication of the foregoing for the distribution of power in the social order.

New worlds of telecommunication

Already most commercial organisations which want to advertise themselves display their telephone number more prominently than their postal address, and in most European countries it is already cheaper to make a short telephone call than to post a letter. On the largest scale, it is a truism that needs no elaboration here that advanced telecommunications systems have reduced the globe to the size of a village so far as people's communicating with one another is concerned. These phenomena, however, are really no more than forerunners and precursors of the telecommunications worlds of the coming century.

There are three layers to any national telecommunications system, and each of them is undergoing a major change: the transmission system – the wires, waves, satellites through which the messages pass; the switching system which enables the messages to reach their desired address; and the equipment at the end of the communication process – the telephones, teleprinters, cathode tubes.

That part of the cost of a telephone connection which goes on *transmission* has since the end of the war fallen to one-hundredth of what it was before: an estimate of the Massachusetts Institute of Technology is that the transmission cost of sending a hundred words by wire to any part of the world will be less than two English pence by 1990. The first of the techniques which is making this reduction possible is the coaxial cable, one form of which will enable 80,000 human voices to speak simultaneously along one cable, or their equivalent in television signals, computer data, stereo-music signals, facsimile. It is the coaxial cable which makes possible 'cable television', which would enable every home to receive a much larger number of television channels than at present; but some of these could also work in reverse direction, with pictures and other signals transmitted from the home. An enormous new range of services in the field of information, merchandising, and local politics could also come over the coaxial cable. The helical waveguide – a two-inch metal tube of fine enamelled copper wire protected by layers of glass fibre, carbon and steel – can carry 230,000 telephone calls if the signal is boosted every 30 kilometers or so. Waveguides may come into service within the 1970s, but as they do so another transmission technology, the optical fibre, will start its field trials. An optical fibre is a 'wire' of glass or silicon, of extremely high purity – as pure as a sheet of glass 10 kilometers thick through which you could see perfectly – through which telecommunication signals can pass. One fibre has the thickness of a human hair and can carry between 1,800 to 2,700 telephone calls or their equivalent in other services. The optical fibre has the advantage of extreme cheapness to manufacture (glass not copper) and extreme flexibility.

Another area of development is the microwave; engineers are finding ways to exploit sections of the electro-magnetic spectrum which have hitherto been impossible to use, especially the waves which go down to and below 3 centimeters or even as low as one millimeter. The electro-magnetic spectrum – or those parts of it which are currently exploited – is becoming extremely crowded, but the area being opened up is thousands of times broader than the whole of the area now used. It could be that, in rural areas, a whole battery of communication devices will make their final journey between the local network and the individual home through a single saucer-shaped device sitting on the roof, replacing telegraph wires and television aerials, not to speak of the postman and the newspaper boy. But the most dramatic developments are taking place in the communications satellite: only a few years ago a single ground station for receiving satellite signals would cost £4 million; now some ground stations are as cheap as £200,000 and in one experiment due to start beaming educational programmes to villages in northern India, mass produced village ground stations are being turned out at around £200 a time. The ATS-6 advanced satellite is already beaming educational programmes and medical data across sparsely populated sections of America. The satellite is being thought of as an instrument of mass education in the Third World, as well as a cheap way of expanding international telephone traffic. In practice, it will create the international links in the new global telecommunication system which is evolving, and will help to abolish distance as a factor in transmission cost.

These inventions are not separate methods due to succeed one another: each possesses its own advantages and all are capable of interconnection within the same national telecommunications system: that is why one of the most intriguing of the new techniques is 'multiplexing', a method by which the capacity of the already existing transmission devices is 'stretched' to encompass some of the new services. A digital system is a new method of carrying messages along wires or by radio which can multiply the capacity of many existing wires and cables, improve the quality of every note, picture, word or printed letter sent out, and enable every message sent into a communication system to be stored electronically and turned back into the original message whenever the consumer needs it. Techniques such as coaxial rings are being developed to attach the individual subscriber to high-capacity digitalised routes; and we can imagine at the central core of a modern nation a vast intersecting highway of electronically processed digital information, passing entertainment, news, ‹ telephone conversations, commercial information, and the electronic equivalent of libraries.

But there would be no point in increasing the capacity to send messages if there were no improvements in the methods of switching them. Many of the new exchanges of the next decade will consist of a series of solid-state units; a chunk of computer circuitry which can be assembled into groups, depending on the capacity required in any locality. The routing of each call will be performed by a computer which has previously been 'taught' all the possible routes in the system.

Wholly new telecommunications services are now being developed around the world. In Japan a newspaper is being distributed by facsimile: it arrives directly in the subscriber's home. In the United States a system of direct electronic fund-transfer has started which could make major changes in merchandising and personal banking. In many countries whole newspapers are transmitted from centre to centre for editions to be printed and distributed locally or regionally.

Some of the most important of the new services involve the display on an ordinary TV set of alphanumeric material: the BBC already offers the CEEFAX service, which enables written material – about a hundred pages of it – to be received in every home; and the British Post Office recently unveiled a more subtle device called VIEWDATA, which demands a combination of telephone, a television set and a small decoding unit: the user chooses the information service he requires – from weather, time, recipes, cricket scores, news headlines to material which can normally be obtained only from libraries. VIEWDATA and its equivalents can also send out still pictures with sound: for one television channel forty or fifty simultaneous educational channels could be substituted, running scores of courses in parallel.

The development of these new services depends on the mass production of highly sophisticated electronic equipment, and this is under way. A group of new processes called LSI (large-scale integration) enables complex circuitry to be 'etched' into a piece of silicon; a computer which requires 100,000 transistors can be produced very cheaply on a chip of silicon the size of a postage stamp; and one million 'bits' of data can be stored in a magnetic bubble an inch across. The implications for the future of the kind of communications system these developments are making possible will be spelled out later: but it is obvious even now that the vastly increased amount of information which they will be able to transmit will – potentially, at least – vastly increase the 'bombardment' to which the citizen is even now subjected. The 'traditional' media, moreover, will certainly still be in operation – and may quite possibly still be the quantitatively major dispenser of information.

The media

The development of the current mass media is likely to be a continuation of the present trend towards greater homogenisation on the one hand, and the hunting out of any possible unexplored corner of marketable interest on the other. National newspapers and news-magazines will continue to get more and more alike. News will come from identical wire services or by syndication from the same dwindling group of major papers.

But this will change the concept of the audience: anything written or spoken will have to be intended for almost everybody, consumable in almost every country, in almost any kind of outlet. The writer's or broadcaster's loyalty will be, not to a reader, but to a market, and news and feature material will thus be increasingly theatricalised, *Time*-style. You decide on an 'image' for the person and write everything to fit – a technique close to that of advertising, copy-writing or the public relations handout.

There is unlikely to be a diminution in print: in general, new media are added on to old ones. Certain forms of print will grow and grow: the xerox copy will finally undermine the law of copyright. This, the cost of making books, and the spread of the electric typewriter, will return us to Caxton and Gutenberg in at least one sense: material will be disseminated mechanically, but it will have a more domestic air than the 'factory finish' that later printing technology gave it. Film will by 2000 be purely an 'art' spin-off from television: it will bear the same sort of relation to television that poetry in the nineteenth century began to bear to the novel. The signs are already there in the financing of Fassbinder by West German television, or of Bergman by Swedish television. The standard 'bestseller' will be increasingly a many-sided package, where it will be ever harder to tell which came first – the film or the TV series or the book.

The psychological risk

The development of the mass media in all their forms, and of increasingly efficient and relentless communications systems, has been attended by a growing awareness of the psycho-social risks which this development is bringing with it. The tacit assumption that man's adaptive capacity will enable him to handle the new demands being made on him has gradually given way to an appreciation of the negative effects on the social and psychological level and an increasing concern for the consequences of new developments in communications technology for man as a biological organism and social being.

A highly developed nervous system, with the brain as the master organ, provides man with a wide repertoire of reactions among which he can make deliberate choices: but while technology has transformed his social environment, the structure and size of his brain have remained essentially the same over some 40,000 years. This standstill of genetic evolution and the accelerating pace of social evolution raises the question of man's adaptability: how far can the tolerance of this old biological equipment be stretched? What happens if the limits are exceeded? Can adaptability be measured, its limits predicted, and hence the harmful effects prevented? These are topical problems in stress research.

A common opinion among stress researchers is that the demands of post-industrial society are straining the adaptive mechanisms to breaking-point. Man is exposed to a multitude of stimuli – from the external world and from the organs in his own body – which reach the brain through the sense organs and through nervous pathways. Unspecific stimuli without symbolic meaning – noise – play an important role in arousing the brain so that it can deal adequately with specific information. However, even when the brain is properly aroused by a moderate amount of noise, only a fraction of the stimuli received by the sense organs reaches the level of consciousness – possibly one out of a million messages. The selection of information is controlled by nervous and psychological processes, forming a hierarchy of gating mechanisms. On the whole, signals which have a high degree of symbolic and emotional significance to the individual have a greater chance of reaching consciousness than objectively important but subjectively indifferent signals. Thus, the human being deliberately develops a kind of 'tunnel' perception, a selective inattention to stimuli which he assumes to be of only secondary importance to him. And this will invariably restrict the scope of his existence.

The nervous system of the young child is characterised by a high degree of plasticity – a sensitivity to impressions – which decreases with advancing age. The information received by the young nervous system is thus extremely important to intellectual and emotional development: but it is still debated whether early influences leave irreversible marks, moulding the individual for the rest of his life, or whether early impressions can be erased by later experiences.

A related area is the need for a moderate amount of stimulation from the external world. The concepts *under-stimulation* and *over-stimulation* refer to the inability of the regulatory mechanisms in the brain to maintain an optimal level of functioning at low and high levels of stimulus input. This is the biological principle underlying the inverted-U function describing behavioural efficiency at different levels of stimulus input (Figure 8.1). The optimal level of mental functioning is located at the midpoint of a scale ranging from very low to very high stimulus loads. At the optimal level, the central nervous system is moderately aroused, the organism's resources are mobilised, full attention is paid to the surroundings, and the individual performs to the best of his abilities.

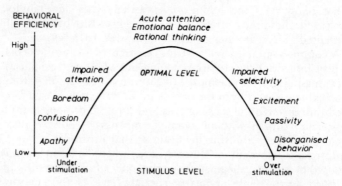

Figure 8.1
The inverted-U relationship between behavioural efficiency and stimulus level.

Source: M. Frankenhaeuser, unpublished paper.

When the input to the brain is either very low or very high, the homeostatic control mechanisms break down. At the high level – which is what concerns us here – the central nervous system is over-aroused: ability to select adequate information, to respond selectively to the impinging signals, is impaired; feelings of tension and excitement develop, followed by a gradual fragmentation of thought processes, loss of ability to integrate the messages into a meaningful whole, impaired judgment and decision-making, loss of initiative and, finally, a breakdown of organised behaviour.

Ideally, a person should remain receptive to new information, new events and new situations: however, because of the limitations built into our nervous system, a heavy stimulus load tends to reduce our sensitivity and reactivity, the stimuli lose their emotional impact and reactions are toned down. Consequently, over-stimulation may form part of a general process towards passivity.

This is a crucial point. On the one hand, the communications systems offer an increased output and a greater variety of choice; on the other, the psychological demands inherent in these choices require initiative and active effort. How can these demands be met, when the human nervous system responds to an excessive input by loss of initiative and loss of involvement? Another crucial point is that large groups in society are forced to live and work outside the stimuli zone providing opportunities for active information-seeking behaviour: among them are industrial workers engaged in under-stimulating jobs, the elderly, the handicapped, and the economically weak groups. Whereas the privileged groups in society may have the power to influence their surroundings so as to attain a better person-environment fit, the under-privileged, the weak groups, are forced to adapt to conditions shaped by others.

Stress research provides information about the psychological costs involved in adapting to environmental demands. The stress induced by conditions characterised by underload and overload is reflected in changes of the electrical activity of the brain, of heart rate and blood pressure, and in the secretion of hormones, such as adrenaline and cortisol. By measuring these physiological functions and relating them to concomitant environmental events and subjective reactions, we can monitor the arousing and relaxing influences of the psycho-social environment.

Controllability is a key concept in the various strategies for coping with over-stimulation. Messages disseminated by advertising and the mass media expose people to more attractive stimuli and more opportunities inciting consumption than they are capable of responding to, either because of lack of time or money, or because of psychological constraints. Severe intra-personal conflicts may develop from having to choose between equally attractive but mutually exclusive alternatives. It has been suggested that the problem of 'decision-stress' might underlie manifestations of discontent, apathy, flight from reality, and violence in affluent societies. The dangers of early over-stimulation are now beginning to attract the attention of the behavioural scientists. It has been suggested that an extremely rich, varied environment – the kind of environment created by communications technology – may give rise to a persistent 'stimulus hunger' of such intensity that it cannot be satisfied by the impressions and experiences offered in everyday life. Such a stimulus hunger may lead to a restless hunt for exciting experiences or to indifference and lack of emotional involvement. So far, this is only a hypothesis. The children of today are the first generation exposed to over-stimulation, and we know next to nothing of its long-term consequences.

Information overload may be regarded as a special case of the attractive stimulus overload: and here the distinction made by the Swedish scientist, Lars Gyllensten between overload of information, pseudo-information, and noise is useful (Gyllensten 1974). Noise is the flow of unsorted messages, unrelated, fragmentary and devoid of meaning: to transform sensory inflow from noise to information requires active participation by the recipient. As the noise level rises, information becomes less readily available, and the consumer will have to search actively for the meaningful messages.

The demand for goal-directed effort favours the well-educated, the influential groups, and these are the people confronted with true information overload, constantly challenged to sort out their priorities and to decide how to allocate their attention and their capacity. Among the members of this group we find the politicians and decision-makers, the educators and other intellectuals, as well as the active users of the new communications facilities. Members of this category are motivated by ambition to keep up with new knowledge, to absorb and process the constantly increasing pool of data. Stress, to these people, increases with the discrepancy between their ambition to absorb information and their information-processing capacity.

This is the true information overload, the problem of the well-educated elite, the stress of the privileged. The motives and values guiding their choices will influence the output offered to the less privileged groups, the majority.

To the great majority, the passive recipients of information inputs, the problem is not one of too much information, but one of too much noise. As long as the consumer does not engage actively in extracting information from the flow, this to him will remain noise, regardless of the amount of objective information contained in the messages. A conscious need to be informed, an active effort to process the inflow, are the psychological prerequisites for transforming noise into information.

A great part of the consumers of information from the various media do not fulfil these psychological requirements: to them the flow will remain noise – noise disguised as information, or pseudo-information; and this information gap may widen with advancing technology.

Information, technology and education

Against this set of problems must now be put another: in education systems.* That there is some kind of 'crisis' taking place in education at this moment no one would deny: nor would anyone deny that it affects, not this or that sector of the educational systems of Europe, but the process and idea of education as such. Everyone thinks, of course, that the age in which he happens to live is a turning-point in history, an age of unexampled uncertainty, change, turmoil and what-not: in the case of education, however, it does seem that over a century of steady evolution has at this moment suddenly and without much warning been halted and even thrown into reverse, producing a situation of extreme indecisiveness and bewilderment which, if not literally unexampled, has not been met within any of our lifetimes.

Here are some of the symptoms. Student enrolment has much slowed down compared with what it was in the 1960s: in some countries it is increasing more slowly, in some it is not increasing at all, and in some it is going backwards. Graduates remain unemployed, school-leavers cannot get jobs. Educational budgets are down everywhere. The 'crisis of authority' is even more plainly in evidence on the campus and in the classroom than it is elsewhere. The way in which the total educational process is divided up – pre-primary, primary, secondary, higher – is seen more and more as unnatural, out of phase with the way children and young people develop, and incapable of cooperating with, or pressing into service, the educational activities and potentialities of the mass media. The question of the place of education within society is now wide open: it is possible to ask 'what is education for?' and receive no straight answer. This is a selection of symptoms: everyone concerned with education at any level and in any capacity has his own private collection of 'things that are going wrong'.

So education is in crisis: it needs reshaping. Assuming that it is

* The development of education to the year 2000 is studied in depth in *Education Without Frontiers* (Fragnière 1976), the companion volume to the present volume: we shall, therefore, confine ourselves here to the changes information technology may help to bring about.

reshaped over the next quarter century – and *not* destroyed and rebuilt – what are the current trends which will play the largest and most effective part in reshaping it? We detect four – four drives already operating which will make the greatest contribution to determining the appearance of the educational systems of Europe in the year 2000.

First: the drive to equality of opportunity. There are few who openly assert that equal opportunity in education is undesirable (though there are, of course, many who are privately glad we haven't got it yet). The great increase in the size of all educational systems over the past 25 years has been welcomed in part because it was thought that more places meant a better chance of getting a place and, therefore, a more nearly equal educational opportunity for the hitherto educationally deprived. We do not say that this has not happened, but it has certainly not happened to the degree many people hoped it would: it is still an aspiration rather than something achieved. But the desire for it is there and the trend towards it is strong: it is not likely to let up between now and 2000.

Secondly: the drive towards lifelong learning. This trend originates in the rapidity with which nowadays new knowledge comes into existence and old knowledge becomes antiquated. The situation is analogous to that which obtained in the invention-rich nineteenth century, except that the speed of change is now very much faster and in some regions of knowledge much more fundamental. Even if you conceive of education as no more than going to school and learning facts, you would, with the world as it now is, have to repeat it after you had 'left school' because the 'facts' would have either ceased to be facts or ceased to be of much use to you. Now this necessity for a recurrent education is developing into a trend towards an education which lasts a whole lifetime: so that education comes to be seen, not as something belonging to youth and finished with when you have 'grown up', but as a tutor you never discharge who is always available to assist you in doing what you want to do in so far as this depends on up-dating your knowledge. But lifelong education is clearly going to mean more than this. Education which goes on throughout life transforms not only education but life itself: the tripartite division of a life into youth, maturity and age is much weakened if lifelong education links them all together; and the aim of education ceases to be the acquisition of facts (though that function must always remain to it) and becomes something more like a continual, or at least never finally suspended pushing forward of the limits of your development. It is plain to see that if and when lifelong learning puts on institutional flesh and becomes reality, it will transform the educational system fundamentally: for, just as there can be only one eternity, so there can be only one 'lifelong' education. Lifelong education cannot start 'when you leave school', for in the sense intended, you never do leave school; it starts when you start school and accompanies you thereafter: both the education of youth and 'adult education' will be subsumed in a single education, lasting, if not from the cradle to the grave, at any rate from the crêche to the old folks' home.

Thirdly: the drive to participation and autonomous learning. What used to be called separatism and is now usually called regionalism – fundamentally the desire and willingness to assume more direct control over one's own destiny – is perhaps the strongest political drive now operating: it is the main cause of the 'crisis of authority' and the weakening of centralised control. In the educational sphere this drive expresses itself in the demand on the part of the student body for a greater degree of participation in, among other things, the construction of courses. That this desire will grow seems obvious: that it must grow is evident from the above-mentioned rapidity with which the quantity of available knowledge is increasing – future study courses will have to be highly selective and there is no reason why the student should not participate in this necessary selection of what he is to study. Active collaboration by the student in the design of the programme of studies he will pursue, and then in the organisation of the institutions in which he pursues them, is a feature of current education which is sure to become increasingly evident as the century advances.

Participation opens the road to autonomous learning – assisted independent learning – through the encouragement of which the student assumes more and more responsibility for his own education. It involves a new relationship between student and teacher – a relationship foreshadowed in the fourth of the drives which are remoulding education.

Fourthly: the drive towards transforming the teacher into a counsellor – or at least towards the introduction of counselling as a major aspect of his duties. Counselling means advising the student on all aspects of his education throughout his learning life – which, with the advent of lifelong learning, can mean throughout his entire life. It involves two distinct though allied activities: orientation and guidance. Orientation is the act of assisting the student to an understanding of what he wants to learn and why: it gives him the information he needs to decide on his own education. Guidance acts within this framework: it assists the student to carry out successfully whatever course of study he may choose. In the educational system which this drive is helping to shape, counselling is not a marginal activity – as 'career guidance' for instance is today – but one which goes to the heart of a new outlook on learning.

These four trends or drives taken together imply a much greater continuity in the educational process that exists at present, and, therefore, the gradual flattening and at length disappearance of the walls which divide one educational sector from another. They also imply an opening out of the educational system towards the community at large: present movements in this direction will probably come to seem very tentative indeed compared with the degree of involvement likely in the year 2000.

This opening-out will, we think, be part of a more general widening of the view Europe's educational systems will take of the resources available to them. But, to press into service all the facilities it can find is going to be a vital necessity on another ground, too: the ground of costs. To speak in a paradox: if education continues to be conducted in the year 2000 in substantially the same way as it is now, it will be too expensive to be conducted at all. Estimates of how many people will be involved in the learning process in 25 years' time vary according to the criteria employed, and the dubiousness of demographic forecasts must in any event make such estimates tentative: but there cannot be much doubt that the number will be very large, viewed either absolutely or as a proportion of the population; and that means, of course, that unit costs will have to be brought down. On this question no two opinions are possible: education will in the year 2000 be a luxury possible only for the richest nations unless measures are taken to prevent its cost increasing in step with its expansion. This means that the construction of more and more schools or other educational institutions, and the engagement of more and more teaching personnel, will be really out of the question: some other way of providing the facilities required by the learning process will have to be found. And this necessary new resource is, of course, the new communications technology. It fulfils two requirements which will in the year 2000 be essential: it does not need a special building constructed for and devoted solely to education, and it is, compared with the traditional apparatus of education, very cheap.

The possibility that many of the essentials of the educational process can be provided anywhere and at any time through the transmission, recording and retrieval capabilities of information technology ought to satisfy the essential drives we earlier detailed: towards equality of opportunity, towards lifelong learning, towards autonomous participatory learning, towards the teacher as counsellor. And it can do so within necessary cost constraints. Britain's Open University, and similar experiments, represent a beginning – but a small one compared with what will be needed by the year 2000. The idea of permanent lifelong education for everybody who wanted it – and there will, of course, be very many who do not want it – would be a utopian dream if it had to rely on the traditional educational structures: it is the capacity of information technology to take the education process out of the institution into the home which makes it a realisable possibility. It is true, too, that the already well-educated are likely to benefit from it most, or at least first, and thus enhance their privileged status: but here again the technology which will have to be used offers a heavy counterweight to this perhaps inevitable effect through its relative cheapness: it is, after all, not only the very rich or the very well-educated who posses television sets, telephones or cassette machines.

Electronic surveillance

As we have emphasised strongly enough in Chapter 4, it is not only the obtaining of information by the individual but also the obtaining of information about the individual which presents a problem. Already none of us knows how much is known about him or by whom: but it is quite conceivable that by the year 2000 the citizen will have to assume that almost everything about him is known and that any relevant piece of information can be obtained at short notice from a central data bank. Perhaps it will not come to that: but, if so, it will not be because the central authority lacks the means. Electronic surveillance – the TV eye in the supermarket, the bugged hotel bedroom – is already commonplace, and is objectionable or otherwise depending on whether or not one approves of the end in view: what all forms of electronic surveillance have in common, however, is that they obtain information about an individual without his knowledge. And if, using the term with some freedom, we include the electronic storage and retrieval of information about an individual without his knowledge within the boundary of electronic surveillance, then we can say that already we are electronically surveilled to a degree which would probably appal us if we were ever in a position to find out. That this phenomenon will become intensified between now and the twenty-first century it is hardly possible to doubt – and this is likely to be so whoever is in power. One can as well imagine the abolition of the tax inspector and the filing cabinet as that governments will fail to press the observing, storage and retrieval capacities of information technology more and more strongly into service: for these will be the equivalents of the tax inspector and the filing cabinet and, eventually, of every other functionary whose job it is to know as much about the citizen as the state wants to know.

Information is power

We begin to see that the theme 'access to information' is a large one, and that the problems that arise within it are manifold, and often quite distinct: the area of psychological problems associated with over-stimulation through the receipt of too much information is not at all the same as the area of political problems associated with electronic surveillance. We would, however, maintain that there exists one problem-area in this realm which may in the last analysis in fact subsume them all: that of the influence of information technology on the future distribution of power.

It is in most societies difficult to judge who precisely possesses power – that is, the real capacity to create the conditions he desires to exist. In a primitive form of state one can see that this power usually resides ultimately in a single individual: he may be hedged about with restrictions, but in the last resort it is he who decides. In modern times, the Nazi state offers a simple model of this sort, with – by the final years at any rate – virtually all decisive power residing in Hitler personally. But turn to a state such as modern Britain and you find it far harder to say in whom ultimate power resides, or by what means he (or they) possess this power; and there have been recent periods in the history of the United States when the 'checks and balances' have functioned so efficiently that no-one has had effective power and nothing has happened that could be traced to a conscious decision for it. This situation – the situation in which power is, not concentrated, but distributed (sometimes so widely as to evaporate) – is one into which information technology will intrude with perhaps decisive effect.

How that effect will be produced is well described by Theodore Lowi. 'We assume', he says, 'a direct linkage between information and politics, based on a definition of information as a resource convertible to political power. All resources – human and physical – influence the commitments of decision makers and the composition of elite groups in the social structure. But politics is specially sensitive to information and to significant variations in the amount and character of available information. Politics can actually be defined as a particular type of information exchange' (Lowi 1972). The mechanism through which it will be produced is the ability to use information technology efficiently: an ability which, like any ability, will be possessed by only a minority. It is possible, even likely, that the political power the capacity to use information technology will confer on this minority will not be exercised directly but through a simultaneous enhancement of the power of management in every field and a diminution of the real power of politicians and elected representatives of all kinds. The power elite thus created may resemble a 'meritocracy', but will differ from it in that its power resides, not in any general or genuine superiority to the rest of mankind, but only in its superior ability to use information technology: in every other respect it may be very 'unmeritorious' indeed.

Through the power conferred by this posession of more and more accurate information it may come to control the information technology by which it has acquired power: and thus it will stay in power. The capacity on the one hand to manipulate the mass of the people and on the other to acquire accurate information about the individual citizen is enormously increased by the resources placed in the hands of any ruling order by information technology: so that a condition of affairs is imaginable in which the 'management' knows all it needs to know and everyone else knows nothing.

This condition may be defined unemotively as one in which the power conveyed by information technology is *narrowly based*. But an opposite outcome is also possible: for it is of course the *use* to which this technology is put which determines its influence on human affairs – the thing itself is neutral. A more *broadly based* – that is, more democratic – power structure could be created through the educational employment of information technology. For the mass of the people to check the power ambitions of the kind of elite just described, it is not necessary for them to become as well informed as this elite – a development which is hardly possible – but only *sufficiently* well informed: they do not need to know everything, they need only to know enough. And this 'enough' can, with the technology even now available, be provided if the will to provide it is present.

It is here too that the solution could lie to the problem of simultaneous information overload and information starvation, which is perhaps really a product of insufficient *public* channels of communication. The information bombardment to which the citizen is even now subjected almost all comes from private, and therefore often competing sources: what he is starved of is the kind of information the public authorities ought to be providing – details of local planning proposals is an obvious example – but at present are not, because, even if the will to do so is present, the means of doing so are not. Properly directed, the new capabilities of television and telephone described earlier in this chapter would offer precisely the agency for transmission of this kind of information: not, that is to say, a 'bombardment' which the recipient would be unable to process, but a simple, easily understood and easily available mechanical method of access.

There is thus a dark and a light aspect to the changes in the distribution of power which information technology can be expected to produce: and which of them it will actually produce will depend on policy decisions taken now or in the near future.

An information policy

At present the 'information revolution' is freewheeling: indeed, there seems to be little conscious appreciation that a revolution is in fact under way. The extent to which information technology will be able – and therefore will – control our lives in the coming century is hardly understood by the greater part of the public, who look upon the new resources as basically no more than improvements on the old – better TV reception, telephone systems which break down less often.

The truth, however, is – as we have tried to show – that a very powerful new element is in process of entering the life and social organisation of Europe: one for which there is no real precedent and one for the control of which there are no precedents either. If measures are taken to direct the effects of information technology into desired channels they will have to be taken on the basis of new conceptions of what 'control' means: how it is to be exercised, who is to exercise it, what ends are to be held in view.

The most urgent necessity is for a comprehension of the information system *as a whole*: as Edward Glaser says:

> ... Information technology itself is fractionated and disparate. There is really no such thing as an information industry. People active in computers ... enjoy precious little interaction with people in communications – the broadcasters, the newsmen, and the film-makers. Out on the periphery are the highly successful automated copying, duplicating, photography, printing and publishing industries living in worlds of their own. Still farther out and temporarily lost in the dust raised by technological advances closely related to its concerns is the library fraternity.   (Glaser 1972).

We should add to this list the educational systems, considered as purveyors of information in the widest sense, which are only beginning to employ the resources offered by information technology. No policy to control, or even to understand the coming world of information and its ramifications can be at all effective unless it succeeds in relating the fragments of this world one with another and assessing their total effect.

Only then will the long-term planning which is required become a practical possibility. Without such planning in the public interest the information revolution will not drift or continue to freewheel, but be seized on and directed by those interests strong enough to do so. The outcome could be computerised authoritarian rule, perhaps disguised as 'management', or it could be anarchy; it might just possibly be the rational rule of benevolent despots: but it will quite certainly not be the broadly based democratic control which we think most people want. That will come only from a comprehension of what information technology and the communications systems as a whole are capable of performing, followed by policy decisions based on this knowledge. The time for initiating the process which will lead to this is – as always – now.

CHAPTER 9

Age, Sex and Gender: The Individual and the Family

Families have existed in Europe since the first men and women cohabited in caves. But the family as most Europeans know it today is very recent: it is basically a creation of the Industrial Revolution. The question is whether it could disappear as rapidly as it came: will the present forces of social and economic change transform it into something quite different? And would that be thought desirable by the millions of European family members who would be involved?

The European family: changing role, changing form

Throughout most of European history – the agrarian and craft society that extended from pre-history to the close of the Middle Ages – two features distinguished the European family: it was an extended family of three (or rarely four) generations, including grandparents, parents and children who shared the same table and the same roof; and it was not merely a social unit for the rearing of children and the companionship of husband and wife, but also the basic economic unit, so that social life, work and education were one.

These two features were connected. Throughout most of this time, at least nine in ten Europeans got their living from the land. The family farm was a logical and efficient way of organising agricultural production: it allowed a simple and partial division of labour, in which different jobs could be performed by family members with the appropriate manual strength or skill, but in which also all the members could be united to perform certain critical tasks such as harvesting. And it provided a small-scale version of mutual aid and social security, in which the young, the old and the infirm could be supported by the able-bodied. The same features are found in the typical urban family engaged in trading or craftsmanship.

The life experience of Europeans over most centuries was thus quite different from that which their urban industrial descendants know today. The family was the framework of most social experience: from birth to death, every member was a part of it. During each day, though individual members might separate to tend the fields or to run errands, the family home was the centre from which work was organised. Though there was usually an outside figure with indirect economic power – the feudal lord, the city merchant – in matters of day-to-day economic organisation the family was the basic unit. Such routine features of our everyday existence as commuting, sending the children to school, labour disputes, absenteeism, alienation from work would have been incomprehensible to this kind of society.

It was, of course, the Industrial Revolution that changed all this: it sent the men into factories and kept the women at home – only then, very recently in fact, did the typical woman become a housewife. A little later, it sent the children compulsorily to school. Later still, parents for the first time found that their children deserted them on marriage or even before, moving to another town or even another country. The fragmentation and segregation of modern European society had begun. The family shrank to the primary nuclear family unit: a husband, a wife, and children of pre-school or school age. Other kinds of households appeared: young people living alone in bed-sitters or small apartments, old people whose children had grown up living together or (after the death of one partner) alone. Both were cut off from the nuclear family, pursuing its avocation of child-rearing. Within the nuclear family, the husband and school children would leave each weekday and return early each evening: the housewife was left alone or caring for small children.

We may forget how recent all this is. In its fully developed form, it is really a creation of the middle-class society of post-1945 Europe. Until recently, a substantial minority of rural populations in Europe still lived in traditional style, and working-class communities in the cities retained much of the solidarity of the pre-industrial family: but a number of changes contributed to the fissioning of the family in post-war Europe, and they are still working themselves out.

The first is the greater mobility of the young: as increasing numbers are trained through education to follow a different career from their fathers, they migrate in search of higher and further education and specialised jobs. The second, already noted in Chapter 4, is the longer survival of the old. The third is the tendency for couples to have children earlier: while the typical wife in pre-industrial society might between the ages of 16 and 45 produce a dozen children of whom only four or five survived, the typical housewife of today produces two children between the ages of twenty and twenty-six; by the time she is forty-five they will usually have moved away and probably have married, and she and her husband may face thirty or forty years together, separated from their children and thus from their grandchildren.

Even more recently, women's attitudes to work and family have shown a fundamental shift. They work before they have children and they work again soon after. In some societies, such as Scandinavia, where maternity leave and job continuity have long been guaranteed, they may never abandon their careers at all; in others, they may do so until their children reach semi-independence. This shift appears to be more or less universal across Europe and to be common to all socio-economic groups: it is in part the result of the competitive consumer pressures of the 1950s and 1960s, in part of a fundamental psychological change in the way women view themselves in relation to their husbands and children.

We need to couple these changes with others already examined in earlier chapters. Since World War Two, millions of Europeans have uprooted themselves from the land, passing in a few weeks from an agrarian to an urban society. Many of them have crossed international frontiers to live in a foreign culture, separating themselves even more from their family links. As urban areas have grown, they have decentralised: millions more Europeans, moving their homes from the crowded inner cities into the more spacious suburbs, have paid a price in the greater separation of home from work. The husband – and increasingly the wife – are compelled to spend more and more hours of every weekday separated at increasing distances from their children – the husband in particular may become a shadowy figure to his family. Increasingly, it becomes difficult to build and maintain relationships. The vital social functions of the family – developing inter-personal relationships between adults and children, the task of development – are neglected, so that problems of sexual identity and of marital relationship arise. Those who have left the nuclear family – students and old people – need special services to perform the tasks that were once performed, economically and almost certainly more efficiently, by other members of the extended family.

While we must be careful not to sentimentalise the old order – life was often hard, children were forced into premature adulthood, tensions between generations or incompatible personalities flared out – we do know that the traditional family provided an obvious basis for many of the social-psychological functions necessary for the development of a child: the capacity for intimacy, for personal and sexual identity, for the development of independence. Today, many if not most of these functions have to be relegated to specialists: teachers, child psychologists, youth leaders, counsellors.

There is little evidence of a reversal of these trends: indeed, it seems likely that they are far from having worked themselves through. And they pose two immediate problems, already becoming apparent in many European countries, which must now be examined. The first is the attitude of the old to their forced segregation in retirement; the second the attitude of women to family, children and career.

The revolt of the old

As we saw already in Chapter 3, Europe is ageing: the proportion of people aged 65 and above has on the whole been increasing for more than a century. Around 1950 it varied from 5 to 12 per cent in the European populations; twenty years later it had moved up to between 7.5 and 15 per cent. The rate of change was particularly high in West Germany, Austria, Sweden, Norway and Denmark. Since a proportion of about 15 per cent corresponds to the lower fertility and mortality rates observed, there are grounds for assuming that this level at least will eventually be reached by all European countries and probably surpassed by several. A recent calculation for Switzerland (at present with a proportion of old people of 11.5 per cent) assumes a proportion of 17 per cent by the year 2000 (Bourgeois-Pichat 1972).

These calculations are founded on the assumption that the prolongation of the expectation of life will on the whole come to a halt at the highest levels so far attained: 72 years for males (Sweden) and 77 years for females (Norway), the reason being that the growth of these figures now seems to be levelling off. It seems as if the combined effect of rising material standards of living and medical advance has almost reached its limit. Information is scant, but there is reason to believe that even in the low mortality countries there are considerable differences in expectation of life between different social strata and occupations – but lack of data prevents estimates of magnitudes.

When mortality is viewed in a long-term perspective, one must be prepared to look beyond the thresholds set by present conditions and discuss what could happen if these thresholds were lowered by such factors as new medical breakthroughs, socio-economic changes, or even new lifestyles, affecting rates of survival.

If one takes the main causes of death as the vantage point, some hypothetical calculations concerning a possible future are feasible. What should first be noted is that up to the age of around 50, mortality is now so low in the low-mortality countries that a further lowering will hardly influence the proportions between age-groups. Beyond this age, cardio-vascular diseases and neoplasms (cancer) stand out as the two leading causes of death: successful attacks on these diseases, in particular on the first, would add considerably to average longevity – complete elimination of cardiovascular diseases, for example, would add around 10 years of life to both sexes, yet the difference in longevity between men and women would remain as it is, if not increase (Hansluwka 1973).

An expectation of life of the order of 80 years for men and 89 for women would bring the proportion of the population aged 65 and above to an order of 25 per cent of the total population. It is clear that a proportion moving towards this upper limit would require profound societal adjustments – but such adjustments would have to start long before the age structure had arrived at such an extreme state.

Within national boundaries there is already a big variation in the age-structure of regional and local populations. The process of urbanisation, with younger people moving towards the urban regions and the middle-aged moving to the suburbs, has created top-heavy population pyramids in both large areas of countryside and older housing areas of big cities. In some of these the proportion of people aged 65 and over has already passed 20 per cent: there is thus no lack of cases to demonstrate what it means to have every fourth or fifth member of the population an old person.

With regional and local pockets of imbalance between age-groups, society can continue to function through the transfer of subsidies and services from areas in which the population contains larger active groups, but in a possible future situation of overall ageing the relation between the working and the supported sections of the population will be much more critical.

At advanced age, when health and capabilities begin to deteriorate, the individual is for the second time entering a period in life when support – whether from family or community – is a necessity. Passage into the new dependence is gradual: from retirement age to about 75 most people are today still active and independent, and for the majority their problems are largely economic; but from 75 onwards mobility tends to deteriorate and the need for personal services grows. Above 85 the number of old people who have to be cared for in institutions – given the failure of the family's traditional role – rises sharply.

Prolongation of life has meant different things for different groups. For some, old age, taken both in a biological and social sense, has been no better than a final phase of life; for others, the effects of ageing have been postponed by continuing vitality. The latter experience is clearly to be preferred, and an overriding goal for the future must therefore be to extend it to as many people as possible. What, then, can society do, in terms of planned, collective action, to help the individual to postpone difficulties related to old age as long as biologically possible?

Political influence

In a society in which organised interest groups play a major role in the allocation of resources, the fate of old people will to a large extent depend on their ability to exert a formal political influence on matters related to their condition. As their numbers grow, old people will control an increasingly large share of the votes: how much their support will influence actual policies is hard to tell. With the present tendency for most people to remain loyal to their political convictions, it does not seem likely that old people will constitute a united force in proportion to their numbers, and they will most probably remain divided among many parties: but insofar as they share a common outlook, it will make itself felt throughout the political spectrum. If a political party emerged which made a special point of furthering the interests of the old the situation would, of course, be different.

A second kind of instrument for political action would be interest organisations – 'Old People's Unions'. This device has already been tried in some countries, both at local and national levels. (In Sweden, for example, about a third of all old-age pensioners are members of a national organisation which receives subsidies from public funds.) Unions have the advantage of being able to cut through the dividing lines between political parties. The growth of such organisations seems to be a rather probable development in the future, in particular if old people's needs and interests are ignored: they are most likely to spring up locally, where no large economic resources are needed for meetings. And one must bear in mind that retired people have plenty of time for political activities.

But there are difficulties. First of all, old people's organisations are bound to have financial troubles and will for that reason be hard to hold together on a national level. Secondly, they can never develop the kind of influence exercised by trade unions, since they lack efficient weapons in disputes: they cannot, for example, go on strike. Even a simple activity like communicating information in order to influence public opinion will be a problem: the old are to a large extent also the least well-educated, and the knowledge they do have is becoming obsolete at an ever increasing rate. It will also be hard to avoid a division within an organisation into sub-groups remote from one another: judging from the present situation, it will be men in their seventies who will dominate the scene. Lack of mobility will to a large extent inhibit those who are older from full participation. In the upper age brackets, moreover, women form the majority, and they seem especially to lack the kind of experience necessary for collective action.

In sum, it is hard to doubt that the political decisions which will have to be taken in the interest of the old will require a great amount of loyalty from the younger generation: the strongest force working for them is perhaps the knowledge on the part of the younger groups that they themselves will be old one day. An important part of any political arrangement will be the provision of the financial, physical and institutional means which the old will need for articulating their interests themselves: such aid seems a precondition for their constituting a group on an equal footing with the active population.

Mobility and the lack of it

Mobility is the first necessity for old people if they are to retain their independence and remain integrated with the community. It is as important for them to be able to move and work at home as it is for them to be able to walk in streets, parks, shops and public buildings; they must have economic access to means of transport for daily travel. The present urban environment is unfriendly to the old: traffic lights are not set for the pace of a slow pedestrian; escalators require quick reactions and good balance; it is often troublesome to move between different street levels, not to speak of getting on and off buses and trains. Those who need to read posted information, for example timetables, are hampered by too small lettering and insufficient light. But the difficulties old people face cannot be fully assessed by their behaviour in the streets: the most serious effect may well be that many of them avoid going out as much as they possibly can. It is obvious that driving a car becomes more and more hazardous the older one gets: and the revitalisation of public transport – and perhaps the introduction of forms of transport especially suited to them – is likely to become a strong political requirement on the part of the old.

Work and income

In traditional society the old received direct economic support from their descendants under more or less formal arrangements; cultural norms, and in some countries the law, still require children to provide for needy parents: but the dominant source of income for the retired today is a pension, conceived of either as deferred payment for earlier work or as a general welfare right. It has till now been taken care of by a great variety of arrangements to look after the total picture and to step in where regulations and contributions have been needed: so that by now, in whatever way the money is administrated it is seen as the collective task of society to provide for its older members. But the differences between groups are still great: there is much poverty among the old; and especially exposed a group is that of the elderly single woman.

The overriding economic problem for the future is to maintain the relative value of old people's income: money savings melt away with inflation and to make private arrangements for later life is a very uncertain venture. Pensions, on the other hand, seem to be of two kinds: some countries apply a built-in fixed relation to the average cost of living, so that the old automatically share the fate of society in general, except that their small incomes make them more sensitive in times of change; others reassess pensions at intervals, with the obvious risk that the old will lag behind as their number increases and resistance grows to tax increases.

When considering the future economic situation of the old one must bear in mind that their money income is only part of their total real income, which includes public subsidies for housing, health and care: so that their real wealth is everywhere a matter of potential political conflict. Very little systematic research has been devoted to the ways in which the ageing of the population will influence economic relations between active and dependent groups. This is a complex task, of course, since one has to take into account, not only the demographic shift, but also the development of productivity, inflation, participation rates in the labour force and future standards of living. A recent model calculation for Switzerland, extended to the year 2000, indicates that even with growing productivity at a moderate rate the old will lag behind in income development unless the taxation rate on their behalf is considerably increased. With constant productivity and constant taxation their situation will become dramatically worse as their numbers grow.

But it must not be taken for granted that all is well with old people if their economic support is in reasonably good shape: ironically the fact that old people have emerged as a special social category is to a large extent a consequence of economic measures taken on their behalf with the best of intentions. Work is normally more than a source of income, it is also a way of participation and creation: and, ideally, the old person should be in a position to choose in what way he or she cuts down economic activity from full-time engagement to complete retirement. There exists wide agreement that those who continue in regular work feel greater satisfaction with life and stay healthier than those who withdraw completely (Gilliand 1972, pp. 220-2) – though clearly there are many heavy and boring tasks in industry for which this relationship cannot hold.

Actual trends seem to move in a direction contrary to what would seem to be generally desirable. Retirement schemes in both private and public organisations tend to set a fixed age for retirement: for administrative and financial reasons, it has been difficult to construct systems which permit a gradual tapering off of work, and a rather abrupt retirement is now more and more normal compared with a time when self-employment in farming and small-scale industry covered a larger area of the economy.

A further difficulty is the way in which industry is developing as a labour market. As technical operations change, job experience becomes obsolete; in many instances, industry seems to prefer to draw in new personnel along with new techniques rather than retrain those already at work. This happens in particular when old factories are closed down or when production is relocated. As a result, many workers are forced into retirement before the age of 60.

The present development is the more unfortunate in that there is great variation in the rate of ageing: there exists no scientific basis whatever for applying a fixed cut-off point at 65 – this or any other age is a purely arbitrary choice.

An abrupt transition from regular work to total retirement throws the individual into a leisured existence for which it is hard to be prepared. Nobody has been able to make the role of being retired into an integral part of society: it is considered rather as a reward for services rendered, and the retired person is required to be grateful for this reward. But an important aspect of quality of life is to stay involved in the serious matters of society, and old people – at least those still in good health – must experience difficulty in seeing uninterrupted recreation and therapeutic activity as meaningful.

Health

The configuration of diseases will change with the ageing of the population: acute illnesses curable by a short period of intensive treatment will be less dominant than chronic ailments requiring attention over a long period, and the purpose of treatment in these cases is frequently not to cure but to ease pain and make a situation endurable. A further difference is that old people frequently have more than one illness at a time. Four out of five of those aged 65 and above have at least one chronic condition (Riley et al, 1968-9, I, p.205), and 70 to 75 is the typical age at which existence begins to become troublesome because of failing health. It is an unsolved problem how to make a clear distinction between ageing and disease: the state of an individual is at any time determined by his inherited biology and by environmental influences, and some problems which look like aspects of ageing might on closer analysis turn out to be characteristics of groups exposed to certain environmental risks over a long lifetime. It may be, therefore, that what is today considered an inevitable consequence of ageing can be counteracted by prevention much earlier in life. There has so far been insufficient research on individual health in a longitudinal perspective, in particular so far as the working population is concerned: such research will be much needed in the future to discover the most suitable ways of extending the period of good health. From what is known today one may conclude that three problem areas will require special attention as the ageing of the population proceeds: public health, chronic hospital care and the place of advanced medical technology.

Many signs show that the state of health varies between groups (Edwards, McKeown and Whitfield 1959), and that hazards and long-term exposure to disturbances in working environments are important factors behind the variation: it is as if the infectious diseases of yesterday had been replaced by chemical pollutants, noise and strained time-schedules. Of course, one finds these stresses throughout the environment, but they are especially concentrated in workplaces: these, and working procedures, are thus the strategic points at which to start systematic attacks on health risks.

For the old, two other sides of public health will be of importance: nutrition and home accidents. Today many old people have a diet which is very unsatisfactory from the point of view of health. Part of the explanation is poverty, but part of it is lack of knowledge and motivation and practical difficulties with the purchase and preparation of food. The Stockport survey (Brockington and Lempert 1966) found that in the over-80 group only about a half had one hot meal daily and around one-fifth had only two hot meals a week or fewer. Serious deficiencies in vitamins and proteins resulted. A conclusion of interest for the future handling of nutrition was that 'the best protection against an inadequate diet for those living alone appeared to be someone coming in to cook the meals'. Services for cooking meals or providing cooked meals from central kitchens under public supervision seems likely to become an instrument for maintaining health in the upper age groups.

Fatal accidents frequently occur in the homes of old people, and risks could be reduced by suitable physical arrangements: an ageing population will require a whole set of reconstructed household equipment and layout principles.

Whatever is done to maintain health, it is finally unavoidable that a growing number of old people will need hospital care over very long periods: they already occupy a very large proportion of all hospital beds, and some have to stay for up to eight to 10 years. They represent a very critical group in the health planning of all countries: in Sweden, for instance, 50 per cent of hospital investment goes on 4 per cent of the population. Two things will be especially needed for this group in the future: a general upgrading of the standard of care and that of resources.

Nursing the old is very hard work, and it is difficult to get sufficient staff at least as long as the job is regarded as exclusively female. Nurses have little time to give patients the kind of personal attention they need. Large institutions located at a great distance from their former homes tend to isolate patients from the people they know – another problem which will require much imaginative effort in the future.

Finally, the advance of medical knowledge itself when combined with longevity is bound to magnify certain problems already discernible. It may be that the way medical treatment is carried out today to maintain health and prevent death in younger groups will lead to unforeseen long-term effects: frequent use of antibiotics, for example, may cause resistent bacteria to develop; preventive treatment of one kind of illness – cardio-vascular disease for instance – might increase the incidence of cancer.

A less speculative prediction is that much serious thinking will soon have to be devoted to death itself and to the handling of those situations in which machines can maintain the biological life of an individual long past the point at which hope of recovery has disappeared. Science and technology have created dilemmas here. What is the responsible course of action for the individual doctor in a given situation? And what way of allocating medical resources is more humane: to concentrate effort on the mere survival of a few or to distribute effort over the population as a whole? Should old people themselves be given the choice of when to die – which current medical ethics forbid?

Housing and social relations

Most elderly men (65+) live with their wives (about 67 per cent). Most elderly women have no husbands (again about 67 per cent). This asymmetrical distribution goes back to two circumstances: the difference in longevity between men and women and the fact that in most marriages the husband is older than the wife. Old couples do better than single old people in many respects: but both groups need a decent place to live in and to have their isolation – which to a certain extent comes with ageing as a matter of course – consciously counteracted as much as possible.

Until recently, as we saw, it was a widespread custom for parents to live with their adult children, and this is still particularly so in agricultural areas and certain occupational groups where the old continue to take part in the family enterprise. But with increasing urbanisation and mobility, and with the development of formal pension systems, the tendency has grown for generations to live separately: this is now the quantitatively dominant pattern in most of Europe as long as the old are able to manage their own households. At higher ages, when the need for daily care arrives, the first option seems to be for the old person to move into the household of a child. This happens in large cities: a recent investigation in Paris showed that by the time of entry into old people's homes 34 per cent of men and 22 per cent of women had been living with family members (Mayen 1972). Despite what is frequently believed about the social isolation of the nuclear family, it seems that the kinship environment is still fairly tight for most people, and this means that a majority of old people with children have them living not too far away: a comparative study from 1962 revealed that in Britain, the USA and Denmark, between 80 and 90 per cent of those aged 65 and above had a child living within an hour's travel. At least weekly visits were common (Shanas et al 1968). But in the future, with fewer children per couple and perhaps increased geographical mobility, the degree of isolation from relatives could easily increase.

The problem arising from the general ageing of the population must therefore be seen in a context wider than the economics and physical planning of health care and social services: it has to do with how the family will develop. Discussion of the future of the family and the future place of women in society tends to forget the needs of the old and the role performed by non-employed women in attending to them. Yet the majority can rely on aid from kin and neighbours: such aid may not be very time-consuming in terms of hours, but it must be carried out by people who are reasonably free to spare time exactly when it is needed and who can travel for visits even in the middle of the day. In other words, fixed working hours, as required in employment, are a hindrance to this kind of socially valuable task. If married women gradually opt for more and more formal employment – something they are likely to do – serious consequences for the old are bound to appear: those who can still manage on their own will become more cut off from a younger generation than they are today; for those in any sort of trouble, the pressure will increase on the community to take over more and more of the care. In other words, there are strong contradictory tendencies in the trends which emerge from present population development.

Old people living in institutions form a rather small fraction – around 3 and 4 per cent – of the whole population of 65 and over: they are predominantly single. There seems to exist a very sharp break in the ability of the old person to manage a home at about 80, which is the average age for seeking entrance to an institution. In France, for example, 15 per cent of all single men and 22 per cent of all single women above 80 live in old people's homes (Mayen 1972). Of all old people above 90 years of age, 30 per cent are in the care of an institution.

The general prolongation of life expectancy means that the population above 80 will grow in number. A simple, if expensive, political measure to meet this situation is to enlarge the capacity of institutions. But most people do not like living in institutions and this attitude hardens with age. Open care, which helps the old to stay in their own homes, might be harder to organise because of the problem of coordinating different administrative departments, but it is probably cheaper in the long run and it is certainly much more satisfying to the old people themselves.

Old people's relationships to their dwellings are not only a practical and economic matter: they also have psychological and social dimensions of great importance. In Europe at least it seems that, when entering retirement age, people prefer to retain their home if at all possible: this means that the sudden change in life-style which comes with retirement is limited to workplace relations.

Reluctance to change dwelling thereafter seems to increase with age. With the tendency to remain settled, it follows that old people frequently live in old houses, inconvenient because of out-dated equipment. Even when a move is made – possibly a move forced by economic circumstances – there is a very high probability that the new home will be a cheap and old-fashioned dwelling: in both urban and rural areas there is a high correlation between being old and living in an old and heavily-worked dwelling.

It is evident that the habituated space, with its well-known objects and faces, is of high positive value: not only is it less stress-creating to move about in a familiar environment, but the space itself, with its content, is impregnated with memories of past times. After the age of seventy, dreams about past times are in important preoccupation of the old person (Riley et al 1968-9, I, p.343), and the environment itself helps to recall events when memory fails.

It is important for the planner working on housing programmes on behalf of the old to keep in mind that to provide convenient modernity is far too narrow a rationality: everything indicates that moderate modernisation – 'conservative surgery', to use Patrick Geddes' term – (Stalley 1972, p.55) which leaves people where they are is a far more humane strategy than wholesale clearance of slums with drastic relocations or scattering of old inhabitants.

The obvious conclusion is that many of the developing problems of the old could be solved, in a fashion both efficient and humane, if more of them could continue to live in or at least very near their families. State care can never give the old the kind of love and regard that would come from children and grandchildren. By segregating them in institutions it reduces the possibilities of communication between the old and the young: children may grow up in a society where old people to all intents and purposes do not exist, and they may in consequence receive a very distorted picture of the range of human responses and of social values. The justification which educationalists give for the comprehensive school apply equally to the need for a comprehensive society – one in which children learn how to live with other humans of all ages as well as of all classes and abilities. But the question is whether, realistically, the family could ever come to take on that role again – thus reversing two centuries of development. Before trying to answer that, however, it is necessary to look at the other evident problem area: that of the role of women in the contemporary family.

Women, children, career and society

As the Industrial Revolution segregated the old, so it imprisoned the female in the family: but there is strong evidence very recently of a possible radical reversal. Judging from trends among the younger age groups radical changes are quite likely. They cannot take place in isolation: a transformation of society in general is both a precondition and a consequence. The process – if it comes about – will not be limited to the social sphere: it will also have demographic, economic, political, cultural and physical ramifications.

Men and women at present represent a kind of social class which cuts across the other social classes: there exists an all-pervading disparity between the sexes in terms of economic status, political participation and tasks to accomplish. When defining social class, sociologists frequently lay stress on the existence of a class consciousness focusing on common economic and political interests: in this sense, the 'class' distinction between men and women is implicit rather than explicit. Men have unreflectingly taken their position for granted: on the other side, pioneering women have for more than a century built up a movement which has many of the characteristics of a class-conscious political force. This beginning may in future enter quite new areas of reform, in particular if an egalitarian mode of thinking continues to spread and demands for participation in business and public life persist.

The position of women today is defined by two features. First, *domesticity*: women are home-bound by life in the modern nuclear family, which not only defines sexual roles but trains new generations in those roles. More than this, women are restricted to domesticity in their work outside the home: their jobs – secretary, nurse, teacher – are seen as extensions of their family role, and their earnings and right to social security are limited by the convention that they are above all housewives. Secondly, *ambivalence* of role: women are women first, and only secondly human beings. But no woman can have time and energy to be really good at being both, and indeed the task is almost impossible, since many of the necessary personality traits tend to be opposed. 'Men are people; women are women. Men have careers, women look after the house and children (and men)' (Oakley 1974, p.82).

Many efforts to equalise life conditions as between men and women have concerned removal of discriminatory legislation: but a formal right is one thing, exercising it another. While in the short term the objective is to counteract discriminatory rules and regulations, the main problem in the long term is to turn the goals behind these efforts into reality, and in this respect advances have not been so remarkable. Two questions are mainly under debate today: complete access for the woman to birth control devices (including legal abortion), and a totally open labour market, with equal pay and equal career opportunities.

In the longer perspective, the former demand is not very controversial within the European context: given the global population development, it seems inevitable that family planning will soon become generally acceptable and that each couple will choose to have only a few children. In northern Europe this is already generally the case, but there are also powerful signs of rapid change in Catholic countries such as Italy and Portugal. It is also to be expected that medical research will soon render abortion, the most controversial and disturbing issue, unnecessary: it is too costly a way of achieving the overriding goal that only wanted children should be born.

The second question, on the other hand, is bound to be resolved only slowly. As seen in Europe, the labour market question is only the front line in a campaign for the much wider goal of abolishing the separation of male and female roles as normally understood today: its purpose is to break down sexual differentiation entirely in public life, education, work and leisure and in the division of tasks within the family, and with role differentiation preserved only in the biological domain. A transformation of this order has to do, not only with values, habits and legal rules, but with the whole organisational structure of industrial society.

In considering this movement, it is essential to bear in mind that a leading argument in its favour, besides the ideal of full equality, is that it offers a means of meeting a wide range of unfulfilled social needs. There are many functions in society which cannot be drawn into the monetary system and carried out by professionals without losing much of their meaning: unless people are given adequate opportunities to deal with these functions on a personal and mutual basis, they will disappear altogether, with remarkably negative consequences for the quality of life. Many children and many more of the aged undoubtedly suffer from the losses industrial society has already exacted in these realms, and one remedy, it is argued, would be to make every adult capable of performing a wider variety of tasks than at present. Advocates of a move in this direction do not as a rule deny that there might exist fundamental differences between the sexes in 'work styles and interests' (Fogarty et al 1971, p.394), or

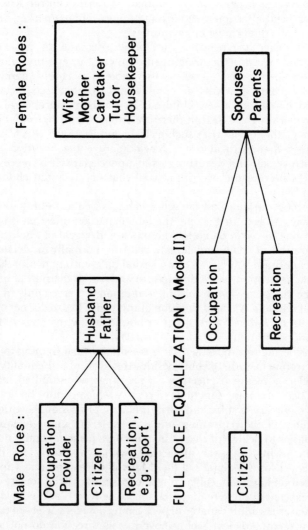

FULL ROLE SEPARATION (Mode I)

Male Roles :

Female Roles :

Wife
Mother
Caretaker
Tutor
Housekeeper

Occupation
Provider

Citizen

Recreation,
e.g. sport

Husband
Father

FULL ROLE EQUALIZATION (Mode II)

Occupation

Recreation

Citizen

Spouses
Parents

Source: DAHLSTÖM AND LILJESTRÖM (1974) (Adaption)

Figure 9.1

that some of these differences ought to be maintained. They do, however, point to anthropological and other evidence to show that in many societies the division of tasks is quite different from our own (Oakley 1974, pp. 163-78). The point is that such differences are not made use of as broadly as would be beneficial for the development of a truly human society.

Described in schematic terms, the two opposite poles of role distribution are as in Figure 9.1.

A wide variety of mixed solutions can be found today, but full separation of roles is probably the most common mode in Europe as a whole, particularly in families with children under school age. During the sixties it was totally dominant in Holland, Norway and Ireland (Fogarty et al 1971, p.110). Full equalisation of roles is found only within very small groups with an advanced education and strong career commitments (a 'creative minority' according to Fogarty et al (1971, p.337). On the whole, it can be expected that the strongest advocates of role equalisation will be the younger, well-educated middle-class women: the working-class seems to prefer to adhere to the former middle-class pattern of keeping the wife at home.

The fact that today a large proportion of married women are employed does not imply a radical move from Mode I to Mode II (Figure 9.1): it is much more likely that what we have got is a rather questionable mixed form which has given some women access to a certain limited range of occupations – principally work of domestic type in low-paying service industry, jobs in small, weakly-unionised units – without releasing them from the traditional task at home, which means a considerable overload, at least for those with full-time employment, and is something very different from the ideals of the advocates of role equalisation. But our concern here is not to describe the existing situation but to explore the problem landscape of the future, and under this perspective full role equalisation is of prime interest: it represents the most radical possible departure from every pattern hitherto.

In pre-industrial agrarian society in Europe, to be sure, men and women were both engaged in well-integrated activities in close relationship to the home: they shared domestic responsibilities, including the job of parenthood, and women played a full role in economic life. But even there, the individual and political rights of women, and their economic independence, were minimal: the business of the larger society was dominated by men much as it is today. (There were, however, important exceptions: the English medieval guilds, for instance, nearly all admitted women on the same terms as men (Oakley 1974, p.18). It was the Industrial Revolution, as we saw, that changed the role of women: first by separating the man from the intimate daily routines of domestic life, secondly by making both the woman and the children economically dependent on the man, and thirdly by isolating housework and the care of children from all other work. Thus the woman became, literally, a housewife, restricted to the home; and the relatively recent return of women to the labour force has not fundamentally altered this, since the psychological division between women and men has not altered. 'The institutionalisation of the housewife role as the primary role for all women means that an expansion of their world outside the home is retarded by the metaphor, and the reality, of the world looked at through the window over the kitchen sink' (Oakley 1974, p.59).

East European governments claim to have achieved full equalisation between the sexes, and it is true that the participation of women in the economy is very nearly total. Much has also been done, both by legislation and in practical terms, to support the working woman with young children. But decision-making at the higher levels is still the exclusive domain of men, and many signs indicate that tasks in the home are still distributed along traditional lines (Haavio-Mannila 1971). In other words, in eastern Europe too the working woman suffers very much from overload and enforced limitations compared with the working man.

It thus seems fair to say that full role equalisation in the four realms of public affairs, employment, recreation and family life would represent a very far-reaching innovation in the history of Europe. A future-oriented perspective suggests three questions concerning it: (1) What are the arguments against the present separation of roles and in favour of full role equalisation? (2) What adjustments in institutions and in the organisation of society would be needed for the inauguration of full role equalisation? (3) What forces for change in this sphere can be observed now? In discussing these questions, we shall predominantly draw on the experience of Sweden, where the most radical position, officially supported, seems to have been arrived at (Sweden 1968): in analysing the conditions and consequences of change it is always the extreme cases which are most revealing.

Criticism of the present situation is directed, not only at the pure case in which the man is the breadwinner and the woman the full-time home-maker, but also at the current compromise. For men and women to work side by side in the sphere of production is often thought of as a positive development, but if one takes a closer look one finds that women are to a very large extent still restricted to a few sectors – teaching younger age groups, for instance, or subordinate jobs in offices, health-care establishments and homes for the old or disabled: in other words, the functions which used to be carried out by women at home and among the family have been moved into the monetary sphere and become large scale. One consequence is that payment is lower than it is for male activities requiring a corresponding level of competence and energy: home work has always been accorded a low value. A second – already mentioned – is overload in terms of hours and responsibilities. More specific criticism concerns the situation of the individual, the family and society at large: the following points turn up again and again in debate.

The woman

The remaining difficulties in exercising birth control make it to a large extent impossible for the woman to take the direction of her life into her own hands in the way in which the man can.

The full-time housewife lacks economic independence. She is obliged to live in a limited world of small children and neighbours, a situation especially obvious in suburbs which have no other function than to provide housing. This isolation becomes still more of a psychological problem when the children have left home and the amount of work to do is too small to fill the day. The latter problem has become exacerbated for two reasons: increased expectation of life and improved health in older ages has created a childless period of several decades with working ability still intact; and geographical mobility has tended to increase the distance the children move from home and made it harder to keep in contact with grandchildren. Few efforts are being made for the return to work of middle-aged women.

The isolation of the mother with small children prevents her from joining organisations through which changes in her condition – for example in terms of urban planning and the provision of transportation – could be worked out politically. It is characteristic that housewives are invited to join 'advisory groups' dealing with such things as kitchen equipment and the design of household goods – in other words, areas which reinforce their segregated role (Östnäs 1971).

The employed woman is obliged to carry the double load of outside job and traditional housekeeping and childrearing. Nursery schools and day centres make it feasible for the mother to leave home for a number of hours, but they do not relieve her of the other innumerable tasks which fall to her in the traditional system of role segregation. The employed woman frequently has also to look after or keep in touch with one or more elderly relatives in her spare time, for which extra travel is usually needed. She is unable to take a very active part in formal or informal organisations at her place of work. Even in labour unions with a female majority the policy-forming congresses and the top elected positions tend to be dominated by men.

The man

The obligation to act as the sole support of a family may lead the man to overtax his capacity: note the striking difference in life expectancy between men and women, and the widespread incidence of what is usually assumed to be stress-related diseases among men. These stresses may pass into the family, since the man may come to regard his home as an emotional haven. It may also mean that for him to leave one kind of work and retrain for another which would give him more personal satisfaction is insurmountably difficult.

In some jobs, overtime has become the rule and this seriously curtails his participation at home. More time with their families and responsibility for children would give men an opportunity to develop aspects of their personality for which the occupational world has no room. An occupation today means as a rule a high degree of specialisation: work in the home, on the other hand, has to be varied, integrative and people-oriented. It would also have a positive effect on the working environment if the man could bring to it his experiences from the less orderly world of the home.

The child

The child is immediately affected if one of the parents is inadequate to his or her role: no substitute is available. Two parents and one or two children in the primary group – not to speak of one-parent families – provide too little variation for adequate training in social and emotional interaction with other people. In what is sometimes called the 'fatherless society', there is a risk of over-intensive contact with the mother and with women teachers: it is assumed to be a serious disadvantage for a child never to be able to watch or take part in the kind of work men are normally engaged in, while the image of what men do comes to a dangerously large extent from TV heroes. Advertising – a very aggressive part of the urban environment today – cultivates a very sharp sexual segregation in which the woman is exclusively a sexual object and the man exhibits a caricature of virility, and it is a very essential purpose of role equilisation to draw men back into the area of family and home, if only for the sake of a well-balanced socialisation of the children.

In families in which both parents are employed, small children must for part of the day be taken care of by other people. (The exception is in the surviving extended families, especially in southern Europe, where grandparents or other older relatives can perform this function, as they once did everywhere.) It is believed to be essential for the general development of the very young child (from perhaps two years) to move between the more intimate home environment and the more lively setting of a care centre or school: he will thus, for example, receive an early training in how to take part in formulating rules of behaviour and obeying them. The day centre or nursery school could, if adequately staffed, have a socially equalising function: children from homes which are at a disadvantage in certain respects find some degree of compensation here.

The family

Two providers give the family greater economic stability than one. Employment of the wife tends to influence the marriage in a positive way, and the children will enjoy the benefit of a mother with wider experience. As soon as the father finds it natural to deal with all sorts of problems in the home, internal delegation of tasks becomes much easier. At the same time, the family as a whole finds more areas of joint activity.

Society

Under present circumstances the potential capacity of the population is not fully employed: technical, managerial and scientific talents among women, for example, can find only partial expression. The same is the case with social and caring talents among men. Investments in education are under-used to the extent that women drop out from the labour market .during the child-rearing period and frequently do not return to it. Younger women in the lower echelons of employment cannot be expected to feel involved as long as they are unable to see good chances of promotion ahead: employers, on the other hand, are not likely to change their attitudes towards the career ambitions of women unless they become convinced that women are not bad business risks.

Because of the strong differentiation between male and female occupations, local labour markets are unnecessarily rigid: with greater equality of choice of occupation, local industrial changes would become more easily manageable. When all adults are active in the labour force, working days could be shorter and vacations longer without loss of productive capacity; more shared free time would benefit both family life and the whole spectrum of political, social and cultural activities.

Minimally, a change in the present role of the sexes would entail an end to the strictly defined task of the housewife, which gives women neither the chance of self-actualisation nor any individuality. Payment for housework, which some have suggested, would merely recognise and cement the subservient position of women, though payment for childbearing would not. Some would argue that a proportion of women like housework: liberationists declare that they are induced to do so by powerful conditioning, which needs to be broken. But, some radicals continue, the housewife role will be abolished only if the nuclear family disappears too, since it is by this means that women transmit their oppression to further generations. And it is not merely the name that needs abolishing, but the whole relationship: in this sense, a commune may be just as restrictive as the traditional bourgeois family.

The radical critique, however, goes further: gender roles must finally be abolished too – women must liberate their life styles from the constraints of gender. This is held to entail no change in sex roles: the two are quite distinct. Not all critics would go so far: nevertheless, it is clear that full role equalisation will demand some such radical change of outlook, and that valuations and deeply rooted habits will have to be revised as well as rules and regulations. The ramifications are so many that only a sample can be dealt with here.

In considering necessary reforms in the economy and society, one point needs stressing. An innovation can be introduced into a social system and work beautifully up to a certain level: after this critical point, however, there may be increasing difficulty in accommodating the innovation to other legitimate claims on resources. Some dilemmas which may result will be developed in the remainder of this chapter.

To recapitulate: the fundamental assumptions of full role equalisation are that men and women are equally committed to continuous and lifelong employment, that every kind of occupation and position is open to all irrespective of sex, and that each spouse is able and willing to deal with tasks in the household and neighbourhood on a similar footing. It will be convenient to discuss reform in terms of: (1) social demands on husbands and wives emanating from sources other than their employment, (2) demands on their part for external resources (personal and material), and (3) the timing and placing of activities in the daily and the longer-term perspective.

Demands on husbands and wives

Children need a great amount of attention: the first years are very time-consuming, since the small child requires continuous access to an adult, but even the older child needs almost 'random access' to parents for emotional and intellectual support. Old or disabled relatives need contact for emotional as well as for practical reasons, and institutional arrangements are too limited and impersonal to deal with much more than physical care. In discussion of the family almost all the attention has been concentrated on parents and small children: a complete picture must take account of the interaction of three generations. The irony today is that the older generation is condemned to institutions instead of being allowed to pursue its traditional role of childminder. Political, educational and cultural factors, and even certain forms of recreation, should also come into the picture, and in particular the need of adolescents for organisational and other help.

Demands of families for external resources

During part of the day outsiders have to replace parents in taking care of the children. The traditional way, of course, is for them to come to the home to live there but, the considerable cost of this solution apart, it evades the important objective of getting the children integrated into a larger group at an early age. Public service facilities – self-service laundries, for example – arrangements for the occasional minding of children, and a reception office for the running of day-to-day affairs would be alternative ways of meeting this need. As in pre-industrial society, a working parent must sometimes be allowed to bring children to work.

Men should be taught how to deal with children and with other practical matters in the home: women will need similar training in more technical kinds of repair work. School curricula will have to take into account that boys and girls have equally to be prepared for employment, child care and household work.

Time and place of activities

We have been speaking as if societal events were not distributed in time and space or subject to budget limitations. The fundamental consideration must be how the supply and demand of human time interact, and simple arithmetic is not adequate for dealing with this. First, production and consumption take time, and we can rarely do both simultaneously. Personal services, for example, cannot work at full capacity for any particular length of time unless they have customers who are in a position not to participate in production or leisure for at least the same amount of time. Thus every dentist or barber who works for 8 hours uses up at least 18 hours of the total time-income of the population in his catchment area and, indeed, more, since time for transport and waiting must be added. Secondly, a large number of activities take place in groups of differing sizes, and as long as a group is in operation its members are not available for joining other groups in other places. What this means is perhaps best illustrated by a small-scale example: if 15 children in a playground decide to play a game which involves 10 participants, then as long as this game lasts the remaining children are prevented from playing any other game which involves more than 5 participants. Society is full of this kind of interdependence. Thirdly, most actions are part of sequences which have to be carried out in a logical order if they are to make sense: we must buy food before we eat it and not *vice versa*; a parent must bring a child to the day centre before going to work, and not the reverse. Such sequences are at every moment very strong determinants for what we have to do next. Fourthly, some kinds of human activity exhibit an odd sort of asymmetry with striking organisational consequences. A person can speak to many others simultaneously, but can as a rule listen to only one at a time, so that the emitting of messages can make use of economies of scale in a way which is impossible when it comes to receiving and digesting them: hence the information overload – which, by the way, is perhaps one of the major reasons bureaucracies grow in size, without seemingly being able to become more efficient. It is this principle which makes the small family group so important for the developing child: many questions can be answered by a parent in an hour, while in class the teacher can listen to and answer an individual child perhaps only once or twice an hour (Carlstein 1975).

These and many more factors mean that the argument for full role equalisation is in fact an argument for removing certain kinds of constraints from people's integrated action spaces and imposing others. No reform can abolish the basic limitations on social existence: the crucial question is how the proposed set of contraints interact with fundamental and unavoidable constraints.

The daily round and the local range

The number of hours worked is perhaps the strongest constraint which can be collectively determined. Today the most common gross number of working hours (work plus travel) is 9-11 hours (Sweden 1968): the second most common is 7-9 hours. These two figures cover 72 per cent of the working population: 14 per cent work more and 14 per cent work less. In a system of full role equalisation, it would be contradictory to have the majority of the adult population at work or commuting for around 9 hours each day: there would be too little time for the other functions foreseen, and the children would have to be away in group activity for too long. Some would prefer longer working hours organised into a four-day week; others advocate a six-hour day and perhaps a longer vacation. The former suggestion seems to conflict with role equalisation: childcare at home would become next to impossible during the working days, and complete institutionalisation would follow – the long weekend would not compensate unless schools were also on a four-day week. The second suggestion is probably more in line with the intentions of role equalisation. The time-resources for achieving this goal would come from complete female participation and the disappearance of part-time work as known today. Labour unions see advantages in the latter consequence, since they have found female part-time work very difficult to handle with respect to upgrading of wages and other conditions, and part-time employees are usually hard to unionise.

The shorter the working day, the more scope individual establishments will have for deciding when work starts and ends: but it is far from obvious what a really good solution would look like in a fully-fledged role-equalisation society. For the bulk of establishments – factories, offices and schools – to operate during the same period of the day as they normally do today would seem to provide the maximum freedom for family life and other commitments, but in other respects this solution would not function well. Present scheduling is based on the assumption that families have segregated roles: the wife is supposed to do the shopping and such service visits as can be delegated to her, while the husband is bound to his place of work. In a situation where everybody is employed – and a growing number in service establishments – there would be no customers to serve. In the bigger cities, where double employment is already very common, it can easily be seen that a large proportion of shoppers are people who have taken time off from work, which is in principle uneconomic. Staggered hours which will be a compromise between a given population's double function as producer and consumer is a more likely solution.

The possibility of realising role equalisation is closely bound up with the design of future transportation systems and with the principles adopted in regional and urban planning. The opening up of the nuclear family which is intended will greatly increase the number of journeys between various premises and they will be more spread out over the day than they are now (Ellegard, Hägerstrand and Lenntorp 1975). This means that private journeys will be preferred to those governed by a timetable, which cause too great losses in time and flexibility.

But these conclusions say nothing of the kinds of vehicles or the distances to be covered. If future technology permitted a variety of small workplaces, with work coming to people rather than people going to work, one could imagine the emergence of an urban texture where life and work were intermingled according to a kind of 'campus' principle. Journeys, though frequent, would be short, and walking and light, slow vehicles would suffice internally. The great advantage of this undoubtedly very utopian solution would be that mobility differences between various groups of the population would be slight and unproblematic. More likely, of course, is a continuation of the present spread-out urban texture, with concomitant long journeys. Under these conditions – and if no energy-limitation interferes – the population would remain divided between a mobile group (car owners) and a next-to-immobile group. Role equalisation would require that families had two cars: for those who cannot achieve this, the range of options would remain severely limited, even if public transport were sustained by subsidies. It can easily be shown that public transport as organised today, will not be able to equalise conditions – not because of questions of price or speed, but because of the rigidity in the way it operates. But clearly, improvements could be made: a certain minimum standard could be guaranteed and the careful location of household services would help.

The long-term period and the wider range

Even if a continuous life in employment is assumed for everybody, men and women, shorter and longer periods away from work have to be provided for.

The first case is 'maternal leave' during the period when the child is very young, perhaps up to two years. For this purpose, economic provision is needed, and it is already provided for varying periods in many countries. With role equalisation, it should be up to the parents themselves to decide which of them is going to do the job or if they prefer to take it in turns. (Recent Swedish legislation guarantees 'maternal leave' for the father as well, though it is not yet known how many fathers have made use of this right – probably not very many.)

The really difficult problem is to maintain contact with the place of work, or at least with the occupation, during the period of leave. The disappearance of mothers from the labour force is largely explained by the fact that it is difficult for them to resume work (Fogarty et al 1971, p.430). But this problem could at least partly be overcome by some sort of systematic briefing.

The second case for longer breaks would be for continued education. Whether arrangements of the above-mentioned kind are employed or not must depend on the relevant circumstances.

The movement to new, more attractive jobs poses a special kind of problem when both spouses are employed. A step in a career is frequently connected with moving to a new town: and the Swedish experience is that wives who follow their husbands to a new residence either leave the labour force or take a worse job than they had. A reasonable conclusion is that, in a society with full equalisation of roles, migration would be held back because of the difficulty of making successful double shifts. Again society could step in and help with labour exchange facilities.

Less geographical mobility is not necessarily a disadvantage in every respect, even if economic doctrine favours a mobile labour market. A geographically stable population means stable social networks, which in turn is one of the prerequisites of well-functioning democratic institutions. Investigations have shown that a person must on average have lived about seven years in a town before he begins to move upwards in local political organisations. In addition, old people will not be so isolated in a more stable population as they tend to be in a very mobile one.

It is not difficult to see that a society with full equalisation of roles is not waiting just around the corner, even in countries where special efforts have been made to move in that direction. Objections to it abound, predominantly concerned with two closely related valuations: doubts about the natural capacity of women to perform what are traditionally considered male tasks, and a strong positive valuation of a continuous and intimate relationship between mother and child which the equalisation movement is assumed to endanger.

The radical position is that '*a priori* arguments that women are incapable of handling this or that type or level of work have again and again collapsed under the test of experience' (Fogarty et al 1971, p.483). Periods of war, for example, have invariably increased the range of female participation. The fact that women are few in many occupations, and in particular that they are seldom found in leading positions, is founded on other reasons than lack of capacity, the foremost being lack of support by husbands and by other men.

As to the relationship between mother and child, a peculiar fact is that almost no studies have been carried out to estimate the importance of the father to the development of the child. Nor has there been any investigation of what it would mean for the man, and through him for the general social climate, if he was obliged to deal with practical and human problems in a closed environment, as women have always done. If we ask where the forces that make for change are to be found, we find that, generally speaking, innovations seem to proceed through social systems along three dimensions. One is the social class: innovations diffuse from upper to lower socio-economic strata. A second is geographical: certain centres of change create an outward spread moving from area to area. The third dimension is demographic: a young generation adopts new ways which become more and more widespread as the older age groups disappear. As a rule, all three dimensions are discernible simultaneously but with differing force.

The filtering-down process applies very little in this particular field: it is true that certain pioneers are to be found among highly educated people, but apart from them, the wives of men in the upper strata seem to be conservative and negative towards a reinterpretation of sex roles (Haavio-Mannila 1971). The geographic influence (the neighbourhood effect) is an obvious factor on the local scale. The psychic load of accepting change is always more and more easily borne as the numbers of other innovators grow in the immediate surrounding. But at a larger scale – for example with respect to diffusion between governments – vicinity cannot be an especially powerful factor: institutional and cultural differences are strong counteracting forces.

The case for the equalisation would seem to be predominantly bound up with the demographic dimension. It is a fact, for example, that an increasing number of young husbands in the Scandinavian countries are prepared to deal with all kinds of housework, even the nursing of their newborn children (Haavio-Mannila 1971), in a way that their fathers would never have accepted. In Britain, too, the evidence is that roles are shared especially among younger, middle-class families: the symmetrical family (Young and Willmott 1973). More important probably is the rising number of well-educated girls. They belong to a generation which has learned how to make visible its problems and wants, and they must be well aware of the long childless period which they can expect later on, particularly if they marry early. It seems thus highly probable that a growing number of women will demand a new order of things: yet, since we have to deal with a process in the demographic dimension, the pace of change is bound to be slow.

Towards a redefinition of the family

Summing up, it is clear that throughout this chapter a whole variety of considerations have all pointed towards the same general conclusion. The problems of the old and of women can be resolved by creating a number of new bureaucratic institutional arrangements: more intensive care in old people's homes, more paid home help, more public transport, more meals on wheels, more old people's housing, more day-care centres for children, more reception offices and self-service laundries. Or they can be resolved by reversing the whole trend of the modern world, and restoring the extended family to its traditional role – so that many of the so-called problems disappear, being resolved by mutual aid among members of the extended family.

There can be no doubt of the attractiveness of the idea of the extended family. It could provide support for the old and, more important, a set of continuing functions for the old: there would be no retirement, merely an appropriate form of work. It could be much more efficient in use of real resources than a set of bureaucratic solutions for the care of old people, besides being essentially humane in a way that institutional solutions could never be. Thus it could provide a way of husbanding scarce public resources at a time when this may be a critical social priority. And it could provide a whole variety of supports for the working mother – not merely through the help of old people, but through a new division of tasks between men and women.

For the extended family to be fully effective in this role, however, a simple return to traditional patterns would hardly be sufficient, for modern economy and society are simply not organised in the old way – least of all spatially. For this solution to operate, it would at the very least seem necessary to return a great deal of paid work to the home base, so that this work and unpaid household tasks can be mixed in a much more flexible way. Freelance professionals or workers whose hours are flexible – university teachers or publishers, for instance – already enjoy this freedom: the question is how far the rest of the economy could operate in a similar way. The problem of the family thus becomes basically a problem of the family economy and its relation to the wider economy.

The other point is that the old extended family was held together by blood relationships and by rigid tradition: these constraints have broken down and will not easily be re-erected. So the new-style extended family would need to be based on voluntary recognition of the need for mutual support and mutual aid. It is not at all clear how this could operate, and in particular how it could become reasonably universal. It would perhaps be easier if the family were based, not on an exclusive blood relationship, but rather, at least partly, on other kinds of affinity. And this might help deal with the associated problem: that a blood-related, economically-based extended family is difficult to combine with any remaining notion of social or geographical mobility.

As things stand, therefore, the extended family solution appears fairly utopian: the thread that connects it with present-day society and its evolution is a tenuous one. But there are possible signs of a change. Women's attitudes to their social role are clearly changing; they constitute probably one of the fundamental social transformations of the twentieth century. A minority of young people, and some older ones, have begun to live communally on a fairly stable basis. More generally, small community groups have begun to proliferate on a great variety of issues in almost all European countries, generally on a very local basis. All these may be harbingers of a very different future: and to this point we shall return in our final chapter.

CHAPTER 10

Class and Inequality

If the family is still the basic smallest unit of European society, the largest next to the nation state itself is the social class: and the continued existence of the social class guarantees that one of the largest macro-problems of a future Europe will be the problem of inequality and class relationships. How great is the difference now between the share one man has of life's goods and opportunities and the share another man has? And will the European of the year 2000 be content to see this distance maintained? What degree of inequality exists between the different nations of Europe? And will the European states of the future seek to alter this balance? These are the questions we shall first consider in this chapter. We shall then go on to analyse what we take to be the nature of 'class' as it is now and what this may mean for the future.

Types of inequality

What is designated by the single word 'inequality' turns out on inspection to be by no means a single thing: it is a complex of different types and orders of inequality. But a large general division does suggest itself and we shall employ it here: between inequality originating in economic causes and inequality originating in causes which are not economic. And in order to concretise a problem which can easily evaporate into generalisations and complaints, we shall examine it in connection with a single country – France – which is mid-way between any extremes to be found in Europe and for which ample documentation exists.

Economic inequality

Because it can be expressed in numbers, economic inequality has always been the first to be noticed and analysed; it has sometimes led observers to forget that other forms of inequality exist, or has even been considered the root cause of these. Today we know that the real situation is much more complicated. We also know that even economic inequality cannot be reduced to simple differences of income.

Income is not in fact as easy to pin down as one might suppose. Wages are only one part of the resources of a household (42 per cent in France in 1965, when 80 per cent of the active population were wage-earners). If wages do constitute an important proportion of the income of socio-economic groups, inadequate wages are only partly compensated for by social benefits in the case of the worst-off; conversely, for the better-off wages are supplemented by other resources.

Then again, wages are not determined simply by the socio-economic group in question; they also reflect disparities between regions or different economic sectors; they are affected by considerations of age and sex. The situation in the 'typical' country, France, can be simply illustrated by ratios. There, in 1972, wage differentials ranged from 1 (unskilled worker) to 6 (upper management), including 1.21 (semi-skilled worker), 1.49 (skilled worker), 2.8 (middle management), 5.16 (engineer) (cf Hatchuel 1972). But these figures should be corrected to take account of possible benefits in kind. For family incomes (as distinct from individual wages) the differentials are obviously wider, running from 1 (unskilled worker) to 25 (chairman and managing director). But such figures need modifying, to distinguish between income that must by law be declared to the Inland Revenue, income that really is declared, income that can be accurately checked and net income after tax. Then one should add the various benefits that can be received through social legislation.

We must also rule out very exceptional cases if we want to find meaningful ratios. We should compare the average income of the richest 10 per cent with that of the poorest 10 per cent (a ratio of 28.5 to 1 in France in 1970), or the bottom end of the first group with the top end of the second (a ratio of 10 to 1 in France), or the average of the richest 10 per cent with that of the poorest 30 per cent (7.7 to 1 in France in 1965). These figures refer to pre-tax income; the last should read 4.43 after redistribution via tax.

But all this quantitative information does not by itself give a proper idea of economic inequality: social milieu, sex and age have their effect. The ratio of periods of activity to periods of inactivity (school, retirement) is higher among the liberal professions, farmers and, to a less extent, unskilled manual workers, than it is for others; it is lower for paid intellectual workers. Whether a woman works depends on her age and on the socio-economic position of her husband. Young people enter active life at an age and level of qualification that depends greatly on the social position of their family. Job security varies according to socio-professional status – though here the situation is changing rapidly, and any extension of job stability to new sectors, such as immigrants and contract labourers, would certainly affect it. Finally, equality in work can by no means be reduced to the certainty of obtaining a regular salary: one must take into account the number of hours worked, the physical and moral conditions in which work is done, the risk of injury; and here again the inequalities are vast.

The gap between the manual and the intellectual job is a familiar one. It may seem odd, to future generations, that our society should downgrade the hardest and most dangerous tasks and as a result allot them to immigrants whose inadequate training makes them more vulnerable to accidents. And many jobs created in the tertiary sector often possess a much higher status than certain 'manual' ones, although the fatigue and boredom they involve are just as high.

A study of patterns of consumption also reveals – if the fact needed revealing – that we are still a long way from an egalitarian society. But it also serves another purpose: for consumer patterns – in the widest sense, including the acquisition of durable goods – highlight family expenses and inequalities of inheritance. It is only lately that economists have begun to take account of family expenses: yet, if we are to get an accurate picture of inequality, we have to compare not only wages (linked to individuals) or incomes (linked to the family, considered as the basic tax unit), but also the satisfaction of needs by those 'consuming units' into which any family can be divided. If we do so, we find other patterns of inequality that are experienced very directly and which have given rise to the debate as to how direct taxation should allow for family commitments – by a straight allowance, irrespective of income, as in many countries, or by a sliding scale of allowances according to family circumstances, as in France?

In nearly all countries, less is known about the distribution of wealth than about the distribution of income – a serious gap in our knowledge. But a reasonable picture can be constructed by comparing available data sources. In the United Kingdom, the National Income Blue Book tables show that in 1972-3 the top 10 per cent of income recipients received 26.9 per cent of total income before tax and 24.0 per cent after tax; but adjusted Inland Revenue data show that in 1973 the top 10 per cent of wealth-holders had 67.3 per cent of the total wealth (and the top 1 per cent had 28.1 per cent). These figures are greatly changed if state pension rights are included; for instance, the share of the top 10 per cent falls to 45.7 per cent. Here as in other countries, it is certain that the distribution of wealth (like that of income) has become more equal over time: in the United Kingdom the share of the top 1 per cent of wealth-holders fell from 69 per cent in 1911-13 to 42 per cent in 1960 and has fallen substantially since then. The explanation of these differences in wealth is still unclear, but in the United Kingdom it is clear that the influence of inheritance is substantial and that there had been no marked change in its pattern, at least up to the mid-1960s (United Kingdom: Royal Commission on the Distribution of Income and Wealth 1975, pp. 156-8).

Non-economic inequality

Social and cultural inequality have been the subject of numerous studies, which have shown that such forms of inequality are resented more than the purely economic variety. The latter is in general under-rated by public opinion; further, if social and cultural inequality is sometimes a direct result of economic inequality, public opinion today refuses to see the connection as inevitable.

To consider first the question of education: the time spent in full time study by young people of 16 to 18 varies according to the father's profession – 30 per cent for the sons of agricultural labourers, 90 per cent for the sons of senior managers and similar categories. Access to university education is also extremely uneven, with managers' and professionals' sons and daughters disproportionately over-represented and manual workers' children as decidedly under-represented with variations of degree. This is true of every European country – including the socialist ones of Eastern Europe.

Such facts need careful interpretation. Poor people's children tend to leave school early to earn money; but their cultural background, too, makes them disinclined to stay on at school, and in any case hardly encourages them to succeed if they do. The average IQ of socio-economic groups in France, in 1973, ranged from 94.8 for unskilled and semi-skilled workers to 108.9 for higher groups. It seems that our society is far from granting equality of opportunity. As a result, social mobility is low: the son of a top manager has a 33.3 per cent chance of becoming a top manager himself, as compared with a 5.2 per cent chance if mobility were perfect. One tends to think that social mobility has eased greatly since the war, but there is no evidence of much movement today.

Inequality of opportunity in the obtaining of information – considered in detail in Chapter 8 – should also be noted here as being of crucial importance to any consideration of social inequalities: active participation in politics or cultural activities largely depends on availability of information. Inequalities in this regard can be traced to differences in age, social milieu, sex and the kind of urban environment one lives in. Thus variation in interest taken in politics, measured either by surveys or by electoral abstentionism, is considerable. For reasons that are often very different, farmers, retired people, shopkeepers, unskilled workers and low-paid manual workers play scarcely any part in community affairs; and similar variations could be found in regard to participation in professional life or trade unions.

Apart from educational programmes on radio and TV, there are many other services theoretically available to all which are in practice used by only a few. But here inequality stems, not only from economic inequality (in terms of leisure time available) or cultural inequality (in terms of life-style), but also from the unequal distribution of services among regions, towns and rural areas. Yet it can be shown that for cultural or sporting amenities – theatres, libraries, swimming pools, and so on – the order of use is the same as the order of income. This does not apply to the utilitarian services – crêches, canteens – but it is never the worst-off in society who derive the most benefit from them. Pierre Mercier concludes: 'A low level of education, plus an inadequate income, seem to combine so as to shut out certain groups of Frenchmen from any real participation in community or social life' (Mercier 1974).

Inequalities in respect of illness and life expectancy are the ones our society most reluctantly admits, and understandably so. Although the general picture has improved – reduction of infant mortality, lengthening of life-span – gaps between the different layers of society still exist: manual workers are where clerical staff were 12 years ago, or where upper management was 22 years ago, so far as the infant mortality of their progeny is concerned; at 35 in France, the further life expectancy for unskilled workers is 33.5, for middle management 38.4, for primary school teachers 40.8.

Inequality between nations

Inequalities within one country are compounded by inequalities between different countries: yet Europe is a place where information circulates fairly freely, and there cannot be much doubt that increasing knowledge of these disparities will lead to an increasing demand for their abolition. Harmonisation of social legislation within the nations of the EEC is, indeed, already contributing towards this end. But do we know exactly where we stand on this matter? The statistics of different countries are differently based. In Denmark, for instance, they are based on gross, pre-tax income, in Britain on taxable income plus social benefits. But if we confine ourselves to one detailed case – employees of multi-nationals, whose functions and hierarchy can be compared from one country to another – we learn that the differentials are relatively wide in Britain and Italy, average in France, Germany and the Netherlands, and much narrower in the USA. Taking now total pre-tax income, if we compare the ratio between the top 10 per cent, and the bottom 30 per cent, the following figures result (for 1962-3):

2.54 Norway	4.12 Netherlands
2.79 Denmark	4.14 Germany
3.15 Britain	5.51 Finland
3.28 Sweden	7.67 France

France, which is in the middle of the wages table, does not occupy the same position in the income stakes. But taking the top 10 per cent involves perhaps over-estimating the exceptionally privileged situation.

Variation in wage bills from one sector to another is much greater, it seems, in France than in Germany; and the latter pays clerical staff worse, in comparison with manual workers, than does France, though there are fewer of them. Seniority seems much more important in France; women seem much more penalised in Germany and distinctly more privileged in Sweden, and especially Denmark.

We also need to compare purchasing power: if we compare the number of months a worker of similar age, with similar family commitments and a similar job, has to work so as to afford a similar car, we get the following figures:

7 Belgium and Holland	11 UK
9 Germany and Sweden	30 Portugal
10 France and Norway	33 Spain

These figures are taken from a survey led by Pierre Mercier for *Vision* (Mercier 1976), a study which attempts, notably, to compare qualitative elements, often suggesting numerical criteria to this end. Thus a wage-earner's security is held to be reflected in the

Table 10.1 International comparisons of living standards

	Germany	Belgium	Denmark	Spain	France	Greece	Ireland	Italy	Luxembourg	Norway	Netherlands	UK	Sweden	Switzerland
GDP per inhabitant at current market prices in French francs	5,610	4,650	4,460	1,750	4,900	1,790	2,130	2,410	5,200	4,780	4,410	3,100	6,140	6,190
Energy consumption per inhabitant expressed in tons of oil	4.75	5.38	4.24	1.64	3.54	1.52	2.19	2.57	12.88	4.27	6.01	4.35	4.75	3.17
Telephones per 1,000 inhabitants (1972)	268	240	377	146	199	160	114	206	361	320	299	314	576	535
Animal protein consumed per inhabitant per day in grams (1972)	58	57	66	46	68	45	63	45	57	57	56	56	58	58
Houses completed per 1,000 inhabitants (1972)	10.7	5.4	10.0	9.6	10.5	14.0	9.0	4.7	5.3	11.1	11.4	6.1	12.8	11.5

Source: OECD (1975)

proportion of his wage that he receives after six months of illness or unemployment (for the Nine the figures range from 50 to 100 per cent) and by the number of factory inspectors per 100,000 employees (which is generally low and varies quite a lot: one in Belgium, 24 in Sweden). On the other hand, the growth of industrial democracy in firms is evaluated by purely qualitative criteria, which put Sweden, Holland and Denmark in first place, ahead of Germany and well ahead of France and Britain.

Similarly, discrimination against foreign workers can be measured numerically (time taken to obtain naturalisation, for instance); but it is also affected by subtler factors, such as the extent of latent xenophobia, which are harder to measure. Sweden would seem to be the country with least discrimination, followed by Holland and Italy. Help for the aged and the handicapped can also be expressed numerically (pensions, allowances), but we also need to take into account psychological data showing how far such groups are integrated into society: there are still considerable differences between European countries. Overall there are notable disparities between the Nine, and these become even greater if comparison is extended to other European countries. Some of the data are given in Table 10.1.

Over time, inequality may have lessened marginally. The same phenomena can be perceived in all EEC countries: a narrowing of wage differentials or even of income differentials, increased care for the aged and handicapped, and palliatives to unemployment. Qualitatively speaking, similar trends can be seen towards improvement of the quality of life, towards increased participation by citizens in decision-making on matters that concern them, towards improvement of and greater access to community services. But this has depended to a great degree on economic growth and the development of productivity. It will be much more difficult and painful to achieve in a no-growth Europe, where helping the poor means taking directly from the rich.

Real inequality, perceived inequality and class

These differences may or may not be felt. Once the poor accepted their lot, now they do so much less. Even so, surveys show that the perception of inequality is much less prevalent than real inequality. But wider diffusion of information may make the poor more demanding – indeed, this may already be happening.

Does any social consensus on inequality exist? If so, it seems to be in favour of eliminating inequality at the bottom end of the scale, rather than seeking total equality. As poverty is a relative notion, it must be related to average income: and it is generally held that the poverty threshold lies somewhere below the half of this average income, while privilege begins at double the same amount.

This question aside, public opinion is certainly over-optimistic about the possibility of evening out inequalities. In *Socialisme en Liberté* Alfred Sauvy puts forward the following calculation, valid for 1968 but still not too far out if updated: if all the active population in France were given the minimum wage demanded at that time (1,000 francs per month) and all the inactive population half this sum, the total paid out would be approximately equal to the total of all private income at that period: so it could be done, but only if we got rid of all capital gains, all forms of hierarchy and all types of supplementary pensions (Sauvy 1970). And this again underlines the rule: all redistribution is made easier by economic growth, but radical redistribution will tend to lean most heavily on it. Finally, public opinion is increasingly sensitive to other sorts of inequality, particularly of status – very prevalent in France – and of participation, especially at work. Nations may differ in their nuances of class distinction, with England at one extreme and Sweden and Holland (perhaps) at the other, but most European peoples are interested in the *power* relationships between classes, which are very real in the attitudes of public servants to clients or passengers or supplicants, of the public in general to what the French evocatively call *cadres*, of provincial bourgeoisie towards metropolitan society, above all of managers to workers. As we have seen, in most European countries there has been relatively little movement up or down the social scale: so managers' sons still find themselves giving orders to workers' sons. All that has happened is that structural changes in the economy have created fewer workers and more middle-class technicians. Now, further structural changes threaten the power and the privilege of the managerial groups – especially through worker participation (now advocated by EEC) and the movement towards group work already described in Chapter 7. At any rate, it is to these deeper class relations that we must now turn.

The nature of class

There is evidence in Europe of a gradual reduction in grosser inequalities – at any rate of the kind that originate in economic causes; and the possibility exists that the grosser inequalities between the countries and regions of Europe may prove tractable to the machinery the EEC is capable of developing. But there is no evidence at all that inequality as such is going to disappear within the near future – and the basic reason is that that which ensures its continuance, namely class, is not going to disappear.

Class is clearly linked to the production system: it is a relationship between worker and owner, administrator and administrated; it is likely to persist as long as the productive system requires a division of labour. But since class relations are essentially dynamic, it is already an historical anachronism to talk of a society polarised between proletariat and bourgeoisie; that the concept was archaic even before World War One, let alone now, is not always consciously perceived. Nor need classes be antagonistic or polarised – though they may become so at times of recession or upheaval. To understand the changed nature of class in contemporary Europe, we need to understand the transformations that have occurred to European capitalism since Keynes' seminal *General Theory* was published in 1936.

The first change was the central Keynesian notion that one could spend one's way out of economic trouble – a theory which brought with it ever increasing state intervention and meant transforming the working population into a consuming as well as a producing unit. The second was the growth of large corporations which tended to displace the small owners through mergers and take-overs, and which were governed not by individuals but by managements and boards of directors. These two developments were the principal features of the post-World War Two economy. But Keynesianism and growth created problems at two levels: the interests of the traditional classes it failed to satisfy, and the new contradictions it created among the working classes. The new situation this created required a new concept of class – the notion of 'centre' and 'periphery' as describing the access of different groups or classes to effective economic and political power. In the early capitalism of the nineteenth century, owners were central and workers peripheral, but the new developments weakened class solidarity in the centre. Intellectuals were turned into managers, professionals very often lost their independence, becoming dependent on the state or on the large company. Those most obviously disadvantaged were the small owners, who were turned into satellites of large companies or state enterprises. The state gradually took over the legitimising role formerly carried out by the church, and the rule of law and order for which the army had previously been responsible, so church and army saw their independence eroded. Technocrats and political cadres became the influential force: but in the new world of capital-intensive, planning-based, integrated industry, the unionised worker also assumed a crucial role through the sanctions he could exert on society. This, however, meant a fragmentation within the working class between those in expanding areas of production with a well-organised workforce, and those in smaller, more disparate industries, with predominantly non-unionised workers, such as women or migrant workers. Certain key workers in growth sectors, and above all their union leaders, came to take a central role in the direction of the economy and the social activity of the state – while others, ironically, remained members of a marginal pool vulnerable to labour-saving investment.

Upon this fragmentation of classes can be superimposed that of the middle classes who, because of their mediatory position, tend to reflect tendencies in other areas of society: large numbers of middle and low rank management and bureaucrats become attached to the technocratic *status quo*, others, with more traditional values, tended to reflect the disorientation felt within the centre at the rapid transformation in status and values, while yet others tended to outnumber workers in most socialist and even communist parties in Europe. And some young middle-class workers are finding themselves in the marginal workforce – as, for instance, teachers facing the consequences of Europe's declining birthrates.

These groups, in Marxist terminology, are being 'proletarianised'. They are having their autonomy eroded, gradually becoming wage earners dependent on an employer, whether the state or a large industry. The major illustration of this state of affairs is the growing unionisation of the middle classes. It should not necessarily be associated with radicalisation, however, for in most cases, despite the obvious radical attitudes of the liberal professions and cadres in France in May 1968, it normally consists of an attempt to maintain the *status quo* and defend their present positions or, in those instances when reaction has come late, a return to the *status quo ante*, which tended to favour their cause.

Society has thus become extremely fragmented (see Fig. 10.1): but it is also, at least potentially, highly polarised between a largely corporate administration (and those who work for it) and marginal members of society, mostly dependent on state hand-outs or surviving through 'illicit activity'. The rush to unionisation reflects the situation. Under certain circumstances this polarisation could lead to social disruption, as in France in 1968 or Italy in 1969. However, certain features of modern society seem to ensure a precarious stability: the abstract character of the centre – the state and the corporations, which are all-pervasive yet are difficult to identify with any one individual or group of individuals – and the security provided by liberal democracy through the considerable social benefits it dispenses; participation through the ballot box or through membership of pressure groups – unequal in strength as these may be. There thus exists no radical challenge to the *status quo*, and this means a change in the class emphasis: polarisation between classes is defined by the mutually exclusive roles of ownership/employee or administrator/administered, and class becomes a determining factor in the distribution of resources

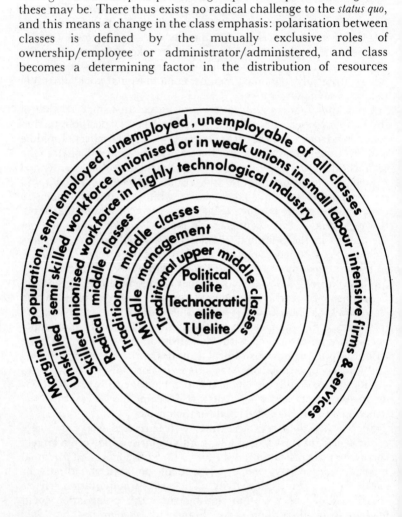

Figure 10.1
SOCIAL CLASSES ACCORDING TO THE CENTRE PERIPHERY MODEL 1945-74

according to already existing schema. But bargaining power based on one's contribution to actual production in turn determines the division of classes: therefore, classes still remain, geared not to income, but to their function in the means of production and to the culture this function produces. This is even true in socialist Eastern Europe and the USSR, where the middle-class command of key positions gives them continued security and prevents a backlash.

Alternative future scenarios

Scenario 1: Extrapolation of trends in the 1960s

We might well return to a situation which was already looming at the end of the 1960s and which Carlo Donolo (Donolo 1972) has called 'marginalisation within development'. Development would not be producing a 20-hour week for all and reducing marginal unemployment as expected; rather, as illustrated by Table 10.2, development would lead to increased structural unemployment and the monopoly of work by certain sectors, for instance by working overtime rather than sharing work. The US employment figures – where capital intensification was at its height – are significant.

Table 10.2 Unemployment rates

	1961-65	1966-70	1971
United States	5.5%	3.9%	6.0%
United Kingdom	2.6%	3.5%	5.6%*
Federal German Republic	0.4%	0.8%	0.9%
France	1.9%	3.8%	3.5%

*Excluding Northern Ireland
Source: Glyn and Sutcliffe (1972)

If one considers that an economy at maximum efficiency can operate with only a small percentage of the population working[1] then the prospect becomes quite frightening: it means that the *fluctuating* sector of employable people, which in periods of expansion tends to disappear, becomes a permanent feature. The *latent* sector, composed of hidden unemployment particularly prevalent in low productivity sectors such as agriculture, is phased out, as is the stagnant sector of part-time and temporary workers – though a

[1] It has been estimated, for example, that the US economy could operate with 6 per cent of the population in work (Wolff 1970).

revival in basic crafts and cottage industries as a reaction against mass-production may slightly off-set this trend slightly. To be added are other exacerbating developments, such as middle class redundancy resulting from an over-estimation of the number of 'organisers' and 'intellectuals' required by the productive system; and the high expectations generated in an era of growth, with the encouragement of upward mobility and meritocracy. In France, for example, there is always a glut of 'intellectuals' leaving universities and unable to find employment in the field for which they were trained – a development initially dismissed as poor allocation of resources, but now realised to be *structural*; increased full-time education at first relieves it, but then exacerbates it. Liberated, mobile middle class women now expect to be able to find employment, so that when they are out of work they must now be added to the list of marginals. And this, we assume in this scenario, is structural – or irreversible. Even in the case of expansion, structural marginality is here to stay.

Scenario 2: A structural down-turn in growth

This last scenario is perhaps appropriate to the late 1960s, when constant growth was still envisaged: in the mid-1970s we face a severe down-turn and one which we believe is unlikely to pick up in any significant way. Profitability is unlikely to return to the level of the 1960s due to pressure from wage demands and over-production in key sectors, such as steel; competition is increasing from the Arab world, the Soviet bloc and the Third World – all of which are combining bought-in western technology with cheap labour. Thus, wherever possible, western capital will be attracted to these areas rather than to home opportunities.

This is highly significant for social relationships: the time required to adjust to the new state of affairs – a large marginal population – is short; the transition will be less controlled; a gradual shift of resources to marginal sectors, to ensure stability by at least assuring a certain level of income and employment, will not be possible in time. Strongly unionised groups will defend their jobs, others will suffer. There will thus be an increase in unemployment which will bite deeply into the tertiary sectors – an area which under conditions of growth would have been expected to absorb much surplus labour. There will be a squeeze on family incomes likely to increase marginality by forcing women on to the labour market. A final contributing factor to instability is inherent in the exploitation of education as a means of absorbing unemployment:

education raises expectations which in times of recession it cannot satisfy and is thus in danger of creating a radical anti-system elite, excluded from the labour market by union anxiety to protect the jobs of their members, as is happening in Sweden in the mid-1970s. Thus the process is as in the France of the late 1960s.

Would it be possible then to envisage a revolution among a rapidly-increasing marginal population? We think not. Marginal populations do not create whole-scale revolutions: they are dependent on the productive system, they are highly fragmented. They include cultured 'gentlefolk' whose savings have been eliminated by inflation, semi-skilled workers who feel they have been displaced by immigrants, many of these same immigrants who will have been among the first to be laid-off, one-parent families, school leavers, delinquents and personality failures. They make an oddly disparate army, hardly the stuff of revolution – unless a middle class group could provide organisation. Thus any disruption will take the form of spontaneous uprisings, individual incidents, isolated occupations and sit-ins, posing no immediate threat to the structure of society. A full-scale uprising, moreover, would require the participation of the workforce – but the gap between the workforce and the marginals is increasing. There is thus likely to arise a 'polarisation' around work which will split the marginals into two groups: those whose aim is the provision of work and those who desire the transformation of the entire productive system (Figure 10.2).

The migrant workers

There is one special group among the extreme marginal population that should receive special attention. Since World War Two migrant workers from the Mediterranean countries have become a mainstay of the economic development of Western Europe: between 1960 and 1971, Germany increased its proportion of foreign workers from 1.4 per cent to about 10 per cent, Belgium from 6 per cent to 7 per cent and the Netherlands from below 1 per cent to 2 per cent; by 1968 in France the figure was 7.6 per cent. A very large part of the total additional demand for labour in these countries in these years was met by the migrants. The great majority come from the Mediterranean lands, including both southern Europe and North Africa: together, in 1968, they accounted for 62 per cent of migrant workers in France, 76 per cent in the Netherlands and 65 per cent in Germany; Belgium and Luxembourg, in contrast, draw most of the migrant labour from other EEC countries. These workers come on a

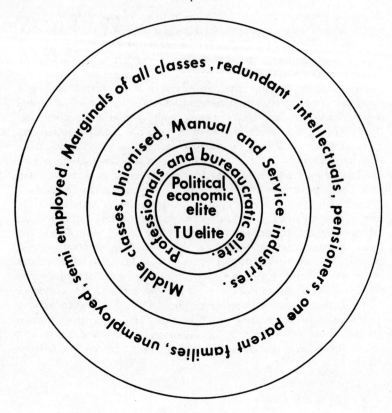

Figure 10.2
SOCIAL CLASSES ACCORDING TO THE CENTRE PERIPHERY
MODEL, 1975-?

great variety of different arrangements: Germany and to some
extent France, have encouraged official organised movements, the
Netherlands have not; Germany prolongs employment from year to
year, while France relates permits to labour conditions; France and
Belgium are liberal on the admission of families, Germany and the
Netherlands discourage it. But what is clear is that the guest
workers are in many cases no longer guests at all: a survey in
Germany in 1968-9 showed that almost a third of male migrant
workers had been there more than five years (Yannopoulos 1974,
pp. 16-18).

Yet in most cases the term guest worker is true in one regard: he is a second-class worker who will be the first to lose his job in a recession. Thus, in Marxist terms the migrants form a new kind.of industrial reserve army which can be employed or not employed according to the state of the market. If they lose their jobs, they automatically go back to their own country, which has to deal with the resulting problems. And they have no political status in either country. Thus to get a job, the migrant has to trade in most other basic rights: to vote, to change jobs, to be regarded as a full member of the labour force, to lead a family life, to live in a decent dwelling (Ozkan 1975).

The migrants create additional problems for their homelands. Though in some countries their remittances have aided the balance of payments, their departure has now left many of these countries actually short of labour, so that in turn they need to import workers from the neighbouring countries of North Africa – and perhaps eventually from West and Central Africa too. These territories thus become locked into the West European economic system, as the Mediterranean countries already have been. Some countries, such as Italy, have the paradox of simultaneous export of labour, import of labour and high unemployment. One reason, as in north-western Europe, is that the immigrant labour performs jobs which the indigenous labour force prefer not to do at any price (Nikolinakos 1975a, 1975b).

The migrants pose a problem now and an even bigger one for the future. If the mid-1970s recession proves to be structural rather than merely cyclical, it is likely to lead to a massive return of migrants to their homelands, since previous studies in Germany had indicated that in these conditions migrants are between five and seven times more likely to lose jobs than native workers (Dirick, Freiburghaus and Sertel 1974, pp. 34-5). If, on the other hand, there is a continuing need for them (as in low-status jobs rejected by the indigenous labour force), there are likely to be social strains due to ghetto formation, leading even to violent demonstrations, such as those seen in Rotterdam (1972) and Marseilles (1973). In turn this will lead to demands to integrate the migrants with the host community; but this will mean substantial spending on the necessary social infrastructure. One Dutch study, for instance, concluded that if migrant workers' families were allowed to join them, the public expenditure on housing would rise some eight times, and this could be a conservative estimate (Yannopoulos 1974, pp. 25-6).

There is an obvious answer to these problems: it is for western European firms to invest even more in the migrants' homelands and to encourage resettlement; then for western European governments to fill the resulting gap by diverting unemployed or underemployed workers from problem regions within their own frontiers. At the very least, it seems irrational to have encouraged such huge long-distance migrations while supplies of under-used labour were at hand within western Europe, often only a few hundred kilometers from the demand.

Class polarisation around work and structural marginality

Why will there be a polarisation around work? There has always been a certain antagonism between the 'proletariat' and the 'Lumpenproletariat' – Marx (1869, 1935, p.196) noted it in nineteenth-century Britain between the British worker and the Irish immigrants, Macciocchi (1969) noted it in southern Italy in the 1960s – but there have always been close class links in so far as large sections of the 'proletariat' were frequently laid off in periods of recession, and because division of labour was not particularly acute when factory work required no particular skills. Now, however, increased division of labour and growing importance of skills, plus union organisation, has increased the gap – not only between workers and unemployed, but within various sectors of the workforce. Differentials within the factory and within the industry are vigorously defended while the wage gap is rapidly increasing as a result of pursuing percentage rates rather than across-the-board increases. Yet it is not merely a question of wage differentials, but rather one of a conflict of interests, because under a competitive system, to quote Harold Wilson, 'One man's pay rise is another man's price rise'. In a system where growth has stagnated, one man's job security is another man's redundancy.

This is mirrored in the conflict between the interests of workers in large and small factories, in growth and non-growth sectors. Any increase of wages to the better-protected workers is normally passed directly on to the consumer by large industry which, unlike the small firm, has greater monopoly control and capacity to fix prices. Furthermore, the large firm tends to operate with wider profit margins and can afford to raise wages more readily both to attract skilled labour and to buy off potential strikes. The result is that the greater the wages paid to the workforce in a large firm:

(a) the less the small firm can afford to compete for skilled labour, therefore the more precarious becomes the existence of the rest of the employees;

(b) the more the price of equipment produced by large industry increases the tighter become the margins of the small firm which is forced to buy from the large; in consequence it is likely to resort to lay-offs or even go bankrupt.

The process follows the classic mechanism of development breeding underdevelopment: the large swallowing up the small, to which the 'central workforce' contributes its fair share in reducing the peripheral workforce to a satellite position.

This trend even occurs within the central workforce itself, this time in terms of employment and job security. The gap between having a job and not having one is again increasing under strict unionisation. In firms such as Fiat or British Leyland, there have been lay-offs. The response of the unions has been to defend employment while at the same time attempting to raise wage levels or at least keep up with the inflationary spiral. Yet this places them in a paradoxical situation, for in a competitive system overmanning with high wage bills renders a firm inefficient, putting into jeopardy the whole existence of the firm and, therefore, the employment of the whole workforce. More often than not, therefore, the situation is resolved by the sacrifice of the few for the many, or in certain cases the many for the few.

Again a conflict of interest occurs: a polarisation around work between stably employed and potentially unemployed. This situation is even more exacerbated by union perspectives. By pursuing the line of interest groups rather than class representation, the union develops a gap between the responsibility it assumes on behalf of its members in work and that which it assumes on behalf of its potential members out of work or its redundant ex-members. As a result, union attitudes towards unemployment become extremely narrow. Unions tend to criticise unemployment when it threatens to affect its present members, but they tolerate the absolute level of unemployment which does not affect their membership, which has fluctuated between $2\frac{1}{2}$ and 6 per cent in western Europe and which is growing at a steady rate. Even the possible policy of wage indexing promises to perpetuate this state of affairs, as does a fixed wage limit. Once more it means that one section of the population is protected, but the breach increases between the fortunate few in employment and the unfortunate many without.

In centre/periphery terms one can envisage, therefore, the following relationship: it will contain gradations within each sector, especially among the fragmented periphery. The rift will increase and large numbers will be badly off. However, their plight is unlikely to reach the levels of Third World countries due to the strong ideological links of unions and leftist parties which may guarantee against exploitation of power by the unions in pursuit of their own interests. It is even possible that wider consideration will be given to marginal populations under regimes where there is executive power for unions than they have received under a free enterprise system: Italian unions, for instance, are increasingly pressuring the government for greater investment in the south, while in Britain and France unions are beginning to involve themselves in more social issues, such as pensions and regional development, as well as general economic planning.

A further important reason why marginality will not reach a crisis level in the near future is the obligation of governments, particularly paternalistic social-democrat ones, to respond to electoral needs and to keep up a certain level of demand for industrial goods. Hence, although initial drastic reductions in the social services can be expected (ironically at a time when they are most needed), a certain reorganization of priorities must eventually take place. But unless the economy is planned on a basis of 'needs', both psychological and material – an impossible hope even in a state capitalist economy when supply and demand and political weight must necessarily be the order of the day – social dissolution is bound to take place. In all areas where a large section of the population depends on government handouts and thus on accidents of political change, the response may well take the form of 'irrational' display of violence and terrorism from the frustrated political 'extremes' whose progress is blocked by the polarisation around work. The only alternative may be the beginnings of a new counter-culture among the marginal elements which, if apolitical, could absorb some of the discontent.

Social relations after state capitalism

Could western society then dissolve, as the Roman Empire did under the invasion of the Goths and Lombards? One must assume that western society has the technology at hand to ward off any potential invader: the Roman Empire depended largely on numbers of armed men (rather than merely equipment controlled by a few), which necessarily needs a greater degree of social cohesion; in the age of the atomic bomb, invasion even of a relatively weak nation, not to mention a highly technological one, is becoming more and more of a risky business for the aggressor. The response to the problem of social dissolution must, therefore, come from within.

The monopoly of work by the workforce, the consequent material stability this confers, and the need to defend this position against a large pool of surplus labour, all rule out a socialist revolutionary response. Where society is polarised between state and workers (of all classes) and Lumpenproletariat, not only is there no material contradiction which will upset the *status quo* by involving the workforce, there is also no culture for the state and the bureaucracy to defend. For the bureaucracy in this context is a collection of functionaries who may find themselves operating a system for which they feel no sympathy.

This cultural vacuum may well be the situation that sparks off social change: should wide sections of society become culturally alienated, that could be the point of fundamental transformation. But note that it occurs without massive polarisation between two camps, and it will, therefore, be a gradual process: those in work have no interest in destroying the causes of the *status quo*, only in remedying its symptoms. Thus the likelihood is a search for a new form of identity in order to fill the cultural vacuum, but maintaining the *status quo*, in the productive system.

To understand how this process may come about, we have already examined in detail the phenomenon which is making it necessary: the phenomenon of *alienation*. It lies perhaps at the very centre of the 'problem of Europe' and is the subject of Chapter 11.

CHAPTER 11

The Heart of the Matter:
From Alienation to a New Rationality

To say that a cultural vacuum exists in Europe is another way of saying that a large part of the European population is alienated from the world it lives in. We think that *alienation* is at the root of our troubles: and we have suggested, much earlier in this book, a means by which we think it may be surmountable – through the gradual, perhaps painfully gradual replacement of the existing *rationality* by a new rationality more in accord with the basic human needs of our society, both present and immediately future. In this chapter, therefore, we shall attempt to define our understanding of alienation and why we think it central to our dilemma, as a preliminary to an exposition of our concept of a new cultural rationality and of why we think this desirable.

Alienation as a force for social change

We define alienation as the process by which an individual becomes to such a degree divorced from a true assessment of a given situation (e.g. his relationship with other people and with things) that he either acts self-destructively or is incapable of free action. There is a subjective and an objective aspect to alienation. Subjectively, the individual comes to regard other people only as a means to an end and tends to disregard their individuality. Things come to assume an existence of independence in his consciousness, placing them outside his control. Objectively, the reverse occurs, whereby the individual becomes the victim of other people's alienation, making him become a means to an end. If current values fail to satisfy certain biological or psychological needs, then man will react, not merely in terms of alienated or abnormal behaviour, but also in terms of a social movement.

The origin and present nature of alienation

Alienation in our time, as Berger, Berger and Kelner (1973) argue, originates in the highly systematised, specialised, technological framework of our lives and in the fragmentation of consciousness it provokes, which dictates our attitude both to things and to human beings. Machine-age logic is necessarily founded on a fragmented world view created through the process of specialisation, which requires a constant repetition of the worker's function and a narrowness of the parameters in which that function can be fulfilled. A form of mentality is thus created which, in terms both of spatial contact and contact through common preoccupations, makes it difficult for the individual subjected to a high degree of specialisation to relate to other human beings, so that there arises a psychological isolation which perhaps did not exist, or not to the same extent, in earlier small-scale societies.

But a great deal of working time is also spent in concentration on a specific task, and the major part of the contact which does occur is contact not with people but with objects. This is another area where technological society contrives to undermine the individual. In a situation which constantly repeats itself, as most work situations do, the object does not exist for itself, but is rather automatically stereotyped in the subject's consciousness almost as a defence mechanism against the overwhelming numbers he has to deal with. Thus his every act involving the object is preconceived, and even if each act is theoretically different, its novelty is not grasped as it might be in a more varied situation. The object as it really is, is thus divorced from the individual's consciousness, and he no longer regards it as something he can act upon or upon which he can impose his personality. On the contrary, it assumes an independence from which the subject can only retreat, and the machine takes over control of the man.

Lastly, and very significantly, the organisation of the work process itself exacerbates the problem of alienation. Specialisation reduces human contact within the work situation and repetition tends to narrow and reify world views, but the most overwhelming factor is the complexity of technological production and the resultant compartmentalisation within that complexity, which combine to render the work itself meaningless. Within the plant they obscure the product, to which each worker will have contributed only a minimal amount (which in any case could have been contributed by any other of the workforce). However, it is not only the product which is disassociated in the worker's mind from his role in its production: the social effects of the product are obscure to him too. Thus anonymity prevails, and from anonymity comes non-association and non-responsibility. The social utility of the job is not perceived, or alternatively is given some trite, compensatory form of justification. Functional, yet potentially anti-social or parasitic work, and dysfunctional acts of sabotage, such as wildcat strikes, are both reactions against the feeling of non-association.

In this way there is created the modern man of almost schizoid tendencies; and an incapacity to identify cause and effect within the productive process leads to what may be called a morality gap – the gap between people's declared and sincerely held views, and their objective functions.

Another effect of the organisation of a technological society is that of overlap, which transports the alienation produced within the workplace into the outside world. It occurs both directly and indirectly: directly via the individual through overlap between his working life and his private life; indirectly through the necessity for the rest of society to subordinate its organisation and ethos to the productive process. Take the direct effect first. Specialisation and repetition mean in far too many cases a complete psychological break between the individual's working life and his private life. This does not contradict the theory of overlap, but means that the psychological break is a reaction to the work situation and is, therefore, related to it in an adverse way. Work is not an extension of private life or integration with it; it is a negation of it in exchange for the capacity to buy goods, sometimes from necessity, but often for the purpose of accumulating goods for their own sake. Fetishism alone can thus become the motive for work.

The individual working in technology has no choice as to the form his development shall take, nor as to how to organise his life outside or through his work pattern. He is powerless before the effects which the present form of social organisation exert on him, and his capacity to evolve or even to vent his feelings is repressed. What usually occurs outside the work process is, therefore, not recuperation but escapism – to the easily digestible, to even greater fetishism, to the dream machines provided by media ready to exploit alienation through a process of promise and retractions, followed by further promises. The extension of technological systems to all areas of civil society is almost complete, and there are few areas left into which the reaction it creates can expand. Even those experimenting in alternative life styles in the remotest communes have found it impossible to isolate themselves completely: indeed, failure occurs *a priori*, in as much as they must necessarily take with them a technologically formed thought pattern even if they reject the technological life style.

This indirect effect – the 'contamination' of the rest of society –

produces a fragmented world view: the shop girl exists in your consciousness only when you enter the shop and expires when you leave it; the postman exists only for the moment he slots the mail through the letter box; even neighbours or friends have only a partial existence – one's neighbour becomes no more than someone (often an interchangeable someone) living next door whose significance is merely spatial and functional. The strict contextuality of conversation topics testifies to this: work becomes something to be discussed only at work, politics at political meetings, light topics in periods subconsciously designated for relaxation.

Bureaucracy as the organiser of alienation

Bureaucracy has always existed in western society: it is the form in which the 'intellectuals', in the terms used by Gramsci (1971), organise themselves and society around them. It is thus highly interested in the perpetuation of division of labour; indeed, it is the creator of it. Its role thus varies according to the level of that division and it is perhaps for this reason that the bureaucracy forms an organic part of the technological process. First, it compensates for the failure of the productive process to subordinate itself to the individual and does so by providing a continuity which would not otherwise exist. But the irony of its role is that the bureaucracy is compensating for something it created in the first place – division of labour – which it is obliged to maintain in order to ensure its own continued existence. Its operations are designed, not for the organisation of its own activities, but for the organisation of the activities of others: it is thus living in a permanent future, and its existence is devoted to the creation of plans the primary purpose of which is to guarantee a continuing need for bureaucracy. But it is dominated by the past in the shape of the rules by which it is obliged to operate: thus it cannot adapt to the situation of those it is supposed to help. Those who go to it for guidance must be made to fit into a bureaucratic norm: if this proves impossible, they are either cast aside or another abstract category is created. People thus become files – that which fits the convenience and ideal of bureaucratic neutrality.

This static universe is, moreover, the actual goal of the bureaucrat: the more a person appealing to bureaucracy is treated as an object, the more the bureaucracy is considered to be performing its task well.

The social consequences of alienation

The complexity and fragmentation of western society which are
largely responsible for alienation are more than of transient
importance: they are embedded in its social organisation. Western
society in its present form exists and can continue to exist only if it
treats men as means to abstract (normally quantifiable) ends rather
than as ends in themselves. Not only does industrial society reinforce
problems of anonymity, complexity and subsequent alienation, it
erodes those institutions which act as stabilisers. Science, upon
which industrial society is founded, has eroded religion and the
world view which religion supplied and which was a necessary
counterpoint to individual insecurity: suffering, pain, general
adversity were explained away by religion – science has created here
a vacuum.

Those other bastions of security, the family and the community,
are also falling: the mobility and consequent urbanisation required
by large-scale production has swept away the sense of stability and
identity the family and community provided. A sense of identity has
been sought in political parties and associations embracing the
whole of life, and whether their allegiance was to left or right they
initially provided a sort of substitute for religion: but political views
are now typically converging towards a neutral centre which
precludes a proper sense of identity, for identity is established not
only *with* something but also *against* something.

The latest attempt to fill the vacuum has come in the form of the
social democratic state: yet, based as it is on the ethos (though not
the practice) of neutrality, and working necessarily along highly
bureaucratic lines, it is a poor substitute. Granted it is paternalist –
as all other psychologically stabilising institutions have been – but its
paternalism can extend only to the provision of specific services and
goods: it cannot provide a world view. Indeed, its policy of
neutralism is based on a supposed lack of any world view, on its
supposed role of arbiter between competing attitudes. The only
world view it can provide is nationalism: yet the threat from the
outside which is usually required to crystalise nationalism is now
lacking. Appeals to nationalism thus tend to wear thin – especially if
the tendency of the liberal-democratic state is towards
internationalism, as it in fact is. The liberal-democratic state is,
therefore, thrown back on to the very element guaranteed to erode
even further the stabilising elements in society – individualism (as
opposed to individuality).

The new consensus: A developing solution?

This failure of social relations to act as a stabiliser and as it were, dis-alienator, may, however, prove to be correctable on the social level through the further evolution of one of the very phenomena just mentioned: the growing consensus between elements of the left and right which seems to be latent in large sections of the population of western Europe. It is a reaction against the increasing abstraction and complexity of modern society and its economic workings; at present there is merely a verbal consensus on both sides of the political spectrum, but this could exercise a vital influence on future development. When it comes to closer identification of causes and possible remedies there is, however, still utter confusion: although the villains – the government bureaucracy and the corporations – are identified (quite rightly in our view), not only is there the expected disagreement as to who was most guilty, the arguments put forward by both sides lack internal consistency, and this incoherence obscures the genuine ground for convergence. It consists primarily of a failure to realise that the solution of the institutional left – to nationalise large sectors of the economy to combat the influence of corporations – and the solution of the conservatives – to pursue free enterprise without government intervention – would both produce the same outcome: abstract corporate planning and bureaucratic (or technocratic) rule. Dictates of scale mean that nationalisation can only increase abstraction and complexity, for large-scale institutions create their own ethos against which individuals feel powerless: to attempt to substitute nationalisation for corporation power is therefore tautological. Non-intervention, profitability, and supply and demand is, however, exactly what has created the present situation: growth is inherent in any market system and growth has its own uncontrolled pattern of development – to support the large and to make satellites of the small. Apart from the historical impossibility of returning to an ideal free enterprise system, it would not make sense from a logical point of view either: it would only lead us after a few years back to where we are now.

And this applies, not only to large corporations – with whom many small owners, through ideological attachment to capitalism, sympathise – it also applies to state intervention and the growth of the state itself. The need to regulate the economy for the benefit of business at large, the need to assure stability through expenditure on the social services and to control demand through public spending, is the basis of the role of the state in the post-war, neo-

Keynesian economy: it is, therefore, not surprising that state intervention has grown, nor that, in response to corporate strategy, large-scale trade union organisation has increased, one of its consequences being to force the state to extend its control to virtually every area of civil society.

The state, corporations, the big unions, are historically inter-dependent, whether they recognise it or not: but it is the inter-relationship of these massive institutions that could theoretically unite the small man of whatever political persuasion. The first signs of a reaction transcending traditional political lines can already be seen in the environmental lobby: for what does this express if not an open distaste for the corporate and large-scale, even to the point at which environmentalism becomes anti-institutional for the sake of it? Unfortunately, however, one reason for the success of the environment lobby is that it lacks real political content and its title is sufficiently vague to embrace most political leanings.

It would thus seem that the idea of a united front against corporatism – which necessitates a high political content – is at present utopian: the ideologies of 'free enterprise' on one hand and 'nationalisation' on the other will work against it. Even if a 'dismantling' programme were involved, it would certainly lead to ideological divisions as soon as specific actions were proposed.

We believe, however, that we are historically nearer to a real than to a theoretical consensus. When, for example, during the 1950s and 1960s the small owners felt themselves threatened – and this occurred all over Europe – their reaction was only partly against big business: more often it was directed against unions and workers in general. On the other side, large numbers of workers, and especially their so-called ideological representatives, tended to lump small owners and corporations together, seeing their salvation in nationalisation and unionisation. Now, no one would deny that this is still the case; but the only development which can occur over the coming few years will be an increase in state, union and perhaps corporate power, and when this happens it is quite feasible that the real nature of this trend – that of abstract corporatism – will come to the forefront and serve as a point of political unification. This political reaction may come in the form of a new Poujadism – but it may also be progressive and force some real devolution of power. Which direction it will take largely depends, we believe, on how fast the left gets away from its nationalisation-solves-all approach and evolves a more worthwhile anti-corporate, anti-bureaucratic, anti-centralisation programme.

Before we look at such political consequences, however, we need to go further into the nature of alienation and its causes. To do this, we must invoke the concept of alternative rationalities, which we began to develop at the very start of this book.

The failure to satisfy needs

Throughout this book we have been examining the future European scene very largely as a series of problems, and we have just argued that alienation underlies the other problems. But we must remember that facts, events, situations are not 'problems' until someone insists on seeing them in that light. 'Problems' are facts brought before some bar of judgment. When we judge that a fact, a certain state of things, constitutes a problem we mean that we confront it with certain criteria of excellence and find it wanting.

What are the criteria we propose when we see the development of Europe for the remainder of this century as a 'problem'? As the scope of our study is as wide as the continent itself so the criteria we have to apply must be commensurate: the development we want to see in Europe must be one which efficiently satisfies basic human needs. It is this failure to satisfy needs that underlies the fact of alienation, and is manifested by all the expressions of that alienation: suicide rates, drug consumption, both legal and illegal, a rise in crimes against property and the person.

The concept 'basic human needs' originates in a number of works, now classics in their field, which appeared around the mid-century. The American psychologist Arthur H. Maslow proposed a 'need hierarchy' (Figure 11.1) and others attempted to modify or improve on it (Maslow 1943, Erikson 1968, MacClelland 1960, Etzioni 1968). Exactly how such lists should be formulated, or what they should contain, is not, however, our present point. The argument is that modern advanced societies so organise the lives of their members as to impose intolerable social costs, which, in the interpretation of Etzioni (1968) means the denial of basic human needs. We have rehearsed detailed examples many times in this book: workers out of touch with the goods they produce lack a feeling of social responsibility or of usefulness which is compensated for by an exaggerated need for social esteem and recognition; the operation of the 'free' urban land market condemns millions of Europeans to live on the fringes of the cities, far away from information, communication, cultural centres or other sources of social stimulation: traditional roles and responsibilities are redistributed, resulting in a tendency for families to become more and more disunited through forced migrations. There arises – to emphasise it

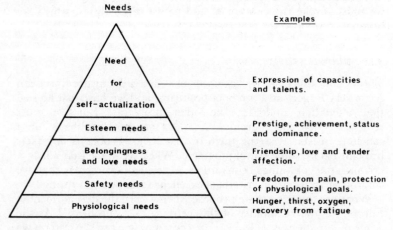

Figure 11.1
MASLOW'S NEED HIERARCHY   *Source:* Maslow (1943)

for the last time – a fragmentation of life and consciousness which is
the basic cause of alienation.

Towards a new rationality

The reason for such a state of affairs and for the existence of
alienation, it seems to us, lies most obviously in the recent
domination of western European society by the principle of
economic rationality. This term, as has already been pointed out,
refers to the logic that reduces all human aspirations and efforts to
the satisfaction of productive ends: it is the logic of the assembly
line, of time and motion studies, of hiring and firing. Economic
rationality packs everything neatly into boxes and thus divides
communal and individual life into separate compartments:
geographically, socially and psychologically.

Now we are not – it should perhaps go without saying – objecting
to economics; society must organise its resources in the most
economic way. But we contend that there may be some critical point
at which the application of economic rationality begins to frustrate
other, equally important human needs and values. And political
rationality – a development of economic rationality – leads to an
obvious stress on a Darwinian survival of the fittest. We are thus
arguing, not for an abandonment of economics, but for a new look at
priorities.

The economic development of Western Europe has brought to the forefront one concept above all: the concept of rationalisation – the optimal employment and coordination of human labour and machinery. But this term is, very significantly, also employed with other connotations. Social psychologists use it to designate a kind of self-deception: a plausible and socially acceptable reason is invented to explain behaviour which is in fact incompatible with prevailing norms; and the German sociologist Jürgen Habermas has defined it as increasing technological command and concluded that the higher the stage of rationalisation, the more likely it is that evaluation of ends will be neglected in favour of increasing command of means (Habermas 1967, p.231 ff).

This suggests that in some ways rationalisation is a distortion, or even the opposite of 'rationality' – the divorcing of rationality from human needs and social authenticity; and it is in this sense that we believe that the rationality of our time is in fact a rationalisation and thus inadequate to our needs.

Recall our thesis, developed in Chapter 3, that every historical era is characterised by a certain type of rationality: that is to say, its own set of priorities and principles for human action and for the production and distribution of goods. If this thesis is sound, to question whether the rationality of a particular era is really appropriate to it, is to ask whether it has taken carefully enough into account all that can be known about the era to which it is applied. If it has not, and men are in fact guided by an inappropriate and thus 'false' rationality, the achievements of which the age is capable would simply fail to be employed or enjoyed: men would feel needs they were unable to satisfy or would try to satisfy them in the wrong way and thus unsuccessfully. Observing the forces which were shaping the socio-economic life of Europe at the end of the last century, Max Weber baptised their tendency with the terms *zweckrational* (goal-oriented rationality) and *wertrational* (value-oriented rationality) (Weber 1964). *Zweckrational* is a rationality directed towards maximum material benefits and is characterised by reliance on quantifiable and calculable considerations: unquestioned basic values and the affective aspects of life play little part in *zweckrational* behaviour. *Wertrational* is, of course, the opposite of this: human relations and values play the major role. Weber considered that these two forms of rationality were adequate for an understanding of the culture of his time – and unquestionably they are still in operation. But if it is assumed that every epoch generates necessarily its own form of rationality – founded on its accumulated technical abilities and social insights – then there is an obvious need for a reconsideration of the sufficiency of the forms of rationality defined by Weber for his time.

From the aspect of our present discussion, we see the main differences between our age and that of Max Weber as twofold: division of labour is far more intensely specialised and institutionalised now than it was 50 or 80 years ago, and priorities as regards human needs are now directed far less at simple physical needs (the provision of food and shelter, for example) than they were then. Over the past two decades especially, the provision of material goods has posed far fewer problems than formerly, but narrower and narrower specialisation and the primacy of economic goals has tended increasingly to splinter society. To update the forms of rationality identified by Weber would, therefore, mean emphasising *social* values and *social* action, and we will, therefore, call this kind of rationality *systemrational*.

System-rationality has a critical relation to alienation and its avoidance. For while Weber's *zweckrational* behaviour related only things to other things (which gave it the quality of mathematical calculability), and while *wertrational* behaviour relates people and things (thus requiring deliberate human evaluation either by groups or people), *systemrational* behaviour would be centrally concerned with relations between people either as individuals or as groups; so that its central focus must be on social organisation. And, as we have seen, the central characteristic of alienation is its tendency to subordinate people to things – in other words, to reduce them to the status of things. This danger looms much larger today than when Weber wrote; and system rationality provides a way out of it. For it is a system in which there is adequate provision for gathering information, for formulating proposals on the basis of this information, and for combining proposals into decisions (Diesing 1962). 'Adequate' here means 'effective for dealing with problems', and we define this as the greatest feasible reduction in the 'social cost' by meeting basic human needs. This means reshaping social institutions which are at present failing to meet these basic needs.

Malinowski was the first to link the way in which social institutions function, or ought to function, with the concept of basic human needs:

In the first place, it is clear that the satisfaction of the organic or basic needs of man and of the race is a minimum set of conditions imposed on each culture. The problems set by man's nutritive, reproductive and hygienic needs must be solved. They are solved by the construction of a new; secondary or artificial environment. This environment, which is neither more nor less than culture itself, has to be permanently reproduced, maintained, and managed. This creates what might be described in the most general sense of the term as a new standard of living, which depends on the cultural level of the community, on the environment, and on the efficiency of the group. A cultural standard of living, however, means that new needs appear and new imperatives or determinants are imposed on human behaviour. (Malinowski 1944, p.37).

This is a description of a dialectical process: needs and the means by which they are satisfied generate one another. But we have already noted that this is not taking place today: modern institutions are patently not a 'dialectical' response to obviously existing needs; and the solution of this dilemma may lie in examining more closely what Malinowski means by his term 'cultural standard of living'.

From economic rationality to cultural rationality

It is plain from the above text that Malinowski regards 'culture' and 'civilisation' as the same thing, a fact revealed by the phrase 'cultural standard of living' itself. Max Weber (Weber 1920-1), however, proposed a distinction between the two, and maintained that 'culture' and 'civilisation' are related differently to the process of social development. According to Weber's conception, 'civilisation' is essentially a steady process along an ascending line, while 'culture' is a chain of events, each event unique. The process of civilisation is essentially related to the idea of 'progress', and as long as it is proceeding always means an increasing *rationalisation* of human existence. In contrast to this, the basic category of 'culture' is creation and its end is not progress, however understood, but individual self-fulfilment. If we accept this distinction, it will be plain that western Europe has plenty of 'civilisation' but that most of the deeply felt needs subsumed under the rubric 'culture' are very ill served by our 'civilising' social institutions.

We can thus see what is fundamentally wrong with the prevailing rationality: it signally fails to take into account the vital importance of individual self-fulfilment and human self-esteem. A type of rationality adequate to present-day Europe could only be one which gave full weight to these neglected things – recognising at the same time the unquestionable advantages of high civilisation: and it seems obvious to us that it should be a restored cultural rationality (Lederer 1975). In other words, *system rationality would necessarily be cultural rationality.*

It is not to be supposed – we, at least, do not suppose – that the changes which would have to occur if economic rationality were to give way to cultural, are in any sense inevitable: they are not a 'historical necessity', though historic conditions contribute to them. We do not envisage any kind of breakdown of society which would compel a shift of emphasis of the kind we have described. Cultural rationality is, as we see it, a desirable response to the problems we face: but we recognise that a will and a historic effort would be necessary for such an accommodation of culture and civilisation to one another.

We are able, however, to suggest three principles, the application of which would further a change of rationalities in the desired direction. First, the emphasis on average figures and indicators, which means homogeneousness, should give way to consideration of the differences between the situations of the groups which make up society: cultural rationality involves *differentiation*. Secondly, it should be borne in on us that nobody can offer more certain evidence of the people's real needs than the people themselves once they have learned to reflect on and to articulate them, and that this can be achieved by a reinvigoration of the institutions of participative and representative democracy. Only thus, we believe, will the second desideratum of cultural rationality be attained: *planning adequate to needs*. Thirdly, we believe that differentiation and an enhanced and reinvigorated democracy would teach society as a whole much more than it now understands about how the various spheres of life within it interact with one another: action founded on this knowledge would, we think, greatly reduce alienation and social stress. Cultural rationality, therefore, also involves *increased sensitivity*.

These are abstract bases for action, not yet proposals for specific action: it will be the task of our concluding chapter to see whether such proposals, specific 'solutions' to the problems we have been discussing, are in any way possible.

CHAPTER 12

From Ideology to Utopia: Towards Feasible Solutions for 2000

The central problem of all forecasting and all planning, which has provided a central theme of this book, was pinpointed by Karl Mannheim in the 1930s: it is to try to bridge the gap between ideological and utopian thinking. Ideology, in the sense used by Mannheim, focuses on the here and now: it sees history as an unfolding of possibilities constrained by an established system of order; it views the world as a relatively fixed place, and the burden of the past hangs heavily. In practice it concludes that there exist only marginal possibilities at most for changing the *status quo*. Utopian thinking, by contrast, sees the world in terms of a preferred future: it creates a new reality that represents a sharp break with the past; and it can thus be used, and almost certainly will be used, by those who desire radical change. Utopians will accuse idealogists of being justifiers of the *status quo*; ideologists will accuse utopians of being historically unrealistic (Friedmann 1973, p.27).

In fact, and as Mannheim recognised, neither of these modes of thought can by itself give us a total perception of how social change, even fundamental social change, can come about; yet we know that it does. Utopianism fails adequately to explain how social change arises out of the existing historical situation – it is insufficiently historicist in the sense in which we have used the word throughout this book. And neither mode of thinking can explain the central dilemma of planning: how to get from here to there, from the existing state of affairs to the desired state of affairs; nor does either provide an explanation of sudden reversals of trends or attitudes, the arrival of new questions on to the political or scientific agenda, the unexpected influence or power of new social groups.

Anyone concerned to influence the course of social change, therefore, must try to bridge this gulf. Marx did it with a theory of history resting on the metaphysical principle that any historical trend would produce its antithesis. Marxism, like any historicist theory, is confronted by the dilemma: if history unfolds according to its own rules, what influence on events can the individual have? Marx was the first to recognise the way out of this dilemma: the individual could influence events by being the first to understand the laws of social development, and thus equip himself to help the process. In Marx's words, the individual could not bring about the birth of a new social order, but he or she could shorten or lengthen the birth pangs (Marx 1867, 1961, I, p.10).

That dilemma has faced sociologists of planning ever since. Mannheim's answer is not very different from Marx's: it is to find what he calls the *principia media*, the vital development processes that lead to structural change within society – or, as John Friedmann puts it in modern systems language, the strategic system parameters. They are the levers that effect social change; they cannot be reversed, but if the forecaster-planner can discover them early he can help in the process of guiding social change. This, for Mannheim, was the planner's critical task. It demanded that he made a bridge between the ideological and the utopian thought modes, reacting between the one and the other (Friedmann 1973, pp. 32-3).

We accept that argument. But it creates for the planner-forecaster a daunting task. He must possess in large measure what C. Wright Mills calls the 'sociological imagination'. He must analyse economic, social and cultural history to try to isolate the mainsprings of social change. Above all, he must have the quality which Max Weber called substantial or value-orientated rationality (*Wertrationalität*): he must have intelligent insight into complex social systems, including their final ends. If we accept the argument of the previous chapter, contemporary European society is itself moving haltingly towards this higher kind of rationality. Dominated since World War Two by economic and political forms of rationality – themselves classic forms of the more limited functional or goal-orientated rationality (*Zweckrationalität*) concerned only with the relating of means to given ends – society is now showing the first signs of accepting a wider cultural rationality. At present these signs are few, but they are particularly associated with key groups of society who could be expected to spearhead social change. If this analysis is plausible – and we shall develop it further in this chapter – then the forecaster-planner must himself attain such rationality in order to guide society in that direction.

Since World War Two, the argument in previous chapters has run, the dominant thought mode in western society has been ideological in a very special sense. We can distinguish it by the label *scientism*. It is superficially rational, but it is not historicist, since it assumes that historical trends do not offer any fundamental constraints to human action. Rather, it asserts that once the planner has discovered how society or the economy works now, then he can mediate or regulate it in any desired way. Thus, if there is a problem of unemployment, it can be dealt with by classical Keynesian regulators; if there is a problem of alienation on the shopfloor, it can be resolved by more effective participation; if there is a problem of student revolt, it can be met by curriculum reform or membership of Senate. Our argument in this book is that measures like these may be effective as palliatives, but that the approach will be completely misleading and unreliable for long-term planning: it ignores just those deeper forces of social change which can cause sudden reversals – in mass values, in the direction of scientific research, in the political agenda – that in a wider historical context can be seen as the most important.

Historicism, we argue, provides the route out of scientism. But we are not therefore committed to one theory of historicism, nor are we asserting that complete knowledge of historical forces will ever be possible. As far as the individual or groups of individuals are concerned, historical reality will always contain a great deal that is incomprehensible and unpredictable.

Along that road we come to the notion of contradiction. The word is almost automatically associated with Marx: but it has a long history going back to Plato and Aristotle. In the course of history, it is only natural that any trend – whether in the facts of economic and social development or in the history of ideas – should in time produce a challenge, a counter-principle. Firms, political parties, individual politicians, classes in society, encourage rival groups to compete for resources or power. Left-wing ideologies will stimulate the emergence of right-wing ideologies, and vice-versa. Suburban neighbourhoods produced campus revolutionaries and campus revolutions may in turn produce a reaction in favour of the values of suburbia.

Contradiction is particularly important for planner-forecasters, for it is just what conventional planning modes, tied to the notion of trend extrapolation, tend to ignore. If one really wishes to move the levers of social change, as Mannheim advocated, one should look first at the developing counter-eddy under the apparently smooth wave of history: the disaffected group, the radical ideology (whether of right or left), the rival product or firm or nation. And that is what we have tried to do in these pages: to follow present trends just so far as to illuminate the contradictions, the conflicts, the possible counter-reactions, that may result from them. It is time now to try to bring these into some broad general structure of social change.

Key trends

First, we have to return to the central dilemma that has recurred throughout this book. In seeking to develop an historicist view of the future, do we start with the material facts of the evolution of economy and society, or with the evolution of ideas? Our answer has been that history is a seamless web: facts create values but these in turn help shape facts. Nevertheless, since we believe that values essentially arise in response to facts, there is a strong case for starting with economic and social evolution.

From the detailed accounts in the chapters of this book we believe that we can isolate six broad trends which will pose acute problems – perhaps even apparently insoluble problems – for European society of the 1980s and 1990s.

First and foremost among these is a deepening *international economic crisis*. The European economy has been developed to a unique degree on the basis of mass-produced industrial goods, a large proportion of which are sold internally within the frontiers of western Europe, but which also have to provide the payments which are needed for imports of vital food and raw materials. Increasingly, the production of these goods has come under the control of multi-national corporations. Aided by modern well-equipped factories and by pliant workers recently recruited from agriculture, European producers of consumer durables have achieved high productivity levels and an enviable standard of quality control, enabling them to compete vigorously in world markets. But more recently, our analysis has suggested, European competitive power has been threatened. On the one hand, as the oil crisis shows, European producers are dangerously dependent on imported raw materials from countries that may decide to develop their own manufacturing outlets – as is already occurring, for instance, with the car industry in Iran. On the other hand, recently industrialising nations (such as Iran, Korea and Brazil) have in even greater measure all the advantages that Europe possessed a quarter-century ago: modern factories equipped with automatic machinery, plus a highly-disciplined and weakly-unionized workforce. At the same time, mounting evidence demonstrates that in the advanced industrial countries themselves – not merely in Europe but also in North America – young industrial workers are becoming growingly disenchanted with the monotonous, soulless character of assembly-line production. Thus the advanced industrial nations are finding it increasingly difficult to compete with their new competitors. For them, it seems, the post-industrial age is truly arriving. But the question remains: how do they now make a living?

The signs of this crisis, it must be admitted, are as yet partial and faint. Profitability in European industry is everywhere declining; that can be interpreted as a mere cyclical phenomenon of the mid-1970s, not as a deeper structural phenomenon. Our argument is that it is in fact structural, that this can already be seen in weaker economies such as those of Italy and Britain, and that within quite a short time it will affect the stronger European economies also. Shortages of raw materials are not yet acute: again, our argument is that these shortages will begin to bite only later, sometime in the 1980s and 1990s, as the newly-industrialising countries begin to demand materials and energy on an exponentially-rising curve. In any event, as observers like Robert Heilbroner have eloquently argued, such an increasing rate of resource consumption would inevitably lead to ecological breakdown sometime in the next century (Heilbroner 1975, pp. 47-55). So in one way or another, world industrialisation must lead to world conflict – not only in the economic sphere, but also, as critical supplies of materials and energy become more and more scarce, in the political and military spheres.

This, then, is the second problem area: *world conflict concerning resource use*. We have suggested that it will not take the form of a world conflagration: the prospect is rather one of limited wars associated with guerilla armies – on the model of the Viet Cong or the Angolan MPLA – in areas of the world, such as the Middle East or the Zambian copperbelt, that contain critical concentrations of industrially vital raw materials. The pattern of such conflicts will be by no means simple, since nationalist movements will often be at war with each other in the same country (as in Lebanon or Angola), and world power blocks will be found to give moral or even material support to one or the other. There seems a strong likelihood, though, that all such movements will be tempted to put pressure on the nations of the advanced world by acts of terrorism and sabotage. The prospect, then, for the countries of Europe is one of increasing personal insecurity (Heilbroner 1975, p.43).

The third problem has already been mentioned in the discussion of industrial prospects; but its ramifications extend far outside the industrial domain. It is the apparently *increasing alienation** of many

---

* Here 'alienation' is used in its general sense (cf. page 50).

people, especially young people, from the whole system. Essentially, they are rejecting the scheme of values that sustained their parents and grandparents. They are no longer willing to sell themselves to an organisational machine – whether to stand on an assembly line making industrial goods, or to sit in a typing pool producing standardised letters – in order simply to make money to pursue the goals of an acquisitive society. Rather, they are saying that their central objective is to live a satisfying life – which includes satisfying work. Again, the signs here are partial and vague: they include the behaviour of younger workers in countries such as Sweden, and the evidence from the United States that the values of college youth are now diffused far into the young blue-collar working population. We would argue that they are the auguries of a possible mass movement.

The fourth problem is almost the antithesis of the third. It is *the decline and even the collapse of the older agrarian society of Europe*, with its stress on the mutual aid which members of the same extended family provided for each other, and on the security and trust that was only feasible through the face-to-face acquaintance of all in a village. The result of that collapse is that vital functions, once performed naturally by family members or fellow villagers for each other, now come to be identified as problems to be resolved only through professional bureaucracies. Education and preparation for life become the province of the nursery school, the school system, the college or university plus their supporting bureaucracies. Health becomes the specialised province of doctors, nurses, hospitals and again their supporting bureaucracies. Production of food and other necessities becomes the monopoly of agricultural or manufacturing industries and their supporting distributive networks. Increasingly, stages in the life cycle come to be defined as problems – the child development problem, the problem of the young mother, the geriatric problem – each requiring a professional bureaucracy to cope with it. The family, now redefined as the nuclear family of husband, wife and children, ceases to exist as its members find more and more of their satisfactions outside the home (Commission of the European Communities 1977). Old people are isolated in senior citizens' colonies or institutions, young people in campus towns. As women assert their right to liberation, career and family maintenance come ever more into conflict.

Related closely to these problems is another: that of *access to information*. There is widespread dissatisfaction with the traditional structure of education, which was inherited from an elitist society and which seems ill-adapted to a rapidly changing world. At the same time, the quantity of information received by the ordinary citizen appears almost out of control; but he has little chance of regulating it or using it for his own advantage. Whether he considers˘ his own newspaper or television set or his child's education, this typical citizen may well think that the control of information is again in the hands of a professional bureaucracy responsible to almost no-one.

Lastly, there is perhaps a growing threat of *polarisation of the entire society*. Though all to some extent feel alienated from real contact with their fellows and from society, some groups – the immigrant workers, the unemployed school-leavers, the low-skill workers who cannot find jobs, the old – may come to feel permanently and irretrievably excluded. As we have emphasised, it is hardly in the nature of such groups to unite in some kind of revolutionary movement. But if their discontent continues to simmer beneath the surface, we should expect it to erupt from time to time in demonstrations, revolts, occupations and general petty disorder. In this way, as in others, the immediate future is hardly likely to prove serene.

Formative ideas

These are some of the key problems of the coming decades as we see them. The list, it may well be said, is hardly an original one. With that we could only agree. The more one explores the literature of future speculation, the more one is struck by the remarkable similarity of the analyses contained there. That might indicate simply a tired and conventional quality of thinking – though that is a charge hard to prove against writers such as Illich, Mumford, Schumacher, Heilbroner, and Friedmann. We would prefer to argue that it shows how clear the broad underlying trends are.

It is the same with the answers. Again and again, one is struck by the similarity of the basic ideas for the transformation of society to meet the challenges ahead. The precise terminology may differ from author to author, but the essential concepts are the same. We find ourselves in substantial agreement with them.

Many of these ideas could be attacked, and have been attacked, as utopian in the pejorative sense. They seem to suppose a reconstruction of society that is too radical to be realistic. In terms of the analysis earlier in this chapter, they do not show how it would be possible to get from the here and now to the desired future. We are by no means convinced of that argument, for two reasons. First, we think that it ignores the vital principle of contradiction, or reaction. As John Friedmann tellingly suggests, anyone in 1960 who would have forecast that by the mid-1970s California would have seriously considered legislation to ban the private car would have been regarded as eccentric if not a lunatic (Friedmann 1973, p.130). Yet such a thing happened. Secondly, we are not asserting that such changes, or any changes, could come overnight. What we are talking about is a process of diffusion of ideas from thought-leaders to followers and then to the general public, whereby – as we argued earlier in this book – ideas emerge into Good Currency. Therefore, we think that these ideas – unconventional though they may be – need to be taken seriously.

The first is that society, above all in the advanced industrial world, will need to become much more *resource-conserving*, particularly in relation to energy supplies. We do not know, nor do we believe anyone now knows, what such an energy-conserving society would be like. But we can develop some partial notions first from the few studies that exist of energy consumption patterns in different urban societies, and secondly from speculations by some of the more utopian writers in this field. We know, for instance, that different cities now have very different energy consumption levels, ranging from 25 Megajoules per head per year in Singapore or 34 in Hong Kong to 328 in Cincinnati, 331 in Los Angeles or a record 740 in Fairbanks, Alaska (Kalma and Byrne 1976, p.5). These differences at national level seem to be related clearly to Gross National Product per head and to population density, though the relation is less good for cities in the same country. Tropical cities seem to have lower consumption levels, per head, than temperate cities, though different per capita incomes confuse the comparison; island economies seem to have low consumption levels (compare West Berlin with 67, against Nordrhein-Westfalen with 287).

Some tentative conclusions can be drawn. The first objective should be to increase thermal efficiency: to get greater energy expenditure out of a given input. At present, an official American study suggests that overall three-quarters of all energy inputs are wasted, and in domestic heating this may be as much as 99 per cent and more. Home heating and transportation should be the main targets here. Secondly, energy consumption can be drastically reduced by cutting down the amount of transportation of both people and goods, and by transferring to modes that use few energy resources – especially bicycles, which according to Illich will triple the mobility of the unaided human being while posing no threat to the mobility of others (Illich 1974, pp. 29-30, 74). This last point is particularly important; for above a certain critical average speed, which Illich claims to be 15 miles per hour (24 km/hr), greater mobility to some will mean reduced mobility to the rest. Thirdly, as a corollary, the aim should be to optimise the size and distribution of facilities in terms of the social objectives they are designed to serve. It does suggest that in most circumstances, small units well-distributed among the population are preferable to large units requiring long journeys to reach them. Offices, shops and factories should all be planned so as to be readily reachable on foot or by bicycle; the era of the giant factory, the huge office, even the great urban complex is perhaps over (Heilbroner 1975, p.139). This, as Kalma and Byrne recognise, may involve a clash with existing patterns of human behaviour; but that behaviour has been grounded in a period of apparently unlimited cheap energy, so that here as elsewhere a major psychological adaptation may be needed (Kalma and Byrne 1976, p.14).

Lastly, the strong suggestion is that, as far as possible, low-energy communication needs to be substituted for high-energy transportation. Clearly, this can be true only of the transportation of information, not of the movement of goods. But, given the stress on service activities that automatically follows from a resource-scarce economy, this becomes an important consideration. It underlines a point made by Illich and others: that the aim of a new resource-conscious technology is not to return to some medieval or rural arcadia where the innovations of the last two centuries are eliminated, but rather to use those pieces of technology appropriate to the new situation. That could include the conscious development and encouragement of new communications devices to substitute for bodily movement and face-to-face communication across long distances, such as the conference telephone, the videotape and closed-circuit television, and the home computer. But these devices have other roles than the saving of energy, and we shall need to return to them.

The resource-saving society, therefore, is likely to be a great deal more efficient than now. Thus it can be fully competitive with other economies still based on economic rationality, even though its decision-makers have regard for social and ecological factors. It will use some resources more generously (building materials) in order to use other resources a great deal more frugally (energy for home heating). It will substitute energy-saving for energy-consuming machinery (small cars with less performance but more economy). It will stress less transportation, above all less long-distance transportation. It will plan cities so that many more activities can be combined within walking or bicycling distances. It will develop communications devices to the same end. And almost certainly, it will make a massive shift away from the production of things to the production of services, ideas and entertainment, in activities like justice, health, education and the arts (Heilbroner 1975, p.87). In a literal sense, it will be a post-industrial economy. But notice here that services, too, can lay massive claims on resources: consider the education programme. What is needful, first of all, is the calculation of economic input-output tables that show the energy and resource needs of each economic sector. For this is an essential prelude to development of cheaper ways of doing the same thing.

A second major feature of the future society, to borrow Illich's phrase, is that it will be *tool-using* rather than *machine-used*. Or, in Schumacher's equally celebrated words, it will use *intermediate technology*: a set of instruments vastly superior to the primitive technology of the past but much simpler, cheaper and freer than the present technology of the affluent world. Schumacher also calls it self-help technology or people's technology, since it can be readily accessible to all; and for him its first use must be in the countries of the Third World (Schumacher 1973a, p.154). This also is very much Illich's notion; but for both authors, the idea goes further, to affect the quality of work everywhere. For Illich, the essential feature of tools is that they allow what he terms convivial work:

> ... autonomous and creative intercourse among persons, and the intercourse of persons with their environment; and this in contrast to the conditioned response of persons to the demands made upon them by others, and by a man-made environment (Illich 1973, p.11).

Tools, in other words, liberate the individual and allow him better to work to shape his own environment, in contrast to machines which enslave the individual to labour for money. They did this once before, in what Mumford calls the polytechnic craft society of the Middle Ages, in which

> ... Playful relaxation, sexual delight, domestic tenderness, esthetic stimulation, were not spatially or mentally separated completely from the work in hand (Mumford 1971, p.137).

All that was destroyed in the course of the Industrial Revolution, when a vast cultural resource of craft skills was wiped out. But there was no need for this; and, as Illich argues, the time is now ripe for its return. The point is that quite recently new technologies have arrived which again give the individual autonomy. Tools can now be given to laymen to allow them to cure sickness that formerly needed the expertise of professionals and their attendant bureaucracies.

Simple public trucks, or bicycles, can give everyone mobility. Self-built do-it-yourself housing can allow everyone to be reasonably housed at a minimum cost. Voluntary learning, or access to information, allows everyone to acquire appropriate skills without elaborate formal education and the attendant ritual of certificates and qualifications. Many quite new tools – the typewriter, the copying machine, the camera, the tape recorder – are essentially convivial, in Illich's meaning, though they may often have been used for non-convivial (or anti-convivial) labour up to now (Illich 1973, pp. 33-40, 64).

The idea of a resource-conserving society based on parsimony (Heilbroner 1975, p.139), and the idea of a tool-using society seeking autonomy for the human being, come together in yet a third key concept: *Quality.*

> ... If you want to build a factory, or fix a motorcycle, or set a nation right without getting stuck, then classical, structured, dualistic subject-object knowledge, although necessary, isn't enough. You have to have some feel for the quality of the work. You have to have a sense of what's good. *That* is what carries you forward. This sense isn't something you're born with, although you *are* born with it. It's not just 'intuition', not just unexplainable 'skill' or 'talent'. It's the direct result of contact with basic *reality*. Quality, which dualistic reason has in the past tended to conceal (Pirsig 1974, p.284).

This notion of quality comes from within, and the quality of society can be made right only if individual values are first of all right:

> ... if we are going to reform the world, and make it a better place to live in, the way to do it is not to talk about relationships of a political nature, which are inevitably dualistic, full of subjects and objects and their relationship to one another; or with programmes full of things for other people to do ... The social values are right only if the individual values are right. The place to improve the world is first in one's own heart and head and hands, and then work outward from there. Other people can talk about how to expand the destiny of mankind. I just want to talk about how to fix a motorcycle. I think that what I have to say has more lasting value (Pirsig 1974, p.297).

For Pirsig, quality has disappeared from the 'primary America' which is the modern industrial nation of 'freeways and jet flights and TV and movie spectaculars' because there people have become objects, isolated in lonely attitudes of objectivity. It is only in the older America that people still relate to their environment. Yet – here Pirsig makes a point similar to Illich's – technology can actually be used to attack the problem:

> ... technology could be used to destroy the evil. A person who knows how
> to fix motorcycles – with Quality – is less likely to run short of friends
> than one who doesn't. And they aren't going to see him as some kind of
> object either (Pirsig 1974, p.357).

'Quality', for Pirsig, is thus a philosophical concept, and those
who connect with it have what the Greeks called *enthousiasmos*, filled
with *theos* or God or quality. It is almost the same as Illich's
conviviality. It has to do with people's relation to their work and with
their simultaneous relation to other people. It is close to what
Schumacher identifies as the first two principles of Buddhist
economics: to give a person the chance to use and develop his
faculties, and to join others in a common task (Schumacher 1973a,
Ch. 4). Thus, coming from very different starting points, three
people – a British economist working for the National Coal Board, a
Viennese-born priest working in Mexico and an American
philosopher-novelist – have arrived at almost identical notions about
the essential principles of social reconstruction.

These notions, again, connect with another: the idea of *social and
economic life reorganised in small-scale units*. Partly this follows naturally
from earlier considerations. A resource-conserving society, since it
must minimise movement of people and goods, will naturally be
small and as far as possible – in a modern world – self-sufficient. A
tool-using society will allow the dismemberment of large
bureaucratic structures, and so will allow production to occur in
small units again. If people are to discover the principle of Quality
for themselves, they are more likely to do so in small groups. But
above and beyond this, small-scale organisation is needed to reduce
alienation and to allow people to come autonomously to grips with
rapid change.

Thus, in the proposal of the psychiatrist Ivor Browne, the only
way of restructuring society to allow adequate personal development
of the individual is to find some scale of organisation between the
isolated individual and the mass collective society. This could be a
group of adults and children of all ages, not necessarily blood-
related: people or whole families might move freely from one living
group to another, so long as this conformed to a basic cellular
network. (The *kibbutzim* of Israel, as well as traditional bodies like
colleges and less traditional grouping like modern communes, offer
possible examples.) Such a society could evolve logically and
naturally out of the women's liberation movement, Browne argues,

because that movement must cause the traditional nuclear family to disappear. Within such a small-unit society – echoing Illich – the techniques and skills for living would no longer be monopolised by professional or technical bureaucracies, but would be freely and flexibly available to groups of people. Many jobs now done by specialists, ranging from garbage collection to social work, could be done by ordinary people perhaps on a part-time basis: the notion of a job as a separate full-time activity would disappear from many walks of life (Browne 1975).

Such a basic unit for a reorganised society would, in Browne's view, be one small enough to allow people to relate to each other as individuals, but big enough to perform essential functions such as education, housing, welfare and employment. It might contain between 30,000 and 50,000 people – the size recommended by Ebenezer Howard as long ago as 1898 for his proposed garden cities, which were realised many years later in the British new towns programme (Howard 1946). It should be divided up (again as Howard proposed) into units or cells that provided for direct face-to-face contact. And it should have some definable barrier or membrane – not merely physical but also socio-psychological – differentiating it from the outside world, a function Howard supplied by a wide green belt. A concept like this might be thought utopian, and indeed that charge was brought against Howard. But his concept has proved anything but utopian: in practice, as Howard always argued they would, the British new towns have proved exceptionally good social investments.

The idea of small-scale organisation can, however, be taken further, into the whole structure of decision-making. For John Friedmann this is the essence of what he calls Transactive Planning: a style based on translating knowledge to action through an unbroken series of interpersonal relations. It demands the capacity for dialogue, of a kind now only generally found among members of the same family or close friends. Transactive Planning, for Friedmann, would be organised through a cellular structure of working groups consisting at most of twelve people and connected through flexible channels of communication (Friedmann 1973, pp. 171-97). Such groups would be temporary, self-appointed or representative in character, self-guiding, and responsible for a certain sphere of action. They would be readily permeated by new members, but once they become too big they would automatically subdivide. They would be based on effective, continuous learning, which constantly confronted theory with the reality of experience – within which the professional planner would merely be a kind of

gentle educator basing his style on that of the Tao: bend (not
destroy) social rules, appear to do nothing (but learn), do not
compel learning, lead but do not be master. It requires an
extraordinary leap of the imagination to see such a self-guiding
society in practice. And the details – especially of conflict resolution
where parts related to wider wholes – are as yet unclear. Indeed, one
of the critical unanswered questions about all such utopias is that of
hierarchical organisation and the transmission of decisions up and
down. True, in a low-energy low-movement society, some of these
kinds of conflict might have lessened or even disappeared – but not
surely altogether.

Such a society would depend very greatly on the communications
linkages between the many small units. They alone could provide a
way of aggregating or disaggregating the many decisions or
suggestions that must be passed up and down the hierarchy. Here
we return to a central notion of Illich: that many recent
technological developments, now used as machines, could become
flexible tools giving people greater control over their environments.
Television, now organised on a one-to-many basis, could be
reorganised on a many-to-many basis by the development of video-
recording machines and cable television. Thus many different small
groups could present their views and argue their points, and the
responses of whole societies could be fed in via telephone responses –
or, eventually, through two-way cable television. Home computers,
drastically reduced in price by the late twentieth century and
communicating over ordinary telephone lines, could achieve an even
more sophisticated many-to-many set of communications channels.
In this way, small groups of people could, for instance, begin to
design their own built environment:

> ... The reason why film and traditional television have been unsuccessful
> as design tools is that they operate one-way, and in the case of television
> (with the exception of closed-circuit educational systems and amateur
> television clubs) the public is prohibited from access. In the UK and in
> other countries operating 'public TV', the medium is not public but
> private. As a creative medium it resembles the state of the printed word
> in England in 1643 when the public was compelled by law to obtain a
> license for the printing and sale of books (Nicholson and Schreiner 1973,
> p.44).

Active community decision-making, as Nicholson stresses, is
possible only where communities have access to, and locally
originate, live programming. A two-way communications system is
for him one in which there is a dialogue where all parties have equal

access to the medium and where the user can assemble his or her message out of loose parts (such as words or visual images). We are a long way from that ideal in contemporary European society.

Correspondingly, as we have seen in this book, we are a long way from decentralised community control – whether in the city, the factory or the school. Indeed, in the last few decades European society seems to have been moving in the opposite direction. So it is not very easy to know what it would be like to live in a society where power over the human environment was given back to small groups:

> ... We can answer this by looking at the societies and communities where this is so, such as the many historic societies, and some modern tribal societies, and the communes and the *barriadas* to which we have referred, but it is more difficult to imagine the adaptive changes that would be needed in a contemporary city which is largely fixed (Nicholson and Schreiner 1973, p.22).

As witness of that fact, notice that most descriptions of a decentralised society are either placeless, in that they seem to exist in a locational vacuum, or follow the traditional utopian pattern in being new communities. As with a resource-conserving society, so with a decentralised decision-making society, *we cannot easily imagine what it would be like.*

Indeed, perhaps there is an impossible contradiction: perhaps the whole notion is after all utopian in the perjorative sense. Robert Heilbroner has argued that, in a society of resource crisis, the most obvious response would be not a freely and locally democratic society, but a highly centralised and autocratic one appealing to a childlike belief in leadership and perhaps based on the nation-state as a psychologically-valid surrogate for the family (Heilbroner 1975, pp. 106-9). But he offers one intriguing possibility: that such a society could, as in China today, be highly egalitarian-structured in small groups while still being intensely conformist. Indeed, the dream of the democrats – that their local groups could somehow achieve harmony by a process of rational discussion – seems to ignore the fact that, in an era of scarcity, the rich would be defending the *status quo* while the less rich would still be committed to getting more of the material good things. To overcome this would seem to need some mass psychological transformation in a very short time – a transformation that is not easy to conceive of without a very highly centralised control over communications. So we come back to our starting dilemma: the missing connection between the here-and-now and the imagined future.

That connection could come only through a change in

consciousness resulting from crisis. A society based on the principle of parsimony would necessarily be somewhat puritanical, though not in a joyless sense: it might resemble some experimental communes of the present time. It would rely heavily on inner discipline and harmony among its members. The right parallel perhaps is seventeenth century New England, though without the bigotry and intolerance which marked that society at its worst. Europe 2000 may be some way on the road towards such a society.

Could such an economy compete with other parts of the world still based on economic rationality? The argument is that it could, because in a wide sense it is more efficient in use of resources. By this time, indeed, the more recently industrialised countries may be paying a fearful price – and may in consequence be willing to follow the lead set by Europe. But first a change in values, expressed through political action, would have had to occur. We cannot posit how that would happen because we do not know, nor does anyone. One of the objects of this book is simply to put the possibility on to the political agenda.

Towards 2000

We now have to make the effort to think the unthinkable. It may be easier if we stress that the Europe of the year 2000 promises to be a *transitional* society between the one we know and a quite different one – at least as different, perhaps, as ours is from the society of the middle ages. The reaction against our present organisational forms and our present social priorities will have gone a good deal further, but it will be no means be complete: too many people gained too much from that older society, too many more people still wanted to join in the gains, to give it up without a struggle. And nostalgia may be a very prevalent emotion in Europe 2000. Just as to the bourgeoisie of Europe the years immediately before 1914 seemed a golden age, so the wide strata of society may come to regard the 1960s as the apogee of a certain kind of civilisation. But events will surely have exerted their own logic.

The first change is that, whether through the operation of market forces, governmental intervention or a combination of both, many of the basic resources of life promise to be more expensive, more hard to obtain, in 2000 than now. That particularly applies to energy and to other non-renewable resources. So new homes everywhere will be designed to produce their own energy, and to conserve what they produce or bring in, to a much greater degree than now. Similarly transportation will be reduced in amount and changed in character.

People will live more of their lives in small place-bounded societies. When they do travel it will be by economic modes, such as small cars or airships. They will communicate more by electronics and less by face-to-face contact.

The second is that within these societies they will tend to work in rather small units, such as workshops or small offices of a few people. A number of such units will be found within a local community, offering the possibility of a wide range of work without moving them far from home. Indeed, partly for energy-conserving purposes, homes and workplaces will probably tend to be combined under one roof (or one set of roofs) rather as the different functions of the traditional farmstead were combined in contiguous buildings. The group of people living together and manning these various workplaces could be described as an extended, non-blood-related family or a commune group. It will contain a nucleus of nuclear families which dissolve and combine for different purposes, plus a number of more transient members.

The third is that these groups will necessarily use a rather different technology from that which we recognise today. Though many of the basic elements will be identical – machine tools, presses, lathes, typewriters, copying machines, tape recorders – they will be used as ancillary aids to work rather than substitutes for labour. And many people will do more than one job, combining intellectual work with craft skills and with work of general social value (such as looking after children). This general sharing of work will serve to break down the present barriers of class and sex. But, in any event, the end products of such work will be quite different from those today. A much smaller part of total human activity will be applied to making mass-produced consumer goods, which will be scarcer and made to last. Conversely, more people will be involved in craft industry using minimal materials and maximum labour; in the arts and entertainment; and in education. These will be the basic skills which the advanced nations of Europe sell to the rest of the world, since by then their capacity to compete in mass-production industry will be minimal.

The fourth is that the nature of both rural and urban life will change. Though a large part of European agriculture will continue to follow the path of mechanisation and higher productivity in order to meet the challenge of world hunger, there will be a powerful movement in the opposite direction. Greater understanding of and sensitivity towards ecological damage by pesticides and other chemical aids will lead to a new concern for natural regeneration of the land – and thus to a return to mixed farming, with a greater demand for labour. This will be especially the case on the medium-grade lands less suitable for mechanised farming in the upland areas of Europe. Here there may well be a large-scale return to the land by people who combine part-time farming with a range of other activities, including crafts and services. The new communications technologies, with their opportunity to perform a wide range of jobs away from the cities, should be a powerful stimulus here.

The cities will continue to decentralise as they have for the past two centuries. But there will be both a quantitative and a qualitative change in that growth. A stable population, plus a concern for qualitative economic growth, will lead to a lessening of the demand for land, and the new emphasis on ecological considerations will lead to a much more cautious policy on the release of land for urban development. It is more likely that many urbanites will migrate some distance from the city, where the new technologies will allow them to work in close contact with it. Within the city, there will be a much greater emphasis on rehabilitation and regeneration of the existing stock of buildings. The pace of physical change in European cities will therefore be much slower than in the quarter-century after World War Two.

The fifth change is that the nature of industry will subtly alter. Qualitative growth will mean an actual speeding-up of the process whereby European industry specialises in the lines of production, and in the productive methods, which it is best suited to supply. That means a greater emphasis on service industry, which is a generous employer of labour and an economical user of material resources; on science-based industry, which employs a great deal of skilled labour to work on rather valuable semi-processed materials and components; on research and development of all kinds, but especially focussed on the new resource-conserving 'soft technologies'; and on craft industry. A central feature of all these kinds of industry is that they can be decentralised – and indeed may best function when decentralised – into rather small units having a great deal of autonomy over such matters as productive emphasis, production methods and charging. These units may or may not remain members of larger productive organisations; whatever the case, such large organisations will almost certainly tend to be reorganised on a federal basis by the year 2000. Within each small productive unit, all members will have their say in the management of the enterprise, and may indeed have a great deal of responsibility for keeping it viable. But, at the same time, the present narrow emphasis on economic rationality will have been replaced by a wider social responsibility enforced through regulation or changing systems; and some at least of the entrepreneurs within each organisation and unit will need to have special regard for these wider matters.

The sixth is that this will be rather a serious, concerned society. It will be very concerned with its own survival in the face of unprecedented challenges. Though there will still be joy, there will be little frivolity. Though it may be quite highly decentralised in its decision-making structures, there will be a considerable degree of inner conformity. Above all, the society will be puritanical in being intensely concerned with the pursuit of individual quality in man's relations with his work, his environment and his fellows.

One day in Europe 2000

We have said that we cannot imagine exactly what it would be like. But nevertheless we should try.

There will be no typical European family of the year 2000, because the European economy and European society will be in a state of transition. Many Europeans in the year 2000 will lead lives very like the lives of 1976: one has only to compare the life styles of 1952 with those of 1976 to see that. The chief difference between those two dates, twenty-four years apart, has been one of material affluence. A few more or less new technologies have appeared – the computer for instance. But most of the story is the diffusion of material goods, already invented and available by 1952, from the richest members of society to the less rich. Accompanying that diffusion has been a spread of mass education and a marked increase in expectations. Everywhere, the net result has been a more egalitarian society based on mass consumerism. But for most people the change has been fairly imperceptible.

We expect the same to be true of the twenty-four years from 1976 to 2000. No cataclysm will occur. Many people will find their lives changed subtly and imperceptibly. Having already identified the key changes, we should now stress change in what follows. But in doing this, we should again repeat that for many the transition will bring more of what has already been occurring to them in 1976.

One typical European family of the year 2000 – we can call them the Dumills or the Deuxmilles or the Zweitausends – live in a converted eighteenth-century farmhouse on the edge of a hill area between 70 and 150 kilometers from a major city: we can imagine them in the Peak District or the Pentlands, or the Ardennes or the Eifel or the Monts de Morvan or the Sierra de Guadaramma. Built in an energy-conscious age, this farmhouse has properties of insulation which make it very apposite to a new age of conservation. But, with the aid of a government grant under the EEC Energy Conservation Act 1982, our family have converted it into a Low Energy Living Unit (LELU). They have further insulated it to reduce heat loss. They have installed a windmill for electric power, though they can still draw from the electric grid. The recycle farm refuse for fuel. And in summer they can draw on solar energy.

The farm is one of a group forming a small rural hamlet. It is occupied by a number of families that moved into them and reoccupied them after they were abandoned in the late 1950s, during the great age of European agricultural depopulation. Lower down the valley are other such family groups, forming a loose cluster of about fifty nuclear families or about two hundred people. Together with other such clusters and the nearest village they form a sufficiently large group to support a village primary school and community centre.

To speak of families, though, gives a wrong impression. Many of the children have broken away during adolescence and have joined other groupings, sometimes with other adults, sometimes with each other. The main point is that each person has a number of primary affinities: with a blood-related group, with a work-group, with one or more groups of like-minded people. He or she may shift groups from time to time, depending on individual needs and on personal development.

During the day almost every member of every living group is involved in some kind of work: this applies to the youngest and to the oldest in the community. The young may be involved in a pre-school group in the care of an adult, who may perform that role only one or two days a week. The old may be indeed performing that very role, or doing ancillary work in shops or offices. Some very old people are still employed in positions of responsibility, as are some surprisingly young people – for age has less significance in this society, where retirement has been abolished. The critical point about these groups, and about the whole society, is the extreme flexibility of the roles. People do not follow lifetime careers. Very few do just one job from nine to five. Instead, people mix different roles. They may be postmen or milkmen in the mornings, students in the afternoon and entertainers in the evening. Similarly, they may be managers at 25, students again at 35, and craftsmen at 45.

Consequently, this is even less of a stratified society than was the European society of 1976. Not only have traditional barriers like middle-class/working-class or white-collar/blue-collar been broken down; traditional skill categories have gone too, because the emphasis is on adaptibility and free entry. Anyone who chooses, provided he or she has the talent, can aspire at any time to become a craftsman or a master chef, a professor or a long-distance truck driver. And, consequently, not only the prestige but also the differential payments for different jobs have been largely eroded. The differentials are related only to the disagreeability of the job on the one hand, the length of training required on the other. So, over a lifetime, given that everyone shares the more and the less agreeable jobs, earnings are roughly equalised. So are prestige and interest; and in this way, alienation is sharply diminished.

Most of these jobs can be done locally. There are a couple of distinguished restaurants which employ a score of chefs; there is a research institute serving as an input channel to the Open University of Europe; there are a great variety of small craft workshops which work up wool, leather, locally smelted metals and a variety of other indigenous materials. But one critical point is that most activities are now freed from locational constraints. The two restaurants serve some diners directly; they serve many more by exporting their deep-frozen gourmet meals, which are famous across Europe and beyond. And their boast is that they largely depend on locally-produced farm materials. The university teachers write course material in their own homes; they broadcast from the local television studio; and they conduct seminars and tutorials by conference phone and videophone. All of them can communicate directly from home with the Eurodata network, which can supply them with microfiche facsimiles of any book or paper within seconds. Similarly the craftsmen get technical information from the same source, and can communicate with the National Crafts Centre when .they want advice. The master chefs write textbooks in their spare time, and similarly broadcast cookery lessons both to the general public and to apprentice chefs in schools all over Europe. And all this without leaving the local community.

This is thus a more service-oriented economy than the Europe of 1976. But it still contains a considerable volume of manufacturing. However, much of this work is carried out in a radically different way. Because of increasing discontent in big urban factories in the 1970s and early 1980s, expressing itself in strikes and disruptions and poor quality, the big multinational companies have decentralised many of their operations to small workshop units consisting of between ten to fifty people, which are given a great deal of autonomy; in many ways they represent a return to the domestic system of industry characteristic of the age before the Industrial Revolution. Many of these workshops are in the new rural communes, where they employ a variety of people – students taking time out, women with small children seeking part-time employment, older people, people who want a holiday from urban life and who are combining farming and factory life. Many of the workshops are indeed parts of farm communities. Most of them produce goods of high quality and great durability which indeed is a requirement for European industry under the EEC Industrial Quality Law of 1992. They have varying degrees of freedom to buy their own materials from sources outside the organisation. Some, indeed, have been given virtual independence, and produce their goods simply to the specifications of the manufacturers – specifications which come from Eurodata via the microfiche system – selling them to the main manufacturers in competition with many other small rural works. Most of the components for the car industry, for instance, are now made in this way. And in this particular commune there are assembly plants which produce Fords and Volkswagens by craft methods. The final products, known as Craft Cars, cost more than the factory-made product but are preferred by many customers on the ground of their reliability. Because they have exceptionally long life, these cars are given preferential tax concessions under the Materials Conservation Act 1988.

Most members of the community do some work on the farms, especially at peak periods such as harvest, when there is a general custom that other work stops. Farming in an area like this is necessarily mixed farming and it is quite labour-intensive, so that overall more people work on farms in the year 2000 than in 1976. Further, as with industry, farmers must now have regard to the wider consequences of their work. The use of pesticides and other chemical aids is carefully regulated, and there are incentives for farming methods that maintain or restore the ecological balance. Under these regulations there has been a strong emphasis on natural farming methods and on reafforestation, for instance. And these farmers meet more of their own needs and those of their neighbours than did the farmers of the area in 1976.

Such a dispersed rural pattern of life, it might be thought, must place big demands on resources for transportation. But those demands have been limited in a number of ways. First, because of the varied character of the rural population it is able to satisfy so many more of its social and cultural needs locally. Secondly, the development of information technology has been so rapid that many needs are met in this way without having to travel at all. (And because the new technology is two-way, the people have much greater control over the information they receive than the less information-rich society of the 1970s). Thirdly, because the age of expensive energy has created its own response in the form of more energy-conserving vehicles and organisational arrangements. To move about locally, most villagers use small mopeds in which the motor is used only as a supplementary device. To move longer distances, they rely on a system of shared rides whereby anyone leaving the village is under an obligation to offer seats in his car, truck or van. In return, he receives tickets for a national lottery – a system developed in Poland as long ago as in the 1970s. In this way, *Europe 2000* actually manages to generate rather more person-kilometers of travel than the Europe of 1976 with fewer energy demands.

Perhaps the most striking change about this society is that it marks a partial return to the extended family, or caring group, of earlier ages. It is in a real sense a community. Within it, very many more tasks are performed by people simply as members of the community, often on a part-time basis, without the need for an exclusive professionalism. There are many more people in this society who can be a teacher, a nurse, a policeman if the need arises. Roles are less well-defined; people are again generalists rather than specialists. And nowhere is this more important than in the division of responsibilities between the sexes. Women and men share the task of child-rearing to a much greater degree than today – and this involves not merely the immediate parents, but a great variety of other helpers of all ages. Indeed, this becomes a most important responsibility for the older members of the community.

Half an hour or an hour's drive away by shared taxi or truck, life in the city continues on a more traditional track. But here, too, the tendency is to stress much more the local neighbourhood and the group. The urban economy, too, has been deeply infused with the idea of small, autonomous, self-directing production units. People are organising their urban lives round the local ward or commune. Physically, the city has seen much less change in the last quarter of the twentieth century than in the period 1950-1975. The slower population growth, the emphasis on qualitative growth of the economy, the new concern for ecological impact and for conservation of the urban fabric have all tended to restrict the amount of urban destruction and reconstruction. That means that the city feels an older place than in the 1960s and 1970s. It could in consequence be a drabber and a more dilapidated place – unless positive attempts were made to restore its fabric.

Many trends, in fact, have worked to the city's disadvantage in the last quarter century. Transportation costs, especially by public transport, have risen. Housing costs and pressures have not greatly diminished, due to the tendency of the population to split into smaller households. Above all, terrorism and guerilla warfare have caused gradual demoralisation causing many people and businesses to flee the city. Among those who remain, there is a disproportionate concentration of dysfunctional groups, some of whom present acute social problems in the form of unemployment and crime. So many have left the city, taking their work with them. The difference is that they have no longer gone to nearby suburbs of the city; they have fled into the countryside. Some, as we just saw, have gone right outside the city's sphere of influence. Even headquarters offices have begun to decentralise to small country towns within easy reach of the white-collar workers who prefer to live in such places. Others have migrated shorter distances, to smaller towns still within the city's sphere of influence. There they live in what are, in effect, poly-nuclear urban clusters of towns, very much on the model that Ebenezer Howard suggested in his pioneer book on Garden Cities (Howard 1946, 1898). So, within every European country – the south following a trend set earlier by the north – large cities have lost people and jobs relative to medium sized and small towns.

These people live in European nation-states that are for the most part recognisable from the Europe of the 1970s. But there may well be some significant changes in the political map, formed by newly-independent states in the peripheral frontier zones of Europe. An independent Scotland or Pays Basque or Corsica is by no means an impossibility. Each will be led by a highly nationalistic government representing a former set of freedom fighters; and some at least are likely to be strongly left-wing in composition. The same applies to several of the countries of southern Europe. These countries are by no means automatically likely to line up with the eastern bloc – which by then is likely to be considerably more fragmented. Rather, they may well be neutral in a strategic sense, aligned with a wider EEC in an economic sense. For almost certainly, all European countries – both old and new – will find it necessary, in order to preserve their competitive stance in a difficult world, to surrender even more of their power to supranational institutions. So it is by no means inconceivable that by the year 2000 we could find a neutralist left-wing Scottish government next door to an English government still aligned to NATO; or a Communist Italian government as a member of EEC.

This picture, we stress, is a caricature that stresses change; it underplays the elements of continuity. Not everyone will live like that; this is a society only some way along a certain path. There will still be industrial mass-production, mechanised agriculture, streams of traffic on multi-lane highways, big cities, elements of the candy-floss society. Indeed, some of the quantitative indicators by the year 2000 may well be higher than those of 1975 – though we would expect many to be already lower. Change in society, even fundamental change, is always a matter of degree.

The cultural rationality which we have posited as a desirable response to the needs of our society may, almost certainly will, experience difficulty in asserting itself. Internal politics – a majority may not want it – and external opposition from nations still adhering to economic rationality which may therefore be more efficient will ensure that. The political dimension could be decisive: organised working class governments – the Labour Party in Britain, the Communist Party in Italy – may very well be insensitive to the demands of cultural rationality and in fact resist them.

But, just as there was no one day when feudal society gave way to capitalist or when an aristocratic order gave way to a liberal-democratic, so there will be no one red-letter day marking the end of the era we live in and the start of another.

Yet since millennia are always intrinsically memorable, the year 2000 may well prove to be the historian's closest approximation to it.

Last words

This is the end of *Europe 2000*. But it should be the start of cooperative research into Europe's future.

The countries of Europe devote countless resources to grappling with the problems of the present – problems that sometimes appear to be overwhelming them. They devote miniscule amounts, in comparison, to trying to anticipate problems before they arrive. That perhaps is why they seem to be overwhelmed. Their approach resembles a medical system that pours money into building hospitals and dispensing drugs, but spends nothing on preventive medicine. In government as in health, that is bad practice. For it needlessly wastes scarce resources – including the most precious resource of all, human creative ability.

If, hopefully, this book has shown something, it is that speculative anticipation of future problems is both possible and useful. To pursue that activity further in depth, Europe should now have an International Institute of the Future.

References

Arndt, R. (1975) *Die regierbare Stadt, Warum die Menschen ihre Stadt zurückgewinnen müssen.* Stuttgart: Bonn Aktuell.

Bacon, R, Eltis, W. (1976) *Britain's Economic Problem: too few Producers.* London: Macmillan.

Bell, D. (1964) *The End of Ideology.* New York: The Free Press.

Bell, D. (1974) *The Coming of Post-Industrial Society: A Venture in Social Forecasting.* London: Heinemann.

Berger, B., Berger, P., Kelner, H. (1973) *The Homeless Mind.* Harmondsworth: Penguin Books.

Blondel, J. (1969) *Synécologie des Passereaux résidents et migrateures dans le Midi mediterranéen français.* Marseille: C.R.D.P. d'Aix.

Bourgeois-Pichat, J. (1972) La deuxième conférence démographique européenne de Strasbourg. I. Le vieillissement des populations. *Population, 27,* 209-239.

Bracey, H.E. (1963) *Industry and the Countryside.* London: Faber and Faber.

Brahtz, J.F.P. (1972) *Coastal Zone Management: Multiple Use with Conservation.* New York, London: John Wiley.

Brockington, C.F., Lempert, S.M. (1966) *The Social Needs of the Over-80s: The Stockport Survey.* Manchester: University Press.

Browne, I. (1975) *The Family in Modern Society* (mimeo). Dublin.

Buchanan, J.M. (1975) *The Limits to Liberty.* Chicago: University of Chicago Press.

Carlstein, T. (1974) Gruppstorlek och kommunikation. *Svensk geografisk arsbok.*

Chermayev, S., Alexander, C. (1964) *Community and Privacy.* Cambridge, Mass.: Harvard University Press.

Cohen, S. (1969) *Modern Capitalist Planning: The French Model.* London: Weidenfeld.

Cohen, S. (1974) Human Warehouses: The Future of our Prisons. *New Society, 30,* 632.

Commission of the European Communities (1977) *A Project for Europe.* Brussels: The Commission.

Coomber, N.H., Biswas, A.K. (1973) *Evaluation of Environmental Intangibles.* New York: General Press.

Cooper, R.N. (ed) (1973) *A re-ordered World*. Washington: Potomac.

C.O.P.L.A.C.O. (Comisión de Planeamiento y Coordinación de Area Metropolitana de Madrid) (1973) *Estudio Subregional Corredor Madrid Guadalajara, Tomo 1*. Madrid: Ministerio de la Vivienda.

C.O.P.L.A.C.O. Ministerio de la Vivienda/I.C.O.N.A. Ministerio de Agricultura (1975) *Plan Especial de Prottecion del Medio Fisico*. Madrid: Ministerio de la Vivienda.

Dahlström, E., Liljeström, R. (1975) *Idéer kring familjebildning och fruktsamhet*. Stockholm: Secretariat for Future Studies.

Detwyler, T.R. (ed) (1971) *Man's Impact on the Environment*. New York: McGraw-Hill.

Diesing, P. (1962) *Reason in Society: Five Types of Decision and their Social Conditions*. Urbana: Illinois University Press.

Dirick, Y.M.I., Freiburghaus, D., Sertel, H.R. (1974) *Incidence of the Energy Crisis on the Employment of Foreign Workers in West Germany*. Berlin: International Institute of Management (mimeo).

Donolo, D. (1972) Sviluppo Ineguale e Disgregazione Sociale: Note per l'Analisi de Classe nel Meridione. *Quaderni Piacentini*, Anno XI No. 47.

Dror, Y. (1968) *Public Policymaking Re-examined*. San Francisco: Chandler.

Dupuy, J.P., Gerin, F. (1974) Produktveraltung – Auto und Medikament. *Technologie und Politik, Aktuel – Magazin, 1*, 156-191.

Durgin, F. (1974) What is left for the Market in our Market Economy? *ACES Bulletin, 16*, 41-51.

Edwards, F., McKeown, T., Whitfield, A.G.W. (1959) Incidence of Disease and Disability in Elderly Men. *British Journal of Preventive and Social Medicine, 13*, 51-58.

Ellegård, K., Hägerstrand, T., Lenntorp, B. (1975) *Två frantidsbilder av verksamnetsformer och resbehov*. Lund: Nordkolt.

Elton, C.S. (1966) *The Pattern of Animal Communities*. London: Methuen.

Erikson, E.H. (1968) *Kindheit und Gesellschaft*. Stuttgart: Klett.

Etzioni, A. (1968) *The Active Society*. London: Collier-Macmillan.

European Cultural Foundation (1969) *Europe 2000: Four Studies on the Society of Tomorrow*. Amsterdam: The Foundation.

Eversley, D.E.C. (1975) Regional Devolution and Environmental Planning. In: Craven, E. (ed) *Regional Devolution and Social Policy*. London: Macmillan.

Farvar, M.T., Milton, J.P. (eds) (1972) *The Careless Technology*. New York: Nat. Hist. Press.

Firbas, F. (1949/52) *Spät- und nacheiszeitliche Waldgeschichte Mitteleuropas nördlich der Alpen*. Jena: Fischer.

Fogarty, M.P., Rapoport, R., Rapoport, R.N. (1971) *Sex, Career and Family*. London: PEP (Political and Economic Planning).

Fragnière, G. (ed) (1976) *Education without Frontiers*. London: Duckworth.

France: Datar (1974) *Scénarios Européens: Travaux et Recherches de Prospective*, 47. Paris: Datar.

France: Datar (1975) *La Méthode des Scénarios: Travaux et Recherches de Prospective*, 59. Paris: Datar.

Friedmann, J. (1973) *Retracking America*. Garden City: Anchor Press/Doubleday.

Galbraith, J.K. (1958) *The Affluent Society*. London: Hamish Hamilton.

Galbraith, J.K. (1974) *Economics and the Public Purpose*. London: Deutsch.

Gilliand, M.P. (1972) Le problème des retraites. *Population, 27*, 220-222. In: Bourgeois-Pichat, q.v.

Glaser, E. (1972) Power without Design. In: *Information Technology*. United States: The Conference Board Inc., New York.

Glyn, A., Sutcliffe, B. (1972) *British Capitalism, Workers and the Profits Squeeze*. Harmondsworth: Penguin Books.

Gonzalez-Bernaldez, F., et al (1976) *Estudios Ecológicos en Sierra Morena*. Madrid: I.C.O.N.A. Ministerio de Agricultura.

Gramsci, A. (1971) *La Giungla Retributiva*. Bologna: Il Mulino.

Greger, B. (1973) *Städtebau ohne Konzept. Kritische Thesen zur Stadtplanung der Gegenwart*. Hamburg: Hoffmann & Campe.

Grupo de Analisis Ambiental (1973) *Terrestrial Eco-Survey and Impact Diagnosis*. Madrid: International Commission on Large Dams, XI Congress, Dirección General de Obras Hidraulicas.

Gyllensten, L. (1974) Information, Pseudo-Information and Noise. In: *Man in the Communications System of the Future*. Sweden: Cabinet Office (Secretariat for Future Studies).

Haavio-Mannila, E. (1971) *Könsrollerna och samhällets förändring*. Helsinki: University, Institute of Sociology, No. 169.

Habermas, J. (1967) Dogmatismus, Vernunft und Entwicklung – Zu Theorie und Praxis in der verwissenschaftlichen Zivilisation. In: *Theorie und Praxis: Sozialphilosophische Studien*. Neuwied/Rhine und Berlin: Luchterhand.

Habermas, J. (1971) *Towards a Rational Society*. London: Heinemann.

Hake, B. (1973) *Social Change and Future Development*. (Mimeo). Amsterdam: The Foundation.

Hall, P. (1973) Urban Trends in North-Western Europe 1950-1970: A Megalopolis in Formation. *Seminar on the International Comparative Study of Megalopolis*. Tokyo: Japan Centre for Area Development Research (mimeo).

Hansluwka, H. (1973) Health Programmes and the Prospects for further Reductions of Mortality in Low-Mortality Countries. *International Population Conference, Liège, 3*, 283-300.

Harvey, D. (1973) *Social Justice and the City*. London: Arnold.

Hatchuel, G. (1972) *Le Mechanisme et .les Resultats de la Redistribution des Revenus en France*. Paris. Memoires D.E.S.

Heilbroner, R.L. (1975) *An Inquiry into the Human Prospect*. London: Calder and Boyars.

Hesse, J.J. (1972) *Stadtentwicklungsplanung: Zielfindungsprozesse und Zielvorstellungen*. Stuttgart/Berlin/Köln/Mainz: Kohlhammer.

Hilf, R.B. (1938) *Wald und Weidwerk in Geschichte und Gegenwart*. Potsdam: Athenaion.

Hirschman, A.O., Lindblom, C.E. (1962) Economic Development;

Research and Development; Policy Making: Some Converging Views. *Behavioural Science, 7,* 211-222.

Hochwald, W. (ed) (1961) *Design of Regional Accounts.* Baltimore: Johns Hopkins.

Howard, E. (1946) (1898) *Garden Cities of Tomorrow.* London: Faber and Faber.

Hydèn, H. (1972) The Biological Revolution. In: European Cultural Foundation, *The Future is Tomorrow: 17 Prospective Studies.* The Hague: Martinus Nijhoff.

I.C.O.N.A. (1974) *Estudios Básicos para una Ordenación Integral: Montes de Cercedilla y Navacerrada.* Madrid: Ministerio de Agricultura.

I.C.O.N.A. (1974-5) *Colección de Guías de Parques Nacionales Españoles.* Madrid: Ministerio de Agricultura.

Illich, I. (1973) *Tools for Conviviality.* London: Calder and Boyars.

Illich, I. (1974) *Energy and Equity.* New York: Harper and Row. (Originally published, also 1974, by London: Calder and Boyars).

Isard, W. (1972) *Ecologic-economic analysis for regional development.* New York: The Free Press.

Jansen, A.J. (1975) *Constructing Tomorrow's Agriculture: Report on Cross-National Research in Alternative Futures for European Agriculture.* Bulletin 38. Wageningen: Department of Sociology and Sociography, Agricultural University.

Kahn, H., Bruce-Briggs, B. (1972) *Things to Come: Thinking about the 70s and 80s.* London: Macmillan.

Kalma, J.D., Byrne, G.F. (1976) Energy use and the Urban Environment: some implications for planning. In: *Proceedings of the World Meteorological Association Symposium on Meteorology as Related to Urban and Regional Land-Use Planning,* Asheville, N.C., November 1975. Geneva: WMO.

Klapp, E. (1958) Grundzüge einer Grünlandlehre. *Wiss. Z. Univ. Jena, 7,* 67-81.

Kormoss, I.B.F. et al (1977) *Reflections on the Future of the European Rural World.* Mimeo.

Krause, L.B. (1973) Why Exports are irrelevant. In: Cooper, R.N. (ed) *A Re-Ordered World.* Washington: Potomac.

Krżymowski, R. (1939) *Geschichte der deutschen Landwirtschaft.* Stuttgart: Ulmer.

Lederer, Katrin (1975) Kulturelle Rationalität. *Analysen und Prognosen, 40,* 15.

Leopold, L.B., et al (1971) *A Procedure for Evaluating Environmental Impact.* (Geological Survey Circular 645). Washington, DC: U.S.G.S.

Liapunov, A.A., Titlianova, A.A. (1971) *O Niekotorykh voprosakh kodirovania i pieredachi informatsii v upravliaiushchikh sistemakh zivoi prirody.* Novosibirsk: Fil. Akad. Nauk RSR.

Lichtenberger, E. (1970) The Nature of European Urbanism. *Geoforum, 4,* 45-62.

Lienemann, F. (1976) *Urbanisation: Towards a Human Environment in Europe.* The Hague: Martinus Nijhoff.

Lindbeck, A. (1975) The Changing Role of the National State. *Kyklos, 28,* 23-44.

Lowi, T. (1972) Government and Politics. In: *Information Technology*. United States: The Conference Board Inc., New York.

Macciocchi, M.A. (1969) *Lettere dall'Interno de P.C. a Louis Althusser*. Milano: Feltrinelli.

McHarg, I.L. (1969) *Design with Nature*. New York: The Natural History Press.

MacClelland, D. (1960) *Personality*. New York: Holt, Rinehart & Winston.

Malinowski, B. (1944) *A Scientific Theory of Culture and other Essays*. Chapel Hill: The University of North Carolina Press.

Malmberg, T. (1976) *Human Territories: A Survey of Territorial Behaviour in Man with special reference to Urbanisation in Europe*. The Hague: Martinus Nijhoff.

Mandel, E. (1970) *Europe versus America: Contradictions of Imperialism*. London: New Left Books.

Margalef, R. (1975) *Ecologia*. Barcelona: Omega.

Marx, K. (1869, 1935) Relations between the Irish and English Working Classes. In: Burns, E. (ed.) *A Handbook of Marxism*. London: Gollancz.

Marx, K. (1867, 1961) *Capital*. London: Lawrence and Wishart.

Maslow, A.H. (1943) A theory of human motivation. *Psychological Review, 50,* 370-96.

Mayen, J. (1972) La Population des Hospices et des Maisons de Retraite. *Population, 27,* 69-82.

Menke-Glückert, P. (1970) The Changing Socio-Technological Environment for Political Innovations: New Challenges for Government Decision Making. *Analysen und Prognosen, 9,* 16-22.

Mercier, P.A. (1974) *Les Inegalités en France*. Paris: Centre des Récherches de Documentation Pour la Consommation.

Mercier, P.A. (1976) The Survival Olympics. *Vision*, August, 35-45.

Mishan, E.J. (1968) *The Costs of Economic Growth*. London: Staples Press.

Mumford, L. (1971) *The Myth of the Machine: The Pentagon of Power*. London: Secker and Warburg.

Naveh, Z. (1968) Multiple Use of Mediterranean Rangelands – New approaches to old problems. *Ann. Arid Zones, 7,* 163.

Naveh, Z. (1974) The Ecological Management of Mediterranean Uplands. *Jr. Env. Management, 2,* 351-71.

Nicholson, S., Schreiner, B.K. (1973) *Community Participation in City Decision Making*. Milton Keynes: Open University Press.

Nikolinakos, M. (1975a) *Migrationsbewegungen, Investitionen und Handelsbeziehungen zwischen Mittelmeer- und Westeuropäischen Ländern*. (Preprint Series, Arbeitsgruppe, Internationales Institut für vergleichende Gesellschaftsforschung, P/75-24). Berlin: The Institute. (Mimeo).

Nikolinakos, M. (1975b) *Auswirkungen der Migration auf die Sozio-ökonomische Entwicklung Griechenlands*. (Preprint Series, Arbeitsgruppe, Internationales Institut für vergleichende Gesellschaftsforschung, P/75-24). Berlin: The Institute (mimeo).

Oakley, A. (1974) *Housewife*. London: Allen Lane.

OECD (1975a) Surpluses and Deficits and Related Payments in 7 Major Countries, *Occasional Studies*, 23-35. Paris: OECD.

OECD (1975b) *Economic Outlook*. Paris: OECD.

Orwell, G. (1951) Charles Dickens. In: *Critical Essays*. London: Secker and Warburg.

Östnäs, A. (1971) Bostadsplaneringen och kvinnoras politiska representation. *Sociol. Inst. Göteborgs Univ. Forskn. rapp, 19.*

Ozkan, Y. (1975) *Stabilisierungs faktor oder Revolutionäres Potential? (Politische Sozialisation der Türkischen Gastarbeiter).* (Preprint Series, Arbeitsgruppe Internationales Institut für vergteichende Gesellschaftsforschung, P/75-1). Berlin: The Institute. (mimeo).

Pack, D.H. (1964) Meteorology of Air Pollution. *Science, 146,* 1119-28.

Pahl, R.E., Winkler, J.T. (1974) The Coming of the Corporate State. *New Society, 30,* 72-6.

Pareto, Alfredo (1965) *Allgemeine Soziologie*. Tübingen: Mohr (Siebeck).

Patrimonio Forestal del Estado (1973) *Memoria Anyal 1970-1973.* Madrid: Ministerio de Agricultura. (As from 1973, continued as I.C.O.N.A. Memoria Anual).

Pavlik, Z. (1971) Nombre désiré et nombre idéal d'enfants chez les femmes rurales en Boheme. *Population, 26,* 915-932.

Pirsig, R.M. (1974) *Zen and the Art of Motorcycle Maintenance*. London: The Bodley Head.

Popper, K.R. (1957a) *The Poverty of Historicism*. London: Routledge and Kegan Paul.

Popper, K.R. (1957b) *The Open Society and its Enemies*. Vol. I: *The Spell of Plato*. Vol. II: *The High Tide of Prophecy: Hegel and Marx*. London: Routledge and Kegan Paul.

Poulantzas, N. (1973) L'Internationalisation des Rapports Capitalists et l'Etat-Nation, *Les Temps Modernes, 319,* 1456-1500.

Rawthorn, R. (1973) Internationalisation du Capital et Pouvoir National d'Etat, *Les Temps Modernes, 329,* 964-996.

Reich, C. (1971) *The Greening of America*. Harmondsworth: The Penguin Press.

Riley, M.W. et al (1968-9) *Aging and Society*. 2 Vols. New York: Russell Sage Foundation/Basic Books.

Rosak, T. (1969) *The Making of a Counter Culture*. New York: Anchor Books.

Rostow, W.W. (1960) *The Stages of Economic Growth*. Cambridge: University Press.

Sauvy, A. (1970) *Le Socialisme en Liberté*. Paris: Denoël.

Schon, D.A. (1971) *Beyond a Stable State*. New York: Random House.

Schumacher, E.F. (1973a) *Small is Beautiful: Economics as if People Mattered*. New York: Harper and Row.

Schumacher, E. (1973b) *Small is Beautiful*. *The Observer* (London), June 10, 1973.

Sellers, W.D. (1965) *Physical Climatology*. Chicago: University of Chicago Press.

S.E.T.O. Mission Interministerielle de l'Environnement (1973) *Loisirs sportifs de plein air et Environnement*. Le Pradet: Conference Loisirs Actifs de Plein Air et Environnement.

Shanas, F. et al (1968) *Old People in Three Industrial Societies*. London: Routledge and Kegan Paul.

Stalley, M. (1972) *Patrick Geddes: Spokesman for Man and the Environment*. New Brunswick, N.J: Rutgers U.P.

Stöber, G. et al (1977) *Man and Industry*. Mimeo.

Sweden (1968) *The Status of Women in Sweden*. Report of the Swedish government in the United Nations. Stockholm: Swedish Institute.

Thiede, Gunther (1975) *Europas Grüne Zukunft: Die Veränderung der ländlichen Welt*. Düsseldorf: Econ-verlag.

Touring Club de France (1973) *Loisirs actifs de plain air. Protection de la Nature et de l'Environnement*. Le Pradet: Colloque Loisirs de Plein Air et Environnement.

Tuxen, R. (1950) Neue Methoden der Wald-und Forstkartierwng. *Mitt. florist-soziol. Arb. gem. N.F., 2*, 217-219.

Ucko, P. (ed) (1969) *The Domestication and Exploitation of Plants and Animals*. London: Duckworth.

United Kingdom. Royal Commission on the Distribution of Income and Wealth (1975) *Initial Report on the Standing Reference. (Report No.1)* London: HMSO.

Van Keep, P.A. (1971) Ideal Family Size in Five European Countries. *Journal of Biosocial Science, 3*, 259-265.

Vieille, P. (1974) L'espace global du capitalisme d'organisation. *Espaces et sociétés, 12*, 3-32.

Waltuch, K.K. (1972) *Entwicklungsproportionen und Befriedigung der Bedürfnisse*. Berlin: Verlag die Wirtschaft.

Webber, M.M. et al (1964) *Explorations into Urban Structure*. University of Pennsylvania Press.

Weber, M. (1920-21) Prinzipielles zur Kultursoziologie. *Archiv für Sozialwissenschaft und Sozialpolitik, 47*, 1-49.

Weber, M. (1968) *Economy and Society*. New York: Bedminster Press.

Whitman, I.L. et al (1971) *Final Report on Design of an Environmental Evaluation System for the Bureau of Reclamation*. Columbus: US Department of the Interior, Batelle Memorial Center.

Wilsher, P., Righter, R. (1975) *The Exploding Cities*. London: Deutsch.

Wolff, R.P. (1970) *Critica della Tolleranza*. Turin: Einaudi.

Wootton, B. (1955) *The Social Foundations of Wage Policy*. London: Allen and Unwin.

Yankelovich, D. (1974) *The New Morality: A Profile of American Youth in the 1970s*. New York: McGraw Hill.

Yannopoulos, G. (1974) *Migrant Labour and Economic Growth: The Postwar Experience of the EEC Countries*. (University of Reading Discussion Papers in Economics, A 65). Reading: Department of Economics (mimeo).

Young, M., Willmott, P. (1973) *The Symmetrical Family: A Study of Work and Leisure in the London Region*. London: Routledge.

Index of Names

Alexander, C., 74, 264
Arndt, R., 130, 264

Bacon, R., 16, 264
Bell, D., 35, 140, 264
Berger, B. and P., 226, 264
Biswas, A.K., 93, 264
Blondel, J., 95, 264
Bourgeois-Pichat, J., 177, 264
Bracey, H.E., 93, 264
Brahtz, J.F.P., 94, 264
Brockington, C.F., 184, 264
Browne, I., 250, 251, 264
Bruce-Briggs, B., 64, 267
Buchanan, J.M., 72, 264
Byrne, G.F., 246, 247, 267

Carlstein, T., 198, 264
Chermayev, S., 74, 264
Cohen, S., 73, 146, 264
Commission of the European Communities, 244, 264
Coomber, N.H., 93, 264
Cooper, R.N., 17, 265
C.O.P.L.A.C.O., 93, 94, 265

Dahlström, E., 190, 265
Detwyler, T.R., 93, 95, 265
Diesing, P., 236, 265
Dirick, Y.M.I., 221, 265
Donolo, D., 217, 265
Dror, Y., 150, 265
Dupuy, J.P., 132, 265
Durgin, F., 146, 265

Edwards, F., 183, 265
Ellegard, K., 200, 265
Eltis, W., 16, 264
Elton, C.S., 94, 265
Erikson, E.H., 233, 265
Etzioni, A., 233, 265
European Cultural Foundation, 1, 265

Eversley, D.E.C., 25, 265

Farvar, M.T., 93, 265
Firbas, F., 93, 265
Fogarty, M.P., 189, 191, 201, 202, 265
Fragnière, G., 3, 165, 265
France: Datar, 6-8, 13, 265
Frankenhaeuser, M., 162
Freiburghaus, D., 221, 265
Friedmann, J., 239, 240, 245, 246, 251, 266

Galbraith, J.K., 63, 133, 146, 147, 266
Gerin, F., 132, 265
Gilliand, M.P., 182, 266
Glaser, E., 172, 266
Glyn, A., 217, 266
Gonzalez-Bernaldez, F., 93, 266
Gramsci, A., 229, 266
Greger, B., 131, 266
Grupo de Analisis Ambiental, 94, 266
Gyllensten, L., 164, 266

Haavio-Mannila, E., 192, 202, 203, 266
Habermas, J., 35, 235, 266
Hägerstrand, T., 200, 265
Hake, B., 6, 266
Hall, P., 83, 266
Hansluwka, H., 178, 266
Harvey, D., 66, 266
Hatchuel, G., 206, 266
Heilbroner, R.L., 243, 245, 247, 248, 249, 253, 266
Hesse, J.J., 131, 266
Hilf, R.B., 93, 266
Hirschman, A.O., 122, 266
Hochwald, W., 141, 267
Howard, E., 82, 251, 262, 267
Hydèn, H., 73, 267

I.C.O.N.A., 93, 95, 267
Illich, I., 245-52, 267

Isard, W., 94, 267

Jansen, A.J., 267
Kahn, H., 64, 267
Kalma, J.D., 246-7, 267
Kelner, H., 266, 264
Klapp, E., 94, 267
Kormoss, I.B.F., 3, 267
Krause, L.B., 13, 267
Krzymowski, R., 93, 267

Lederer, K., 237, 267
Lempert, S.M., 184, 264
Lenntorp, B., 200, 265
Leopold, L.B., 94, 267
Liapunov, A.A., 93, 267
Lichtenberger, E., 104, 267
Lienemann, F., 3, 267
Liljeström, R., 190, 265
Lindbeck, A., 146, 267
Lindblom, C.E., 122
Lowi, T., 170, 171, 268

Macciocchi, M.A., 222, 268
Malinowski, B., 236, 237, 268
Malmberg, T., 111, 268
Mandel, E., 13, 268
Mannheim, K., 239-41
Margalef, R., 94, 268
Marx, K., 222, 239-41, 268
Maslow, A.H., 233, 234, 268
Mayen, J., 185, 186, 268
McHarg, I.L., 93, 94, 268
McKeown, T., 183, 265
MacClelland, D., 233, 268
Menke-Glückert, P., 148, 150, 268
Mercier, P.A., 209, 210, 268
Mills, C. Wright, 240
Milton, J.P., 93, 265
Mishan, E.J., 133, 141, 268
Mumford, L., 245, 248, 268

Naveh, Z., 94, 268
Nicholson, S., 252, 253, 268
Nikolinakos, M., 221, 268

Oakley, A., 188, 191, 192, 268
O.E.C.D., 15, 211, 269
Orwell, G., 80, 269
Östnäs, A., 193, 269
Ozkan, Y., 221, 269

Pack, D.H., 93, 95, 269

Pahl, R.E., 46, 269
Pareto, A., 269
Patrimonio Forestal del Estado, 94, 269
Pavlik, Z., 39, 269
Pirsig, R.M., 249, 250, 269
Popper, K.R., 32, 33, 269
Poulantzas, N., 13, 269

Rapoport, R. and R.N., 265
Rawthorn, R., 13, 269
Reich, C., 35, 269
Righter, R., 75, 270
Riley, M.W., 183, 197, 269
Rosak, T., 35, 269
Rostow, W.W., 35, 269

Sauvy, A., 213, 269
Schon, D.A., 53, 269
Schreiner, B.K., 252, 253, 268
Schumacher, E.F., 115, 245, 248, 250, 269
Sellers, W.D., 95, 269
Sertel, H.R., 221, 265
S.E.T.O., 93, 95, 269
Shanas, F., 185, 270
Stalley, M., 187, 270
Stöber, G., 3, 270
Sutcliff, B., 217, 266

Thiede, G., 87, 270
Titlianova, A.A., 93, 267
Touring Club de France, 93, 95, 270
Tuxen, R., 94, 270

Ucko, P.J., 94, 270

Van Keep, P.A., 39, 270
Vieille, P., 110, 270

Waltuch, K.K., 270
Webber, M.M., 114, 270
Weber, M., 132, 235-7, 240, 270
Whitfield, A.G.W., 183, 265
Whitman, I.L., 93, 94, 270
Willmott, P., 203, 270
Wilsher, P., 75, 270
Winkler, J.T., 46, 269
Wolff, R.P., 217, 270
Wootton, B., 59, 270

Yankelovich, D., 55, 101, 270
Yannopoulos, G., 220, 221, 270
Young, M., 203, 270

General Index

access to information, 76-7, 79, 170, 244
adaptability of man, 110, 161-5
agriculture, 2, 9, 78, 85-92, 94, 98, 99-102, 113, 123, 255-6, 260
alienation, 9, 50, 57, 62, 71-6, 80, 84, 150, 225, 226-38, 243, 245, 259

birthrates, 38-9, 82

central notion of community, 112, 125
China, 30
city, the form of, 68, 75, 78, 101, 261
class, 43, 66, 79, 205-25
commune group, 250-1, 255, 260-1
communications technology, 156-9, 161, 163, 168, 173, 252, 260
concept; of Europe, 11; of need, 55; of social indicators, 142
craft industry, 61, 113, 248-9, 250, 255

decentralisation; of industry, 139-40; of population, 67, 101, 107, 114
deconcentration of population, 107, 118, 120, 256
demand, 16-17, 36, 88, 90, 146
development of mass media, 160-1
devolution, 26, 31, 47, 50, 66
discrimination against women, 68-9
distribution of power, 170-2
division of labour, 229, 236
dysfunctionals, 71-2, 262

Eastern Europe, 27-9
ecological factors, 88, 90, 93, 95-7, 99, 111, 118-19, 122-4
economic development, 23, 146-7
econopolis, 110, 113
education, 1-2, 9, 72-4, 79, 156-73, 208, 218-19; lifelong, 166-9
environment; human, 117-19, 122; natural, 91-4, 96, 98, 108, 110-11, 116-17, 122; urban, 106, 108
equality of opportunity, 166, 168

family, the, 79, 174-204, 244, 258; extended, 174, 203-4, 244; nuclear, 175, 200, 244, 251
federalism, 11-12
forecasting, 4-5, 239

garden cities, 82, 251, 262
growth, 35, 78, 86; economic, 14, 28, 36-7, 55, 58, 97, 134, 139, 147, 212-13; industrial, 37, 139-40; population, 37-8, 78, 82-3, 88; suburban, 83; urban, 84
guerilla warfare, 14, 57

historicism, 32-3, 241
human dimensions, 125-7
humanopolis, 112-13, 116
human territorial behaviour, 110-11, 116-19

individualism, 126, 237
individual privacy, 77, 169-70
industrial; expansion, 37; investment, 149-50; production, 141
industrialisation, 105-6, 109
industry, 2, 9, 37, 45, 49, 72-4, 78-9, 116, 132-55, 256-7
inequality, 205-25
information overload, 164, 198
international; competition, 36; economic crisis, 242; power, 10, 21; relations, 14, 18

marginal groups, 42-3, 47, 49, 71, 219, 224
megalopolis, 22, 24, 83, 84, 107
middle-class group, 41-4, 47, 215
Middle Eastern bloc, 30
migrant workers, 219-22
migration, 38, 62, 66, 201
multinationals, 17, 20, 45, 137

nationalisation, 44-5, 149, 231

nation state, 11, 19, 20, 22, 25-6, 30-1, 50, 262
needs; human, 62-3, 74, 127-8, 233, 236; social, 111, 119, 128, 133, 189

old people's organisations, 179-80
old, survival of, 69, 175, 177-87
organised working class, 14, 16, 36, 39-43, 232

peripheral regions, 22-5, 31, 97-9, 100
planning, 239-41, 251; environmental, 96; indicative, 145-8, 151; industrial, 138; urban, 128-31
politics, 32, 80, 170-1
population, 5, 24, 37-8, 78, 82-3, 88, 106
production; factors, 108-10, 124; organisation of, 62-3; potential for, 87-8
prolongation of life, 177-9, 186
protectionism, 17, 20-1, 47, 137
public participation, 128, 130, 252-3

quality, 249-50, 260; of life, 100, 142, 212, 257

rationality; 8-9, 34-5, 47-51, 61-5, 80, 100, 105, 143, 148, 226-38, 240; cultural, 113, 117, 129-31, 263; economic, 35, 44, 85, 99, 106-8, 110-11, 115-16, 118, 121-2, 134, 143, 147, 234, 247, 254, 256, 263; political, 34-5, 39-43, 44
research and development, 134-5, 137, 154
resource conservation, 54, 246-7, 249-50, 253, 260

retirement, 69-70, 79, 182, 186-7, 258
role equalisation, 188-92, 195-6, 198-203, 261

'scientism', 35, 241
security, 56, 58, 78
self-sufficiency, 2, 59-60
separatist movements, 24-5, 27
social; change, 224, 225-6, 239-42, 263; system, 61-2, 130, 230, 240
'stagflation', 36, 63
standard of living, 21, 29, 40, 78, 211
state intervention, 34, 43-4, 62, 145-48, 231-2
stress research, 161, 163
superpowers, 10-11, 13, 20, 30

technical; co-operation, 18, 30; monopoly, 20
technological; development, 134; innovation, 13, 65; leadership, 17
technopolis, 112, 114-15, 122
terrorism, 57
Third World, the, 17-20, 30, 37-8, 57, 122, 136-7, 248
trade war, 22, 137

unemployment, 17, 24, 49, 217, 223
United States, 10-14, 19-22, 27, 46
urban regeneration, 118-21, 256
urbanisation, 2, 9, 85, 95, 103-31
USSR, 10, 12, 19, 21-2, 27

value systems, 54-6, 112, 130, 151, 244

women, position of, 38-9, 188, 192-4
world conflict over resource use, 243